The Last Days of Dispensationalism

The Last Days of Dispensationalism

A Scholarly Critique of Popular Misconceptions

Alistair W. Donaldson

WIPF & STOCK · Eugene, Oregon

THE LAST DAYS OF DISPENSATIONALISM
A Scholarly Critique of Popular Misconceptions

Wipf & Stock
An Imprint of Wipf and Stock Publishers
199 W. 8th Ave., Suite 3
Eugene, OR 97401
www.wipfandstock.com

ISBN 13: 978-1-60899-515-8

Manufactured in the U.S.A.

Contents

Foreword

The United States must join Israel in a pre-emptive military strike against Iran to fulfill God's plan for both Israel and the West . . . a biblically prophesied end-time confrontation with Iran, which will lead to the Rapture, Tribulation, and Second Coming of Christ.[1]

THESE ARE NOT THE views of some eccentric or extremist cult leader, but of Pastor John Hagee, the senior pastor of Cornerstone Church, San Antonio, Texas, a church of more than 19,000 members at the heart of America's Bible belt. Hagee's apocalyptic speculations are disseminated to one hundred million homes via radio and television on a weekly basis. His views are shared by many other evangelical, charismatic, and Pentecostal leaders, seminary professors and television evangelists. Together, they are promoting a deeply pessimistic, confrontational and destructive view of America's present and future role in the world, and in the Middle East in particular.

Perpetuating a dualistic and Manichaean worldview—first Communism and now Islam are demonized as the "enemy"—Bible verses are quoted confidently to explain contemporary geopolitical events leading to the battle of Armageddon. Religious-sounding rhetoric such as "Operation Infinite Justice" and "Axis of Evil" is used to justify a belligerent foreign policy and military intervention against other sovereign states. Huntington's *Clash of Civilizations* is becoming the self-fulfilling prophecy of the Christian Right.

Alistair Donaldson could therefore not have written a more timely or needed book. He rightly insists that "beliefs shape how Christians live their lives. Eschatology is no mere appendage at the end of the Bible with little to say to life in the present. Eschatology is the goal of God from the beginning of time; the Bible is therefore eschatological from beginning to end. The past, present, and future of God's redemptive work is the

---

1. Posner, "Pastor Strangelove," para. 4.

vii

Christian's context for exegeting an understanding of who they are. To get that context wrong is to misunderstand our role in effecting God's redeeming activity."

The church, particularly in America, must therefore rethink its eschatology. For a century or more, the dominant eschatological view held by Christians in America has been dispensationalism. Dispensationalism teaches that God has two separate chosen people, Israel and the church, a heavenly and an earthly people. This has led many Christians to believe that their responsibility is to take sides and support or "bless" Israel to ensure God's continuing blessing of America.

Typified by John Hagee, dispensationalism is deeply skeptical of peacemaking as a Christian calling. It has largely silenced the prophetic call for justice. It has sacralized unilateral military and economic support for a belligerent Zionism. It is exacerbating the deep mistrust much of the world feels toward America and, more importantly, toward Christianity.

Donaldson shows with careful logic that following a literal hermeneutic does not lead to a distinction between God's purposes for the Jewish people apart from other races. Just the reverse; God's purposes for both are fulfilled only in and through faith in Jesus Christ. It is not that the church has replaced Israel. Israel and the church are one people. In the progressive revelation of Scripture through history there is a continuity among God's people. Membership has always been on the basis of faith not race.

Donaldson shows that it is artificial and unbiblical to distinguish between Israel and the church in God's purposes. There has only ever been one people of God. Indeed, there is an organic unity of God's people between the Old Testament church and the New Testament church. Christ has made the two—Jewish and Gentile believers—one (Eph 2).

Donaldson tests the veracity of dispensationalism and finds it inherently defective. He shows that it is inconsistent and selective in its hermeneutic and flawed in distinguishing God's purposes between Israel and the church, that it acquiesces in the face of suffering and injustice because of its pessimistic and determinist eschatology, and that it is therefore confused about its redemptive mission to a lost world.

By contrast, in the New Testament, followers of Jesus Christ are called to be "peacemakers"—indeed, it is peacemaking that Jesus insists identifies the authenticity of those who claim to be his followers;

"Blessed are the peacemakers, for they will be called children of God" (Matt 5:9). The Apostle Paul elaborates on this radical yet intrinsic role of Christ-followers in 2 Corinthians 5:

> From now on, therefore, we regard no one from a human point of view; even though we once knew Christ from a human point of view, we know him no longer in that way. So if anyone is in Christ, there is a new creation: everything old has passed away; see, everything has become new! All this is from God, who reconciled us to himself through Christ, and has given us the ministry of reconciliation; that is, in Christ God was reconciling the world to himself, not counting their trespasses against them, and entrusting the message of reconciliation to us. So we are ambassadors for Christ, since God is making his appeal through us; we entreat you on behalf of Christ, be reconciled to God. (2 Cor 5:16–20)

We are to repudiate worldly criteria that distinguish and categorize people on the basis of wealth, race, color, or creed. God is not willing that any should perish: "The Lord is not slow about his promise, as some think of slowness, but is patient with you, not wanting any to perish, but all to come to repentance" (2 Pet 3:9). The vision of the future found in the book of Revelation is ultimately a message of hope not despair. We see in the closing chapters God's dream not his nightmare: "And I heard a loud voice from the throne saying, 'Look! God's dwelling place is now among the people, and he will dwell with them. They will be his people, and God himself will be with them and be their God. He will wipe every tear from their eyes. There will be no more death or mourning or crying or pain, for the old order of things has passed away'" (Rev 21:3–4 TNIV).

The closing chapter of the New Testament takes us back to the imagery of the Garden of Eden and the removal of the curse arising from the entrance of sin: "Then the angel showed me the river of the water of life, bright as crystal, flowing from the throne of God and of the Lamb. . . . On either side of the river is the tree of life with its twelve kinds of fruit, producing its fruit each month; and the leaves of the tree are for the healing of the nations" (Rev 22:1–2). Surely this is what Jesus had in mind when he instructed his followers to work and pray that God's kingdom would come on earth as it is in heaven.

In this book, Donaldson offers a more robust, biblically consistent, and constructive view both of the future and of the role for the church between now and the return of the Lord Jesus Christ.

> The alternative eschatological view here presented has sought to be faithful to the biblical text and to the far-reaching all-creation inclusive restoration hopes inherent in the gospel of the kingdom; God's redeemed and restored humanity purchased from every tribe and language and people and nation as one people— one kingdom of priests, enjoying restored fellowship with God who is present with them, and reigning in the place that God intended for them to live, the new heaven and earth. This is the good news of the kingdom of God, experienced now in part; the full realization is yet to come.

"Amen. Come Lord Jesus" (Rev 22:20).

Stephen Sizer
July 2010

Preface

DISPENSATIONAL PREMILLENNIALISM, AN ESCHATOLOGICAL belief system developed in the mid-eighteen-hundreds, gained widespread acceptance in the years following 1907 through the publication of the Scofield Reference Bible and later by Hal Lindsey's *The Late Great Planet Earth*. More recently it has formed the basis for the popular Left Behind series of novels written by Tim LaHaye and Jerry B. Jenkins. Despite these being fictional novels, the dispensational belief system on which they are based is claimed to be biblically accurate. It follows that readers of these novels will often understand that the story contained within reflects a terrible future reality yet to eventuate—perhaps in their lifetime.

Claiming to be formed from a consistently literal interpretation of the Bible, normative or classical dispensationalism believes that the Christian church is a heavenly people of God quite distinct from Israel, his earthly people, the latter to whom God has promised a distinct and glorious future. The church is said to be a parenthesis interrupting God purposes for Israel and is brought into being solely due to Israel's rejection of Christ as their Messiah. Due to this rejection, the kingdom of God—understood to be a political and national kingdom for Israel—was postponed until the *parousia*, the second coming of Christ. Further, in order for this kingdom to eventuate, the church (in an event known as "the rapture") must first be removed from the earth. This rapture of the church, it is believed, will initiate a seven-year period of horrific tribulation for those "left behind." This is the period of time that sets the stage for the dramatic content of the Left Behind novels. At the end of these seven years, Christ will return to establish a one-thousand-year-kingdom reign from Jerusalem in which Israel's Old Testament kingdom promises will all be fulfilled. The earth will then be destroyed by fire and a new earth will be created to replace it.

In this book I contest the validity of the dispensational belief system. I begin by demonstrating that the hermeneutical basis for the formation of dispensationalism is seriously flawed and as such gives us reason to question the truthfulness of the entire system and its foremost tenets: (1) the distinction of Israel and the church in relation to God's purposes, (2) the kingdom of God as a future political and national kingdom for Israel, (3) the rapture of the church from the earth in order for God to resume his purposes for Israel and initiating a seven-year tribulation period leading up to the second coming of Christ, and (4) the millennium as a future one-thousand-year earthly kingdom reign of Christ in fulfillment of Israel's kingdom hopes.

After testing the dispensational understanding of these tenets one by one and finding each to be problematic, I suggest that dispensationalism is not a well-reasoned understanding of biblical redemption. Throughout I will present an alternative understanding of these issues and pave the way to very briefly consider, by way of conclusion, God's eschatological and redemptive work in relation to his creational intent, which the entrance of sin has hindered. It will be shown that the dispensationalist eschatological system, including the above-mentioned problematic tenets, neglects to observe the all-creation-encompassing scope of redemption as revealed in the story of Scripture. As such, dispensationalism appears to be not only an inadequate understanding of Scripture, but also serves to advance a distorted worldview that in turn shapes a diminished meaning for Christian living.

Introduction

THE DISPENSATIONAL PREMILLENNIAL SYSTEM of eschatology has significantly influenced Christian thought and practice since its development and systematization by John Nelson Darby (1800–1882) during the mid 1800s. One only needs to observe in our time, some 170 years or so later, the vast array of published writing in bookstores capitalizing on what Gary DeMar has called *Last Days Madness*[1] to perceive just how pervasive this eschatological belief system has become. The widespread acceptance and promotion of dispensational premillennialism through the mediums of television, film, and record-selling novels such as Jerry B. Jenkins and Tim LaHaye's Left Behind series[2] reveals the far-reaching influence this perspective has had at the congregational level of Christianity.[3] These television programs, films, and books build on the legacy of Darby's work, and the more recent Hal Lindsey's 1970s multi-million-copy seller, *The Late Great Planet Earth*. Despite the fact that many dispensational scholars would, and do, cringe at the speculative excesses communicated through these forms of media[4] (though they build on the basic dispensational system), adherence to the belief system expressed within them has for many sincere Christians become the litmus test of true Christianity.[5] This is true at the level of congregational Christianity.

1. DeMar, *Last Days Madness*, 17.

2. This series of novels by LaHaye and Jenkins had sold approximately 63 million copies. Cited July 5, 2010. Online: http://www.leftbehind.com/01_products/details.asp?isbn 978-1-4143-3485-1.

3. The writer experienced this while leading a Bible study recently. A participant adamantly declared that in the book of Revelation John saw twenty-first-century airplanes and that he described them as locusts. When asked how he came to this understanding he responded that he had heard this on television.

4. For example Blaising and Bock, *Dispensationalism, Israel and the Church*, 14. See their footnote #3.

5. I am aware that this is a generalization, noting that there are exceptions to this

However, many, indeed most, within scholarly circles continue to question the soundness of dispensationalism as a reasonable system of thought—whether in its classical form with its offspring of highly speculative and literally novel extremes, or that of the more recent *progressive dispensationalism* espoused by scholars such as Blaising and Bock.[6]

This is no small issue. Belief systems shape how people live their lives on a day-to-day basis. Dispensationalism, as a belief system, has been embraced by millions of people, some of whom have been or are currently in positions to influence the policies of governments and thus to significantly impact the lives of many people, both Christian and non-Christian, throughout the world—the impact of which is felt nowhere more intensely than in Israel/Palestine.

Two truths presented thus far suggest that there is an urgent need to bring to this system of thought an analysis that will test its truthfulness.[7] First, the majority of Christian scholarship doubts the reliability of dispensationalism. Second, this system of thought has an influence on the manner in which millions of Christian people live their lives, often to the support of and at times promoting injustice and oppression in the land where our Lord once walked.

Chapter 1 will address the hermeneutic adopted by dispensationalists to test the trustworthiness of the manner by which they approach and interpret the biblical text. Subsequent chapters will then address some of the key tenets of dispensational premillennialism: Israel and the church, the kingdom of God, the rapture and tribulation, and the millennium. These studies will be somewhat brief due to limitations of space—many books have been written concerning each of these topics, however, I will endeavor to demonstrate the inadequacy of the dispensa-

---

from the mainstream Protestant, Catholic, and Orthodox churches who do not hold to dispensational theology. Clarence Bass, however, notes that despite his affirmation of the cardinal doctrines of the faith some of his dearest friends were convinced that he had departed from the evangelical faith. Bass, *Backgrounds*, 9. Grenz, *Millennial Maze*, 91–92.

6. Blaising and Bock, *Progressive Dispensationalism*; Blaising and Bock, *Dispensationalism, Israel and the Church*. While still referring to themselves as dispensationalists, these writers have made significant movement from their predecessors to a more covenantal view of the Bible and more toward the understanding of amillennial, postmillennial, and historic premillennial interpreters in a number of key elements of eschatological thought. However, adherents of these latter positions still look to see a further progression.

7. Walker, Introduction, 9.

tional understanding concerning these issues. Each chapter will present a view counter to that of dispensationalism and will end with a conclusion concerning the particular tenet being discussed. The concluding chapter will therefore only briefly summarize these and then will merely introduce with a little discussion what I consider to be a further essential component of a more holistic and biblically sound Christian eschatology.

1

The Hermeneutics
of Dispensational Premillennialism: A Critique

WHEN DISCUSSING THE DISPENSATIONAL premillennial system of eschatology with those who hold to this viewpoint it immediately becomes apparent that it is difficult to persuade them to a change of view. Vern Poythress emphatically notes that this "is not at all easy."[1] I have experienced Poythress's point firsthand many times, and I can agree with him when he writes that "nearly all the problems associated with the dispensationalist/non-dispensationalist conflict are buried beneath the question of literal interpretation."[2] Discussions concerning various points of difference in understanding without first considering the interpretive principles employed by adherents of the differing viewpoints will only see the disputants and their discussions going around in circles. For any conversation between dispensationalists and non-dispensationalists to be of value we must first attend to the all-important issue of hermeneutics as it relates to eschatological thought.[3]

For that reason, after giving a brief overview of dispensational premillennialism, the purpose of this first chapter is to identify the hermeneutical principles of the dispensational system, to examine these in order to determine their strengths and weaknesses, and then to make some conclusions as to their value in forming a biblically sound eschato-

---

1. Poythress, *Understanding Dispensationalism*, 52–53.

2. Ibid., 78.

3. Peter Kusmič, "History and Eschatology," 137–38. Kusmič, writes, "Depending on the hermeneutical principles used in interpreting the Book of Revelation, and on the hermeneutics applied to Old Testament prophecies pointing to an era of the restoration of Israel, and an age of peace, progress and prosperity, Christians have decided for or against a millennial Kingdom and have developed elaborate theologies and schemes relating to the parousia, the second coming of Christ."

logical understanding. My focus is primarily on the traditional, early, or normative dispensationalism of Scofield, Ryrie, Walvoord, and others, for two reasons. First, any later developments or modifications in contemporary dispensational thought stem from this form. Second, these relatively recent and significant developments in dispensational scholarly circles (e.g., the progressive dispensationalism of Blaising and Bock) appear to have not yet reached or impacted the understanding of people at a local level of the church; the tenets of traditional dispensationalism continue to lie behind and inform the assumptions and beliefs of many Christian people.

This examination of dispensational hermeneutics will be limited in scope by making primary use of Charles C. Ryrie's *Dispensationalism* (published in 1995)—a revised and expanded version of his 1965 *Dispensationalism Today*. His view appears to be representative of the understanding of most normative dispensational thinkers.[4]

OVERVIEW OF DISPENSATIONAL PREMILLENNIALISM

A Brief Historical Overview

Premillennialism, vis-à-vis dispensational premillennialism, has been on the theological landscape since the early days of the Christian church, with second-century church fathers such as Papias and Justin Martyr believing in a premillennial return of Christ, that is, *prior* to the *millennium*—the thousand-year period mentioned only in Revelation 20.[5] While this is true, Alan Boyd discovered when researching Ryrie's claims to the historical longevity of dispensational thought—by appealing to the longer historicity of premillennialism—that the dominant understanding of the early church was more analogous to what is now known as amillennialism.[6] Boyd concluded his master's thesis on this research by stating, "It is the conclusion of this thesis that Dr. Ryrie's statement [premillennialism is the historic faith of the church] is historically invalid

---

4. As one views the writings of both proponents and critics of dispensationalism one finds in their discussions and footnotes repeated reference to either the early or latter version of Ryrie's book.

5. Mathison, *Dispensationalism: Rightly Dividing*, 13.

6. Boyd, "Dispensational Premillennial Analysis," discussed in Crenshaw and Gunn, *Dispensationalism Today*, 126.

within the chronological framework of this [Boyd's] thesis."[7] Papias and Justin Martyr, while holding to a premillennial return of Christ, should not be referred to as dispensational premillennialists; this designation is to be reserved for those holding to the much later and very different premillennial system of thought formulated by Darby in the nineteenth century. Philip Mauro states that

> The entire system of dispensational thinking . . . a system of doctrine that contradicts what has been held and taught by every Christian expositor from the beginning of the Christian era . . . suddenly made its appearance in the latter part of the nineteenth century.[8]

While this nineteenth-century development of dispensationalism is widely accepted, scholars such as Ryrie have sought to provide evidence of a longer history for dispensationalism by appealing also to the undeniable historicity of dispensational-like concepts espoused by others prior to Darby, who recognized that God has managed his dealings with the world in different ways in different eras—the broad meaning of the term "dispensation."[9] This appeal is misleading, however, as all systems of eschatological thought recognize this understanding of dispensations to one degree or another. Covenant theology, the primary rival of dispensationalism, recognizes at least two economies by which God has administered his world,[10] that is, the covenants of works and grace. Therefore, while crucial to Darby's system, dispensations are not, nor are they capable of being, the defining characteristic of the dispensational system due to this loose commonality with other views and because of disagreement within dispensational scholarship as to how many dispensations there are.[11] This inconsistency within dispensationalism

---

7. Boyd, "Dispensational Premillennial Analysis," cited in Gerstner, *Wrongly Dividing*, 10–11.

8. Mauro, *Gospel of the Kingdom*, 9, cited in Bass, *Backgrounds*, 15.

9. Ryrie, *Dispensationalism*, 63.

10. "Economy" is derived from the Greek *oikonomos*—translated as *dispensatio* in the Latin Vulgate—and refers to the administration or management of a household (*oikos*, meaning "house," and *nomos*, meaning "law").

11. Ryrie, *Dispensationalism*, 46. Ryrie writes, "Most dispensationalists see seven dispensations in God's plan (though throughout the history of dispensationalism they have not always been the same seven). Occasionally a dispensationalist may hold as few as four and some hold as many as eight. The doctrinal statement of Dallas Theological Seminary (Article V) mentions only three by name."

is remarkable in light of Ryrie's insistence that dispensational theology recognizes "definite and distinguishable" distinctions.[12] This raises the question: How can the dispensations be distinguishable and at the same time indistinguishable to the point of there being a multiplicity of views within dispensational scholarship regarding their number? It seems these *definite and distinguishable* dispensations must be in reality *indefinite and indistinguishable*.[13] This inconsistency does, however, raise some concerns as regards to the hermeneutical processes adopted by dispensationalist interpreters.

Ryrie admits, as he must, that "a person can believe in dispensations . . . without being a dispensationalist."[14] In fact, it is true that one can recognize dispensations *and* hold to a premillennial return of Christ and not be a dispensational premillennialist—the term therefore does not accurately reflect the *sine qua non* of the system known by that name.[15] Ironically, the foundational tenets of dispensational premillennialism, as derived from and including the system's hermeneutical principle, reside apart from it being dispensational and premillennial. It is these foundational tenets that make Darby's dispensationalism both a unique and a somewhat recent development in eschatological thought: uniqueness and recentness being further reasons to test the reliability of the interpretive principles of dispensationalism.[16]

Despite the above-noted irregularities, others such as Cyrus Ingerson Scofield (1843–1921) soon accepted Darby's system of thought. He then proceeded to intersperse dispensational annotations into his Scofield Reference Bible—first published in 1909 and followed by revisions in 1917 and 1967, the latter by others after his death. This initial endeavor was undertaken by Scofield despite his having no formal theological training. The Scofield Reference Bible soon became very popular and widespread among the Christian community with the result of disseminating the dispensational system of thought more quickly and

---

12. Ryrie, *Dispensationalism*, 32.

13. It is to some degree incongruous that Ryrie can claim that "Dispensationalism avoids confusion and contradiction." Ibid., 37.

14. Ibid., 38.

15. Ibid. Ryrie states, "Is the essence of dispensationalism in the number of dispensations? No, for this is in no way a major issue in the system."

16. As Ryrie notes, dispensationalism's newness does not imply wrongness. The crucial factor, he writes, is whether it is biblical. Ibid., 67. This writer agrees. However, the fact that this view was unheard of for the first eighteen-and-a-half centuries of the Christian era should cause one to at least bring some questions to examine its validity.

geographically further than perhaps even Darby could have imagined. Its popularity among the theologically uneducated meant that they could now easily understand eschatology—albeit in the dispensational manner—without the discipline of personal in-depth study and without the need to consult with other writers. The result: dispensationalism gained widespread, yet uncritical acceptance.[17] Lewis Sperry Chafer (1871–1952), who was influenced by Scofield's views, founded in 1924 Dallas Theological Seminary—a seminary that would aid the spread and acceptance of dispensationalism through dispensational scholars such as Walvoord and Ryrie.[18] Through Scofield's Bible and the writings of such people, dispensationalism has continued to shape the eschatological understanding of many people, churches, and denominations to the extent that it continues to hold great sway; its effects are presently impacting the lives of millions of people, both Christian and non-Christian. This is so despite the fact that today only a relatively small segment of Christian scholarship adheres to dispensationalism and that it was unheard of for the first eighteen-and-a-half centuries of the Christian church.[19]

A Brief System Overview

Dispensationalism, despite the presence of some internal disagreement, in its most common form regards human history as divided into seven periods (dispensations) of time, each administered by God using differing means to test human obedience according to some specific revelation of the will of God.[20] The present dispensation, the sixth—the period

17. Cox, *Examination of Dispensationalism*, 13.

18. Sizer, *Christian Zionism*, 119. "Dallas Theological Seminary, founded in 1924 by Lewis Sperry Chafer, one of Scofield's students, has probably accomplished more for the cause of dispensationalism and Christian Zionism than any other institution in the world. For nearly eighty years, through its faculty and students, Dallas has contributed to a proliferation of dispensational thinking, from the classic dispensationalism of Scofield and Chafer to the revised dispensationalism of Ryrie and Walvoord; the apocalyptic dispensationalism of Lindsey and LaHaye; the Messianic dispensationalism of Moishe Rosen and Arnold Fruchtenbaum; and the progressive dispensationalism of Craig Blaising and Darrel Bock."

19. Crenshaw and Gunn, *Dispensationalism Today*, 126. Gunn states that Alan Boyd (a fellow student of Gunn at Dallas Theological Seminary), in his master's thesis, explained his finding a lack of evidence of dispensationalist thought in the early church as "an example of the rapid loss of New Testament truth in the early church." Perhaps Boyd should have accepted that his research is more likely to prove that dispensationalism had never been conceived of in order to be lost. One can't prove the loss of something by discovering a lack of evidence for its prior existence.

20. Ryrie, *Dispensationalism*, 23.

between the first and second comings of Christ—is labeled the dispensation of grace. During this time God's purposes for Israel are postponed due to Israel's rejection of Jesus's offer of an earthly kingdom with himself as king. This dispensation will end with seven years of tribulation directed toward the Jewish people beginning immediately after the church has been raptured from the earth to meet Christ in the air, which will in turn allow God's purposes for Israel to resume. The great tribulation— the latter three-and-a-half years of the seven—will reach its climax by ending at Christ's second coming, at which time God will establish the seventh dispensation—the millennium, the kingdom of God. This will be a one-thousand-year period during which Christ will rule the earth from Jerusalem with the Jewish people as the principal nation. Central to the dispensational system, as can be seen from the above description (and figure 1), is the maintaining of a radical distinction between God's two peoples, Israel and the church.[21]

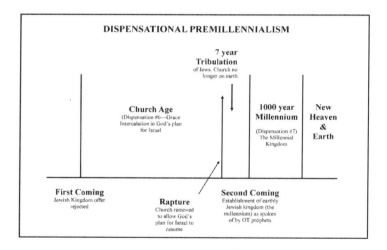

Figure 1: Dispensational Premillennialism

21. This view understands the Old Testament prophecies concerning a future glorious kingdom to have been postponed due to the Jewish rejection of Christ. For a counterview to the postponement theory, see N. T. Wright, *Climax of the Covenant*. As the title suggests, Wright proposes and demonstrates a climax of the Old Testament prophecies rather than a postponement.

THE DISPENSATIONAL HERMENEUTIC

A Literal Hermeneutic

The following lengthy quote from Crenshaw and Gunn (both ex-dispensationalists who trained at Dallas under Ryrie) detailing a description of the millennial period, by drawing from the writings of Walvoord and Pentecost, demonstrates the kind of conclusions that emerge from the dispensational hermeneutic:

> Dispensationalists are expecting literal and cataclysmic topographical changes in the land of Palestine. The Mount of Olives will be split in two to form a new valley running east and west. Mount Zion will be elevated above all the surrounding hills and the rest of Palestine will be transformed from a mountainous terrain to a great fertile plain. There will be an earthly Jerusalem from which Jesus will exercise his earthly Davidic rule and a heavenly Jerusalem hovering over Palestine from which Christ will co-reign with the church. The heavenly city will have a foundation 1500 miles square and will be either a cube, a pyramid, or a sphere that is 1500 miles high. The land in general and the temple area will be enlarged. The land will be redistributed to the twelve Jewish tribes, and the temple described in Ezekiel's vision will be built. The Old Testament priestly and Levitical orders will be reestablished under the sons of Zadok, and the offering of bloody sacrifices will be reinstituted. From the temple a small flow of water will come forth whose volume will progressively increase with distance from the temple, becoming a mighty river within a little over a mile from the temple. The river will flow south through Jerusalem and divide to flow west into the Mediterranean Sea and east into the Dead Sea, the Dead Sea being transformed into a fresh water body full of fish and surrounded by vegetation. Jerusalem will be the center of a world government system, national Israel will be exalted, and the Gentile nations will be subordinated as Israel's servants. This is the millennial situation as described by Dr. John F. Walvoord and Dr. J. Dwight Pentecost, who are influential and respected dispensational authorities.[22]

---

22. Crenshaw and Gunn, *Dispensationalism Today*, 132–33. It will be demonstrated later in this essay that despite the literal interpretation of Scripture evidenced in this quotation, there are occasions when dispensationalists, contrary to their commitment to a literalistic interpretive principle, are willing to interpret in a nonliteral manner. These occasions, as will be shown, appear to be in order to maintain a prior commitment to the dispensational belief system.

This quotation illustrates the dramatic conclusions derived from the literal hermeneutical method claimed by dispensationalist interpreters to be essential if we are to rightly understand the Scriptures. Pentecost writes that

> the original and accepted method of interpretation was the literal method, which was used by the Lord, the greatest interpreter, and any other method was introduced to promote heterodoxy. Therefore the literal method must be accepted as the basic method for right interpretation in any field of doctrine today.[23]

Pentecost's statement, while very strongly worded in a rather accusing manner, is however, debatable at almost every point in regard to its accuracy.[24] Despite this, his statement demonstrates precisely the vigor by which dispensationalists value their controlling interpretive principle. Any interpretive principle other than theirs is, according to Pentecost, introduced with the intention to promote unorthodox teaching. The entire dispensational system is claimed to be built on this *literal* interpretive methodology—equated by Ryrie to the grammatical-historical method[25]—and is claimed to be *consistently* applied to the text. This literal hermeneutical principle is one of the three indispensable conditions of dispensationalism listed by Ryrie, and consistency in the application of it, he writes, is what sets them apart from non-dispensational interpreters.[26] He states, "To be sure, literal/historical/grammatical interpretation is not the sole possession or practice of dispensationalists, but the *consistent use of it in all areas of biblical interpretation is*."[27] Consistency in its application, he says, "is the strength of dispensational interpretation."[28] That this interpretive principle is without doubt, for Ryrie, the core indispensable foundation of dispensationalism is evidenced when he declares that, "the first tenet of dispensationalism is that the Bible must

---

23. Pentecost, *Things to Come*, 33.

24. There are numerous occasions in the Gospels where Jesus appears to use nonliteral language. This will be considered later in this chapter.

25. Ryrie, *Dispensationalism*, 80.

26. Ibid., 38–41. The other two indispensable conditions are the distinction of Israel and the church, and the underlying purpose of God in the world regarded as "the glory of God." The latter being prominent also in non-dispensational thought negates this as a dispensational distinctive.

27. Ibid., 40 (emphasis added).

28. Ibid.

be interpreted literally"[29] and again that "consistent literalism is the basis for dispensationalism, and since consistent literalism is the logical and obvious principle of interpretation, dispensationalism is more than justified."[30] He further writes, "If plain or normal interpretation is the only valid hermeneutical principle, and if it is consistently applied, it will cause one to be a dispensationalist."[31] If these statements are accurate, then by Ryrie's own terms the validity of dispensationalism as a whole system of thought rests squarely on the literal principle of interpretation being able to withstand the critique of non-dispensational interpreters.

From this "consistent" literal interpretive principle Ryrie states that there flows a second indispensable condition that is the "most basic theological test of whether or not a person is a dispensationalist"; it is that Israel and the church must be kept distinct from each other.[32] This belief in the absolute separation of Israel and the church is fundamental to dispensationalism—equal in importance to literal interpretation—and at the same time constitutes its point of departure from historic Christian thought.[33]

This separation of Israel and church as two different people of God leads the dispensationalist to conclude that "God is pursuing two distinct purposes: one related to the earth with earthly people and earthly objectives involved which is Judaism; while the other is related to heaven with heavenly people and heavenly objectives involved, which is Christianity."[34] Each of these two, Israel and the church, have separate eternal destinies—Israel's is on earth, the church will be in heaven.[35] It should be noted that the recent development of progressive dispensa-

---

29. Ibid., 89.

30. Ibid., 90.

31. Cited in Crenshaw and Gunn, *Dispensationalism Today*, 234.

32. Ryrie, *Dispensationalism*, 39.

33. The Israel-church tenet will be examined in detail in chapter 2.

34. Ryrie, *Dispensationalism*, 39.

35. This radical distinction in this essential dispensational tenet appears to be counter to the global intent of God's promise to Abraham that from his seed blessing would be appropriated to all nations (Gen 12:1–3) and the emphasis in Ephesians that Gentile Christians are no longer strangers to the covenants of promise but are in fact fellow citizens with the Jews by becoming one new humanity in the place of two (Eph 2:11–22). Galatians states that there is no longer Jew or Greek for all are one in Christ, and if a person belongs to Christ they too are Abraham's offspring and therefore heirs of the promise (Gal 3:28–29).

tionalism rejects this aspect of classical dispensationalism. However, as stated earlier, the concern of this book is with the prior traditional system of dispensational thought that continues to shape the understanding of many Christian people, despite the more recent modifications by some dispensational scholars.

With this Israel-church distinction in mind, along with dispensationalists' claimed consistently applied literal interpretive principle, dispensationalists propose that all Old Testament prophecy concerning Israel must be fulfilled in the literal nation of Israel, in an exact literal manner. Therefore, there can be no fulfillment of Old Testament prophecy in the church; in fact, say dispensationalists, the Old Testament prophets knew nothing of the church age.[36] God's primary purposes are with Israel; however, due to the Jews' rejection of an earthly kingdom offer by Jesus at his first coming, the fulfillment of prophecy (i.e., the kingdom) was postponed until the millennial period. Consequently, the Christian church era that emerged as an outcome of this rejection is considered a parenthesis, or more accurately, an intercalation—a time period completely undisclosed in the Old Testament—in God's program for Israel.[37]

For dispensationalists, due to their literal hermeneutic, Israel means Israel, and the church means the church—never should the two be brought together. The offshoot of this is that when interpreting the Bible one must first determine if a text is for Israel or for the church. Poythress highlights this dichotomous hermeneutic by quoting Darby:

> First, in prophecy, when the Jewish church or nation (exclusive
> of the Gentile parenthesis in their history) is concerned, i.e.,

36. Cox, *Examination of Dispensationalism*, 38. This will be addressed later in this chapter, however it is of value to note that Peter in his Pentecost address sees a fulfillment of Joel's Old Testament prophecy in the then present outpouring of the Holy Spirit (Acts 2:14–40). On this occasion he tells the Jewish people present that the promise is for them and for all who are afar off, i.e., the nations (v. 39). This indicates clearly that Old Testament prophecy spoke of things pertaining to the church age contra the claim of dispensationalism. It also affirms the global nature of prophecies specifically spoken to Israel.

37. Crenshaw and Gunn, *Dispensationalism Today*, 133–36. A parenthesis is usually connected in some way to the surrounding context. An intercalation is a totally unconnected interruption. This theory again appears counter to the global nature of Gen 12:1–3 and the evident fulfillment of Old Testament prophecy within the very period labeled as an intercalation or parenthesis as noted above from the Joel/Acts promise and fulfillment theme of Acts 2.

when the address is directed to the Jews, there we may look for a plain and direct testimony, because earthly things were the Jews' proper portion. And on the contrary, where the address is to the Gentiles, i.e., when the Gentiles are concerned in it, there we may look for symbol, because earthly things were not their portion, and the system of revelation must to them be symbolical. When therefore facts are addressed to the Jewish church as a subsisting body, as to what concerns themselves, I look for a plain, common sense, literal statement, as to a people with whom God had *direct* dealing upon earth.[38]

This dichotomous hermeneutic eliminates all Old Testament prophecy spoken to Israel from having any application to the church—after all, it was addressing Israel. Further, this quote contains an additional statement regarding prophecy as being a domain where a non–plain symbolic interpretation is acceptable but only when not directed to Israel. This in turn raises several questions: Does the literal principle really determine the Israel-church distinction, as Ryrie says, or does a prior commitment to this distinction determine how one approaches and interprets the biblical text? Why is literal interpretation only permissible when prophets are addressing things that concern Israel, and not always permissible when speaking about Gentiles? (This gives the impression of an interpretive principle originating from a prior commitment to an already adhered-to system of belief in two peoples of God,[39] with some additional assumptions as to how God communicates with each of them.) According to Scofield, however, absolute literalness is found in prophecy, whereas symbols and figures are only to be found in Old Testament history,[40] despite the former genre of prophetic oracle being for the most part written in poetic form—a genre in which symbolism and nonliteral forms of expression are much more likely to be found. This principle of interpretation would appear to be, similar to Darby's above, overly presumptuous and without any literary basis to formulate

---

38. Poythress, *Understanding Dispensationalism*, 17. The 1948 restoration of Israel to land and nationhood provided for dispensationalists a historical verification of the literal interpretive method due to the dispensational belief in the earthly nature of promise for the nation. The significance accredited to this event by dispensationalists in support of their belief system has been convincingly refuted by Don K. Preston in his booklet *Israel: 1948 Countdown to Nowhere*.

39. Ibid., 78.

40. Ibid.

such an interpretive rule, and once again may imply a prior commitment to an already established set of beliefs.

It seems from the above that Darby and Scofield are at odds in respect to their interpretive approach as to when and when not to apply the literal principle of interpretation, despite the latter's heavy dependence on Darby's writings.[41] They are, further, both at variance with Ryrie who, as previously quoted, has claimed that the literal principle is consistently applied by dispensationalists in *all* areas of biblical interpretation.[42] The fact that three leading dispensational scholars each advocate conflicting guiding principles for the application of the literal interpretive principle should again be cause to question the reliability of dispensational interpretation and the theology that emerges from it.

Defining "Literal"

The first difficulty that appears when examining the validity of the dispensational literal principle of interpretation is the word *literal* itself. What does it mean? When should it be applied? It has already been observed that this latter question is answered in different ways within the dispensational scholarly circle. However, before it is applied to any text of Scripture one must first establish what is meant by "literal."

In defense of the interpretive principle upon which the dispensational system is built, Ryrie states that literal interpretation, "gives to every word the same meaning it would have in normal usage, whether employed in writing, speaking, or thinking." He refers to this as the "normal or plain interpretation" that is, interpretation "according to the received laws of language." He further equates his terms "normal" and "plain" with the grammatical-historical method of interpretation.[43]

Difficulty in understanding what is meant by "literal," even with Ryrie's definitions, still remains. His first definition of giving "to every word the same meaning it would have in normal usage" is susceptible to what Poythress has termed as "first thought meaning."[44] That is, the

---

41. Gerstner, *Wrongly Dividing*, 43.

42. Davis, "Hermeneutical Issues," no pages. Despite Ryrie's confidence, Davis perceives the "lack of consistency in definition and application of 'what is literal'" to be "a plaguing issue with dispensational hermeneutics."

43. Ryrie, *Dispensationalism*, 80. This chapter will later address factors related to grammatical-historical interpretation that appear to be ignored by Ryrie.

44. Poythress, *Understanding Dispensationalism*, 82.

meaning most likely to enter one's mind when a word is used in isolation from other words. This could be the meaning of a word as presented in a dictionary or a meaning influenced by the hearer's own circumstances. Someone in prison might understand the word "free" as meaning being freed from jail. For a bargain-hunting shopper it could mean getting something for nothing. Both are interpreting the word by normal everyday usage, yet the two are hearing it differently due to their differing life settings. What is normal or plain for one appears not to be normal or plain to another. When engaging in the task of biblical interpretation, all interpreters bring to the text a pre-understanding from their different contemporary cultures, their immediate life situations and experiences, and from their scope of knowledge or prior perception of the Bible. These each influence in varying degrees what is to them a "normal" or "plain" understanding of a text. Ryrie's definition is therefore unhelpful as we need more than words to understand the intended meaning; the culture, context (both literary and historical) of the original audience are also needed.[45] His term "the received laws of language"[46] is equally vague, speaking of laws that are untold and assumed rather than stated and proven. By equating his use of "normal" with the term "grammatical-historical" Ryrie is adopting a term well understood in hermeneutical studies; this clarifies to some degree what he intends by "normal" and "plain." Poythress describes grammatical-historical interpretation:

> In this type [of interpretation] one reads passages as organic wholes and tries to understand what each passage expresses against the background of the original human author and the original situation. One asks what understanding and inferences would be justified or warranted at the time the passage was written. This interpretation aims to express the meanings that the human authors express.[47]

Thus, when an interpreter utilizing the grammatical-historical method asks, "What does this mean?" the real question being brought to the text is "What *did* this mean to the original author and hearers/readers?" However, from what Poythress goes on to point out, Ryrie's equating this

---

45. Walton, *Lost World*, 9. "Language assumes a culture, operates in a culture, serves a culture, and is designed to communicate into the framework of a culture."

46. Ryrie is quoting Lange, *Commentary on Revelation*, 98.

47. Poythress, *Understanding Dispensationalism*, 84.

method with plain meaning is still unhelpful. "Sometimes," Poythress writes,

> the grammatical-historical meaning is not at all "plain" to us because we must work hard to reconstruct and appreciate the differences between then and now. Moreover, for lay dispensationalists the plain meaning will be the meaning that occurs to them in the context of their already existing knowledge of the prophetic system of dispensationalism.[48]

Ryrie's claim to use of the grammatical-historical method is commendable, but he limits the scope of the interpreter's use of this method by his insistence that they must apply to every word the same meaning it would have in normal usage. Such an insistence confines the interpreter to limitations that may or may not have been appropriate at the time of writing. Important as it is for interpreters to utilize the grammatical-historical method of interpretation by understanding as much as is possible the historical setting in which words were written, the interpreter must give equal weight to the word *grammatical* by asking how the words and sentences are used by the writer and in what way these words were understood by the readers who first read them. Was their normal everyday usage of words the same as contemporary readers' usage? Did their context and culture provide meaning and nuance that is not immediately apparent to twenty-first-century readers? Does the author intend the "normal," that is, the dictionary meaning or first-thought meaning, or does he use various literary tools such as metaphor or metonymy? Even Ryrie would allow for clear or obvious figures of speech, but what about the less obvious uses? Could a figurative literary form be obvious to the original readers/hearers yet not be obvious to the modern interpreter? Could a writer initiate a figurative use of a word that is not common at the time of writing but apparent in its literary context? The use of nonliteral language may be more evident at some times than it is at other times (e.g., dragons and horns as symbols in Revelation), and writers seldom give warning by saying, "Interpret with care, I'm using a metaphor here." Interpreters, such as Ryrie, who promote a flat rule of literal, normal, plain, or obvious meaning assume that a writer's use of words is obvious and agreeably plain in meaning to all. Further, they can fail to integrate

48. Ibid., 85.

much that is widely accepted practice in the field of hermeneutical studies. One such aspect of crucial importance is that of genre.[49]

Grant R. Osborne, in his comprehensive study in the field of hermeneutics, notes,

> The presence of genre is an important point in the debate as to whether one can recover the author's intended meaning. . . . Every writer couches his message in a certain genre in order to give the reader sufficient rules by which to decode that message.[50]

W. Randolph Tate, in his *Biblical Interpretation: An Integrated Approach,* echoes Osborne's view when he writes:

> The most plausible understanding of a text and its subsequent explication is best actualized when the reader has an adequate grasp of the literary genres and subgenres by which an author operates.[51]

Anthony C. Thiselton in *New Horizons in Hermeneutics* also emphasizes the importance of genre when he notes that,

> All texts presuppose code. . . . To make a mistake about the semiotic code, therefore, violates the text and distorts its meaning.[52]

Joel Green in his book specifically on the interpretation of prophecy says,

> Because of the diversity of literary forms, then, it is certainly too simplistic to assert a literalistic method as the one guiding rule of interpretation.[53]

Ryrie does acknowledge that the study of genre "promises a better understanding of the historical and cultural background of the Bible" as

---

49. The writer is aware of the enormous scope for possible discussion having raised the issue of genre, particularly with its implications as it relates to prophetic and apocalyptic literature. Such extensive discussion is, however, beyond the scope of this book. For the immediate purposes of this book it is sufficient to note the force by which hermeneutic scholars stress the importance of genre considerations as it relates to the interpretive task.

50. Osborne, *Hermeneutical Spiral,* 9.

51. Tate, *Biblical Interpretation,* 70.

52. Thiselton, *New Horizons,* 80–81.

53. J. Green, *How to Read Prophecy,* 40.

part of grammatical-historical interpretation but then he immediately states that,

> one of the pitfalls [of genre considerations] is to claim that "each genre represents truth in its own way and makes unique demands for how it should be read," and that "meaning is genre dependant."[54]

It appears that while Ryrie wishes to acknowledge the benefit of genre study as an important element of the grammatical-historical interpretive method he then seems to negate the very reason for that interpretive benefit. He does this in order to assert, counter to Green's warning, that the literal principle is sufficient as a single guiding rule of interpretation. Ryrie is at odds with current trends in hermeneutical studies by not acknowledging the significant influence that the literary conventions of the various genres have when seeking to understand written or oral communication. Further, he has failed to be clear in defining "literal" even when we interpret his words by adopting his own terms (normal/plain) for interpretation; his terms that were written using simple prose are not easily understood even by those who live in a similar time and culture to Ryrie. This in itself highlights the difficulty of hearing what an author is seeking to communicate to readers and also shows that the locus of meaning needs to be found by taking into consideration the whole process of literary communication—the author and his world, the form and content of the text (i.e., genre), and the culture, context, and pre-understanding of the intended readership.[55] The difficulty experienced in understanding clear meaning from Ryrie's words, written in the same historical times as his present readers but nonetheless being unclear in meaning and purpose, should caution interpreters to be slow to conclude what the "normal" or "plain" meaning is when interpreting a biblical text written a very long time ago and in very different historical and cultural settings to the present.

The use of grammatical-historical interpretive principles by dispensationalists is a commendable element of their interpretive method. However, it must be concluded that in itself the grammatical-historical method—especially with the further controls dispensationalists add to

---

54. Ryrie, *Dispensationalism*, 80, quoting Blaising and Bock, *Progressive Dispensationalism*, 77, and Osborne, *Hermeneutical Spiral*, 9.

55. Tate, *Biblical Interpretation*, xxv.

it—is inadequate as a hermeneutical method for establishing meaning. Poythress writes, "Grammatical-historical interpretation is only one moment in the total act of interpretation."[56] There are many other factors that the interpreter must take into account alongside and as part of this method when seeking to find the meaning of biblical passages.

There are other questions that need to be asked: Are dispensationalists faithful to their own rules of interpretation? Do they always interpret with a literal/normal meaning? Do they, as Ryrie insists they do, *consistently* apply this principle in *all* areas of biblical interpretation? Are there examples where New Testament authors do not adopt the literal "normal/plain sense" principle in their interpretation of Old Testament Scripture? To these issues this discussion now turns.

Testing Dispensational Literalism

ARE DISPENSATIONALISTS CONSISTENTLY LITERAL?

It was noted earlier that dispensationalism insists, due to a consistent literalism whereby one gives to each word the meaning it would have in normal usage, that when the Bible uses the word *Israel* it means Israel, that is, the physical nation. However, in the *Ryrie Study Bible*[57] notes for Galatians 6:16, Ryrie explains the meaning of the phrase "the Israel of God" in this way:

> *the Israel of God.* I.e., Christian Jews, those who are both the physical and spiritual seed of Abraham.

Ryrie has in this explanation given the word *Israel* a meaning that betrays the demands of his literal principle of interpretation. He has in fact redefined the meaning of the word *Israel* by restricting its referents to only those who are both bloodline descendants of Abraham and are Christians. Non-Christian Israelites and Israelites not physically of Abrahamic descent are excluded. This is not the normal or plain everyday use of the word *Israel*. Not only has he violated his own interpretive principle and his claim to the consistent application of it, he also appears not to have considered how the immediate literary context clarifies for readers how Paul is using the term "the Israel of God" in this instance—a meaning quite different to what Ryrie suggests. When

56. Poythress, *Understanding Dispensationalism*, 91.
57. *New American Standard Bible*, 1976, 1978.

the context provides meaning in this way we are not at liberty to supply a different meaning. Context reveals that believing Jews have already been included in the words "all who follow this rule."[58] To follow Ryrie's interpretation would have us read the verse as follows: Peace and mercy be upon Christian Jews and Christian Gentiles—that is, all who walk by this rule—and upon the Christian Jews. This makes no sense and in fact makes the phrase under discussion completely redundant. The sad irony here is that the passage containing this phrase is concerned to show that neither circumcision nor uncircumcision (i.e., being Israelite or non-Israelite) is of any relevance. For Ryrie to impose such a distinction is counter to the purpose of the text in that it sets up a distinction whereas the text seeks to remove such a distinction.

It seems that Ryrie's interpretation is concerned to maintain his commitment to the dispensational distinction between Israel and the church and yet to do so he has had to sacrifice his commitment to the basis of his belief system, that is, a consistently applied literal hermeneutic. It appears out of the question for Ryrie to consider the possibility that "Israel" in this context could be a reference to *all* believers—a legitimate understanding whereby the phrase functions as a clarifying descriptor of the "all who walk by this rule."[59] If Ryrie was to be faithful to the literal, normal, and everyday usage principle, he in fact should understand the word *Israel* as a reference to Israel the nation, but this would have the meaning of pronouncing blessing on Christian Israelites, Christian Gentiles, and upon "the Israelites"—yet "the Israelites" would include the Christian Israelites already mentioned. Again the phrase "the Israel of God" becomes unnecessary. Further, it would see Paul pronouncing blessing on the very people he has, in the context of the entire letter to the Galatians, excluded from blessing—that is, those who regarded circumcision as an identity marker of the people of God. In effect Paul would be extending a blessing to as many as walk by this rule (of circumcision not counting for anything) and as many as don't follow this rule (circumcision counts for something)—and would therefore be

---

58. Hoekema, *Bible and the Future*, 197.

59. The Greek word *kai* introducing the clause *kai epi ton Israēl tou theou* can be understood as meaning "even" as translated in the NIV. This interpretation seems preferable in light of the context and supports the idea of the phrase functioning as a further descriptor of the "all who walk by this rule." See Burge, *Jesus and the Land*, 82–84.

both nonsense and contrary to his entire line of reasoning.[60] The "normal usage" meaning is just not possible in this use of the word *Israel*. Its intended meaning or referent must be found by other considerations.

A further betrayal of Ryrie's literalism is seen in his actual definition of the term "Israel of God" in which he speaks of both the physical and spiritual seed of Abraham. By making this distinction of two kinds of seed Ryrie has permitted the word *seed* to have both a literal meaning *and* a nonliteral meaning. Is this being consistently literal in all areas of biblical interpretation? It does appear then that Ryrie himself is in fact inconsistent with the application of his literal method, that the dispensational commitment to two peoples of God has had some bearing on his interpretation and, in effect, demonstrates the dispensationalist's inability or perhaps unwillingness to adhere to a consistent application of literalism. There is, at least to some extent, a selective and inconsistent application of their hermeneutical principle.

Keith Mathison notes a different type of inconsistency by another well-known dispensationalist:

> John Walvoord . . . insists that when an Old Testament prophecy refers to Israel, it must mean the literal nation of Israel; but when the same prophecy speaks of other nations, such as Assyria or Philistia, it refers only to the land once inhabited by these nations. Whoever may be inhabiting these lands may fulfill these prophecies.[61]

Mathison concludes, "This is not consistent literalism."[62] There is no literary or logical reason for Walvoord to simply assert this interpretive rule and once again gives the appearance of selective literalism that is governed by a prior commitment to a controlling belief system.

A further example of Ryrie breaching his literal hermeneutic is seen in his notes for Matthew 24:34.[63] Here he states that the word "generation" can mean race or family, and he understands its use in Matthew 24:34 as referring to the Jewish race and its preservation in spite of persecution until the Lord comes. Matthew's prior and consistent use of the term "this generation" is without doubt referring to the people living at

---

60. Robertson, *Israel of God*, 40–46.
61. Mathison, *Dispensationalism: Rightly Dividing*, 6.
62. Ibid.
63. Ryrie, *Ryrie Study Bible*.

that time. It is a strange form of a consistent literal interpretive principle that applies a different meaning to a term than its writer's consistent usage. Whatever we may understand "this generation" to mean, Ryrie has not applied a normal, plain-sense, or everyday-usage meaning to the word and has once again acted counter to his claim of consistent literal interpretation.

O. T. Allis succinctly points out the inconsistent literalism of dispensationalism:

> The Book of Esther is nowhere cited in the New Testament. As the simple record of one of the most remarkable deliverances of God's people, it is a deeply impressive record of divine providence. But these simple lessons are not regarded as sufficient by Dispensationalist interpreters. Walter Scott, whom Scofield calls "the eminent Bible teacher," gives its typical significance as the following:
>
> "As to the typical bearing of the book Ahasuerus would represent the supreme Gentile authority, and Vashti, *beauty*, the professing church failing to show her beauty; she is then superseded by the Jewish bride, Esther, *star* (Ps. xlv.); while the wicked Haman, planning the destruction of Israel, and in the midst of his murderous purposes signally cut off, would as surely figure the conspiracy of the latter-day enemies of restored Israel (Ps. lxxxiii.); Mordecai would set forth our Lord head of His exalted people in the millennial future."[64]

Allis continues, "Whatever else may be said of this method of interpretation, it is certainly not literal."[65]

It must therefore be suggested that Ryrie's statement that "literal/ historical/grammatical interpretation is not the sole possession or practice of dispensationalists, but the *consistent use of it in all areas of biblical interpretation is*"[66] is inaccurate. Ryrie himself has shown that even he cannot abide by it. Further, when he writes that this consistent use of literal interpretation "is the strength of dispensational interpretation,"[67] he in fact weakens, rather than strengthens, the case for dispensationalism by his own lack of consistency in his application of this principle.

---

64. Allis, *Prophecy and the Church*, 21–22, quoting Walter Scott, *Bible Outlines*, 1879, republished 1930.

65. Ibid., 22.

66. Ryrie, *Dispensationalism*, 40 (emphasis added).

67. Ibid.

He instead shows that it is in reality impossible for any interpreter to adhere to absolute literalism and evidences that at times the intent of biblical writers requires a nonliteral understanding of their writings. It must also be suggested that if literal interpretation consistently applied is an indispensable building block of the dispensational system then that system of understanding Scripture is built on an interpretive foundation that cannot be sustained—even by its own advocates. Subsequently, dispensationalism may be considered doubtful as a reasonable form of understanding.

Do New Testament Writers Themselves Always Interpret Literally?

An understanding based on a strict literalism often caused Jesus to correct and occasionally to rebuke his hearers for their inability to hear what he had really said. In Matthew 16:6 Jesus said to his disciples, "Watch out, and beware of the yeast of the Pharisees and Sadducees." Taking Jesus literally, the disciples began to discuss the fact that they had no bread with them. Jesus responded to this by saying, "You of little faith, why are you talking about having no bread?" (v. 8). He then asks, "How could you fail to perceive that I was not speaking about bread?" (v. 11). It appears that Jesus did not intend his words be understood with strict literalism—in their normal everyday usage meaning—and he seems surprised that the disciples had done so. He then explains what he meant, and we read in verse 12 that they then understood that he was not telling them to guard against yeast as used in making bread, but against the teachings of the Pharisees and Sadducees. In this context *yeast* did not mean yeast, but instead its use and intention was to warn the disciples by means of metaphor and to provoke by the inherent imagery a response or action from them. It should be noted that Matthew has made no significant redactions to Mark's account of this event but appears, along with Mark, to accentuate the disciple's lack of ability to perceive the intent of Jesus's words more than Luke does in his Gospel (Mark 8:14–21; Luke 12:1). Their inability to hear the metaphor is thus highlighted in Matthew and Mark, reinforcing the need for interpreters today to interpret with the possibility of figures and with genre considerations in mind.

In John 2:19 Jesus says, "Destroy this temple, and in three days I will raise it up." His Jewish hearers replied, "This temple has been under construction for forty-six years, and will you raise it up in three days?"

(v. 20). Once again by understanding Jesus through giving to each of his words their *normal everyday* meaning his hearers had missed the point of what Jesus was saying. John explains that, "he [Jesus] was speaking of the temple of his body" and specifically with reference to his resurrection (v. 22).

It is clear from these examples drawn from within Scripture that to interpret in a woodenly literalistic manner, without consideration of (a) the circumstances surrounding the act and purpose of speaking, (b) the progress of the development of God's purposes,[68] (c) the use of various literary devices—particularly genre as noted above—and (d) the multifaceted conventions of language communication, can lead to a misunderstanding of what is said or written. The narrowing of the interpretive process to a single literalistic rule betrays the highly modernist nature of the dispensational hermeneutic. We can therefore propose that these biblical examples suggest that Ryrie's literal principle is unwarranted and in fact is not a principle that Jesus Christ adhered to in his use of language communication.[69] Even if a literalist agreed with my understanding of the above passages, the simple fact remains; interpreters cannot always apply to every word their everyday, normal-usage meaning in order to hear the message of a text. Literalism by Ryrie's definition is therefore unsustainable; the above-mentioned examples—examples that could be multiplied from within the Bible—won't allow for such a rigid principle of interpretation. The temple example from John 2 also highlights the fact that Jesus took an Old Testament motif and reinterpreted it in light of himself. The temple took on greater meaning in the person of Jesus Christ, thereby indicating a fluidity or development in meaning within the context of progressive revelation. To continue to understand temple as in the Old Testament understanding was to miss all that it had and would come to mean as God's redemptive purpose was unfolding in the world. Throughout the New Testament is a pervading continuity between the story of Israel's history, the person of Jesus Christ, and the emerging global church that validates a hermeneutical principle of progressive development whereby many Old Testament themes take on an enlarged meaning.

Paul, in his first letter to the Corinthian church, states that the gospel, which he proclaims to the Gentiles, is "in accordance with the Scriptures" (1 Cor 15:3–4).[70] Consequently, Paul sees continuity between

---

68. Osborne, *Hermeneutical Spiral*, 11.

69. Contra Walvoord's statement quoted above, p. 8.

70. Compare Hays and Green, "Use of the Old Testament by New Testament Writers," 222.

Israel's story recorded in those Scriptures and the inclusion of Gentiles as they respond to the gospel. Likewise, in the second chapter of Acts, Peter recounts Israel's history by way of explaining how this history leads to the Christ event and the fulfillment of Joel's prophecy (Joel 2). This pattern stressing continuity and development of Israel's history in the events surrounding Christ and the emerging first century church is repeated by Phillip in Acts chapter 6, Stephen in Acts 7, and Paul in Acts 13. The Old Testament was interpreted by these early Christians in light of Christ's life, death, and resurrection. These recent historical events advanced and expanded their understanding of the ancient writings of Judaism.[71] It is reasonable to conclude from the New Testament that the early church adopted a Christological hermeneutic as they now read and interpreted the Old.[72] Matthew in his Gospel frequently makes use of fulfillment formulae, for example, "This was to fulfill what had been spoken through the prophet Isaiah . . ." (Matt 8:17), or "This took place to fulfill what had been spoken through the prophet . . ." (Matt 21:4). This linking of present events to the prophets' words indicates that Matthew also saw a continuation, indeed a fulfillment, of Israel's story rather than its postponement as proposed in dispensational thought. Things spoken by the Old Testament prophets were being brought to pass in Matthew's time as they are brought to their *telos* in Christ.

Therefore, a generally accepted and safe principle of interpretation is that of *analogia fidei* with the correlative of progressive revelation—to allow Scripture to interpret Scripture.[73] In view of this unfolding progressive nature of biblical revelation it seems reasonable to permit the New Testament to enlighten our understanding of the Old Testament. Jesus himself stated the Old Testament in its entirety spoke of him.

> Oh, how foolish you are, and how slow of heart to believe *all* that the prophets have declared! Was it not necessary that the Messiah should suffer these things and then enter into his glory?" Then beginning with *Moses* and *all the prophets*, he interpreted to them the things about himself in *all the scriptures*. (Luke 24:25–27, emphasis added)

---

71. Ibid., 231.

72. Snodgrass, "Use of the Old Testament in the New," in *NT Criticism*, 411.

73. Osborne, *Hermeneutical Spiral*, 273.

The Christ event in history therefore should shape an understanding of the Old Testament that Jesus said was about himself. That which spoke of him (the Old Testament) can be more fully understood now that Christ has come in order to fulfill the law and the prophets (Matt 5:17). Many of the institutions and themes of the Old Testament come to a heightened significance in the New Testament and find their ultimate or fuller sense of meaning as Christ brings fulfillment to them.

How then do New Testament writers understand and make use of the Old Testament? Do they apply a consistently literal principle of interpretation? One biblical example often referred to when discussing the literal approach of dispensationalism is the words of Amos 9:11–12 as quoted by James/Luke in Acts 15. In Amos the passage reads:

> On that day I will raise up the booth of David that is fallen, and repair its breaches, and raise up its ruins, and rebuild it as in the days of old; in order that they may possess the remnant of Edom and all the nations who are called by my name, says the Lord who does this.

When reading these verses from Amos at face value there appears to be little reason to expect anything other than a physical rebuilding of David's booth. However, in Acts 15:15–17 James states that the present (i.e., at the time James spoke) incoming of Gentiles (the "rest of humanity," TNIV) into the people of God through the ministry of Peter, Paul, and Barnabas is in agreement (*sumphōneō*) with these words of Amos. "In the NT *sumphōneō* means 'to correspond,' 'to be at one,' 'to agree.'"[74] James's use of this word suggests that there is a complete harmony (symphony) between what Amos the prophet said would happen and what was in fact happening.[75] It appears that "booth" (house) is not a reference to the dwelling place of David but a reference to the people of the kingdom. The connectedness between the events taking place in James's time and the words of Amos is clear—people from the nations are being incorporated into the people of the true Davidic king. There is a direct

74. Betz, "συμφωνέω," 1292.

75. McConville, *Exploring the Old Testament*, 176. James (using the Septuagint translation) applied Amos 9:11–12 to Jesus (the son of David) and Paul's ministry to the Gentiles ("Edom" and "humanity" have the same Hebrew consonants). The promise to restore the fortunes of Israel and David is not fulfilled in a literal manner with the house of David ruling over a restored empire. McConville points out that the promise "is reinterpreted. Edom is no longer singled out, rather the focus falls on the 'rest of humanity,' and the prophecy becomes a prophecy of the world-wide salvation in Christ."

correspondence of the two; therefore, James equates the present events as being fulfillment of Amos's words. In doing so he has interpreted Amos in a nonliteral manner and therefore establishes within the text of Scripture itself an interpretive principle that is in direct contradiction to Ryrie's literalism.

It should also be noted from this example that James is willing to attribute the fulfillment of the prophet's words within the church age despite the dispensational insistence that what is spoken to national Israel must be fulfilled in national Israel. James allows for a fulfillment in the church as Gentiles come to share in its life. It is therefore appropriate to reason that the intended meaning of Amos 9:11–12 included meaning as nuanced by the further revelation of Acts 15:15–17—a meaning that may not be apparent by use of the literal-grammatical-historical method without the proviso of allowing for the nuances of later New Testament revelation to inform our understanding of the Old Testament text.[76] The nonliteral fulfillment of the Amos prophecy, originally couched in language familiar to its first hearers, shows both a connectedness with the expectation but also an exceeding of that expectation. The fulfillment surpassed that which a literal understanding may expect. Joel Green's comment is helpful,

> Given in particular, historical circumstances, prophecy uses words and ideas appropriate to its day. A different historical situation at the time of fulfillment, however, may involve a realization in updated terms beyond the literal meaning of the original prediction.[77]

Despite this evident dimension as regards the interpretation of prophecy, Walvoord writes that, "James was not saying the church fulfills the promises to Israel in Amos 9:11–12. He was saying that since Gentiles will be saved in the yet-to-come Millennium, they need not become Jews in the Church."[78] Walvoord has allowed his literalism and tenets of his dispensational system of belief (especially the distinction of two peoples of God, and the idea of a future millennial reign) to attribute the fulfillment of Amos's words to a time future to James's time—to a one-thousand-year period of time that, it is important to note, is not

76. Davis, "Hermeneutical Issues," no pages.

77. J. Green, *How to Read Prophecy*, 104. Green proceeds to provide a helpful illustration of this principle.

78. Walvoord, "Amos 9:12," no pages.

mentioned in either Amos or Acts—and then to read supposed implications of that future fulfillment back into the church age. That is, because Gentiles will be saved in a future millennium, Paul's Gentile converts don't need to become Jews.

The 1917 revision of the Scofield Bible has this as a heading for these verses in Amos:

> Future kingdom blessing (1) The Lord's return and the re-establishment of the Davidic monarchy.

This heading points its readers to understand Amos as speaking of Christ's return and a supposed subsequent one-thousand-year reign of Christ on earth, neither of which is mentioned, and so to conclude this meaning is, as Walvoord has done, to allow the dispensational system to govern how the passage is understood. By including this heading between the previous verses and those under discussion, Scofield has predisposed readers to understanding the passage in a manner consistent with dispensational thinking. No longer can they approach these verses without this understanding of its meaning in mind. This has been the subtle influence of the Scofield Bible. Readers are influenced by Scofield's interpretive additions within the pages of the biblical text. What this Amos passage does speak of is restoration. How is this restoration worked out? Acts 15 tells readers how (this is a different understanding than that demonstrated by Scofield's heading) and thereby highlights the errors of a strict literalism and of failing to allow the New Testament to inform one's understanding of the Old Testament.

CHAPTER CONCLUSION

We can say that the literalistic hermeneutic of dispensationalism as defined and advocated by Ryrie warrants critique. Is it really a reliable principle by which to interpret Scripture? It was noted earlier that Ryrie stated, "consistent literalism is the basis for dispensationalism, and since consistent literalism is the logical and obvious principle of interpretation, dispensationalism is more than justified,"[79] and "plain or normal interpretation is the only valid hermeneutical principle."[80] Ryrie, by such statements, is making bold claims, claims that categorically place the

---

79. Ryrie, *Dispensationalism*, 90.

80. Cited in Crenshaw and Gunn, *Dispensationalism Today*, 234.

viability of dispensationalism squarely on a consistently applied literal hermeneutic. However, despite such bold claims, the discussion above has shown the following:

1. Consistent literalism is in fact not the logical and obvious principle of interpretation. Neither is it the "only valid hermeneutical principle" as seen in the Gospels and the New Testament usage of Old Testament Scripture, as well as from other studies in the field of hermeneutics.

2. The terms "normal," "plain," and "everyday usage" as used to describe the literal method of interpretation increase the potential for eisegesis—reading meaning into rather than out of the text—due to the influence of a reader's contemporary culture, life circumstances, and the degree and nature of one's pre-understanding. These defining terms open the way for the imposition onto the biblical text an alien framework of understanding—such as the dispensational system.

3. There is substantial disagreement within dispensational scholarship as to when the literal approach should be applied. Ryrie says always, Walvoord says in prophecy directed only to Israel, and Scofield specifies in prophecy but not always in history. If this literal principle is the foundational element for the development of the dispensational viewpoint, then it would seem reasonable to expect a greater consensus among dispensational scholars regarding its application.

4. It is equally apparent that, despite the above point, Ryrie's insistence that dispensationalists consistently apply the literal principle in all areas of biblical interpretation is untenable. All interpreters, including dispensationalist interpreters (even Ryrie himself), interpret the Bible in a nonliteral manner at times—often, it appears, in order to fit in with prior commitments to dispensational tenets and at times counter to the essential purpose of a passage. It has been seen that Ryrie is willing to allow a single word to have both a literal *and* a nonliteral meaning in order to maintain his Israel-church distinction, therefore invalidating his consistent literalism. Walvoord is happy to attribute literalism when prophets speak of Israel but to allow nonliteral interpretations when speaking of

other nations. Both these dispensational scholars are, it seems, inconsistent literalists, thus significantly weakening the validity of their own foundational interpretive criteria for the theological position they seek to construct and uphold.

5. New Testament writers, as shown in the Acts 15 example above, do not consistently interpret using the literal principle as described by Ryrie when they make use of Old Testament passages. Such evidence within the Bible itself of an interpretive principle counter to that which Ryrie proposes suggests that as an overarching principle of interpretation literalism is inadequate.

6. In the Gospel narratives alone, literalism can be shown to be inadequate on a number of occasions.

7. If the principle of consistent literalism is a defining hallmark of dispensationalism and the central principle upon which the dispensational system is built, then the dispensationalists' lack of consistency in its application must call into question the system of thought that is derived from that principle.

8. The second indispensable dispensational condition of a distinct separation between Israel and the church, which, as Ryrie states, flows from the literal interpretive principle, must therefore be potentially invalid. If this is correct the key tenets of the dispensational system that stem from that distinction are also brought into the arena for questioning. Dispensational timelines of God's future purposes depend on the validity of the distinction between an earthly people (Israel) and a heavenly people (the church). We will consider this point in greater detail in chapter 2.

9. Old Testament prophecy spoken to Israel can at times find its fulfillment in the church—as seen in the Amos/Acts example above. This suggests a connectedness between the two groups rather than an absolute separation such as proposed by dispensationalists. This same example also reveals that the Old Testament prophets spoke of things concerning the church age and so demonstrates that the church is not an intercalation interrupting God's plan for Israel but is included as the focus of his redemptive work. Classic dispensational interpreters, however, do not believe that the prophets spoke of this age; it was unforeseen and is a parenthesis in time that will

end with God's resuming his purposes with Israel. This claim has important implications for the interpretation of Old Testament prophetic passages and is directly related to the literal principle.

10. Dispensational literalism fails to take into consideration many aspects that are both necessary and widely accepted practice in the field of hermeneutics. Hermeneutics within dispensationalism is governed by the one rule of normal and/or plain meaning consistently applied and as a consequence neglects the value of many crucial elements necessary for the formation of an appropriate interpretation of a written text. By reducing interpretation to a single principle, dispensationalism has to some degree declared many hermeneutical principles commonly applied to other literary works as irrelevant to the interpretation of the Bible. This inevitably creates a false framework for understanding and perhaps equates to constructing a set of interpretive principles in order to achieve a pre-desired result.

It was noted at the outset of this chapter that dispensationalism has gained a considerable degree of acceptance within congregational Christian thought, but that the majority of those within scholarly circles question its legitimacy as a system of understanding. Much of its early acceptance has been attributed to the widespread use and influence of the Scofield Reference Bible. However, perhaps its popularity may also be due to the apparent simplicity of the dispensational hermeneutical principle along with the sense of the immediacy and relevance of Scripture to a reader's context or immediate future that emerges from that principle. The principle—interpret using the normal meaning of words—has the appearance of being reasonable, uncomplicated, and relatively simple to apply, and therefore attractive as a principle to work from. However, as has been seen above, communication, whether verbal or written, is not necessarily straightforward so as to allow a single principle to govern its interpretation. The simplicity of one's interpretive principle does not necessarily imply its correctness, nor does it mean that it can be consistently applied without encountering complications as noted above.

Comprehensive studies in the field of hermeneutics, such as those noted earlier by Green, Osborne, Tate, and Thiselton have shown compellingly that a single literal interpretive principle claimed to be consistently applied to all areas of biblical interpretation is insufficient if one is to be comprehensive and careful when seeking to understand the biblical writings in their various genres along with the complexities of the conventions that govern them. Bearing in mind all that is deemed to be necessary practice concerning the interpretation of the biblical genres, a one-size-fits-all principle is too restrictive and places inappropriate boundaries around the interpretive task. In light of the effort required to participate in such a careful and thorough study, it is understandably tempting to resort to a simpler interpretive principle such as that proposed by dispensationalism—yet in the end the cost appears to be greater than the gain. Ultimately, that cost may well be the potential loss of truth and the subsequent correlative of living the life of faith based on what may in fact be a nonbiblical worldview.

The inadequacies of the dispensational hermeneutical principle enumerated above suggest that literalism is profoundly problematic as a basis from which to construct a biblically sound eschatological understanding, and conversely they call attention to the need for a constructive alternative. A better interpretive framework for approaching and understanding the text of Scripture, especially the prophetic and apocalyptic books that form much of the dispensationalist eschatological comprehension, is necessary.

2

Who Is Israel? A Discussion of Dispensational and Non-Dispensational Perspectives

THE PREVIOUS CHAPTER DREW conclusions concerning the literal hermeneutical principle of normative dispensationalism as advocated by scholars such as Ryrie, Walvoord, and Scofield. It proposed and demonstrated that the strict literalistic approach to biblical interpretation adopted by such scholars appears to be profoundly deficient as a principle by which to understand Scripture. Despite this, it is a principle that these three dispensational scholars regard as essential to the formation of a dispensational theology, though each suggests conflicting views regarding its appropriate application. My conclusion was that the strict literalism of classical dispensationalism appears to be overly simplistic by reducing interpretation to a single rule of literalism and by failing to take seriously the implications of the diversity of literary genres, the nature of progressive revelation,[1] the use of the Old Testament by New Testament writers, the findings of comprehensive studies in the field of hermeneutics, and last yet most importantly, the significance that the person and work of Christ have for understanding the Old Testament Scriptures.

Regardless of the many apparent deficiencies inherent in a literalist interpretive methodology, Ryrie, as has been noted, claims that a literal approach is the "logical and obvious principle of interpretation."[2] This *plain* or *normal* principle when consistently applied will, according to

---

1. As a system dispensationalism is built on an understanding of progressive revelation as each dispensation builds on the previous. However, it seems that the church age dispensation is an anomaly in that it interrupts the progression of God's purpose for Israel. The seventh dispensation—the millennium—appears to revert back to Old Testament forms including the sacrificial system. In this way dispensationalism fails to take seriously the forward movement of progressive revelation.

2. Ryrie, *Dispensationalism*, 90.

Ryrie, "cause one to be a dispensationalist."[3] We further noted his saying, "As basic as one believes normal interpretation to be, and as consistently as he uses it in interpreting Scripture, to that extent he will of necessity become a dispensationalist."[4] However, if the literal interpretive method that is so crucial in the formation of the dispensational system is questionable (as I have shown), then the dispensational tenets that emerge from that interpretive principle must be similarly doubted. One of these key tenets will be considered in this chapter.

Ryrie states, as one of the three *sine qua nons* of dispensationalism, that "a dispensationalist keeps Israel and the church distinct." He notes also that "this is probably the most basic theological test of whether or not a person is a dispensationalist. . . . The one who fails to distinguish Israel and the church consistently will inevitably not hold to dispensational distinctions; and one who does will." He further states that this separation of Israel and the church is the "essence of dispensationalism."[5] Dispensationalist Stanley D. Toussaint writes, "If the church and Israel become so blurred in dispensationalism that there is no separation between them, dispensationalism will become as extinct as the pitied dodo bird."[6] This Israel-church distinction, as emphasized in these statements from dispensational writers, is therefore to be regarded without doubt as *the* essential element of dispensational thought. Without this distinction there would not be a dispensational system. As the literal hermeneutic (also one of Ryrie's three indispensable conditions) is regarded as essential in the formulation of dispensationalism, the absolute distinction between Israel and the church is its foremost indispensable belief upon which all other dispensational tenets depends.[7] The purpose of this

3. Ibid., 20.

4. Ibid.

5. Ibid., 39, 41.

6. Toussaint, "Israel and the Church," 227.

7. The crucial nature of Israel in dispensational theology is perhaps nowhere more clearly evident than in the title of a book by Arnold G. Fruchtenbaum. His naming of his book *Israelology: The Missing Link in Systematic Theology* shows (according to Fruchtenbaum) the importance of understanding Israel as natural Israel for the development of a dispensational theology. This author recognizes that Fruchtenbaum's work, a work drawing heavily on Chafer, Ryrie, Walvoord, and other dispensational scholars, is a significant work counter to the proposition to be developed in this chapter. Despite this, it will not be directly referred to due to his view being consistent with the overall dispensational perspective of his Dallas Theological Seminary teachers (especially Ryrie as he dedicates the book to him). His view will in effect be challenged within the

chapter is to examine this key tenet of dispensational understanding and suggest an alternative answer to the question Who is Israel?[8]

This question is a crucial one to answer. How one understands "Israel" as employed in the biblical narrative and who it is that constitute this people will shape much of one's eschatological thought. It is therefore essential, if one is to arrive at a biblical eschatological understanding, to consider the outcome that a literalistic method of interpretation has on this issue. The outcome of dispensational literalism in answer to this question, as will be shown, leads to a conclusion very different from that of historic premillennial, amillennial, and postmillennial thought—a conclusion therefore that is at odds with historic Christian understanding.

IMPLICATIONS OF THE WHO IS ISRAEL? QUESTION

Who is Israel? From this question further questions related to dispensational beliefs arise: Is there to be, in Jerusalem, a one-thousand-year period of Christ's earthly rule (the millennium) after his return and before the eternal state and in which Israel will play a predominant role? Will there be during these one thousand years a rebuilt temple in Jerusalem in which, as Thomas Ice asserts, "all that was prescribed and initiated in the Old Testament ceremonial and ritual activities *will come to completion and find their fullest meaning*?"[9] Does God have a future special purpose for Israel as a nation as distinct from his purposes for the church? If so, what does this mean for both the present and future of the Christian church? Is the church to be at-any-moment raptured out of the earth in order for God's purpose for Israel to resume? These are important questions. How we answer these questions is entirely dependent on how we answer the first: Who is Israel? The answer to this question will in turn directly affect to some extent the manner in which Christians live in the present. Many Christians conduct their lives in a way that is governed by

overall presentation of a non-dispensational view.

8. I am aware that the more recent progressive dispensationalism such as advocated by Darrel Bock and Craig Blaising has moved from normative or classical dispensational understanding of this issue. The focus of this work is to describe and evaluate the normative dispensational understanding. The teaching from this view (especially through books such as the popular Left Behind series) still very much influences the understanding of a substantial proportion of the Christian population.

9. Preston, *Israel: 1948 Countdown*, 9 (emphasis added), quoting Ice and Demy, *Prophecy Watch*, 256.

their understanding of both Israel and who they are as Christian people. Are Christians *the* people of God, or are they just one of God's peoples alongside the nation of Israel? What is God's purpose for the Christian in relation to his purpose for Israel? Again, how one answers such questions affects how life is lived as Christian people today.

The ramifications of the Israel-church distinction advocated by dispensationalists are not only potentially enormous but are already enormous in reality. This is true not just for the individual Christian or for the church as a whole, but for all humanity—Christian and non-Christian alike. American politics concerning the nation of Israel have been and continue to be significantly shaped by dispensational beliefs concerning that nation. The May 2003 issue of *Time* magazine reveals that George W. Bush appeared to be under pressure from dispensational teachers regarding U.S. involvement in the Middle East.[10] Condoleezza Rice, the then U.S. National Security Advisor, likewise in 2003, apparently called on dispensationalist Jack Van Impe as an adviser. Van Impe wrote regarding this invitation that, "He [George W. Bush] will know exactly what is going to happen in the Middle East and what part he will have under the leading of the Holy Spirit of God."[11] United States government consultation with dispensationalists is not a new phenomenon. Hal Lindsey acted as a consultant to the Pentagon after his publication of

10. "Today the most influential lobbying on behalf of Israel is being done by a group not usually seen as an ally of the largely Democratic Jewish community: Evangelical Christians. . . . The White House is getting the message. At a meeting on April 10, sources tell *Time*, Senate minority leader Trent Lott informed Bush that Republicans were under increasing pressure from the religious right to back Sharon. The next day, as Secretary of State Colin Powell headed to the Middle East, a group of Evangelical leaders led by the Rev. Jerry Falwell and former presidential candidate Gary Bauer sent Bush a letter demanding that the Administration 'end pressure' on Sharon to withdraw from the West Bank. After Falwell adjured his followers to do the same, the White House was flooded with calls and e-mails. The next day, sources say, senior presidential aides phoned Falwell to reassure him that Bush stood behind Sharon." Ratnesar, "The Right's New Crusade," *Time*, May 6, 2003.

11. "I believe he [George W. Bush] is a wonderful man," Van Impe responded, and goes on to say, "I was contacted a few weeks ago by the Office of Public Liaison for the White House and by the National Security Advisor Condoleezza Rice to make an outline. And I've spent hours preparing it. I will release this information to the public in September, but it's in his hands. He will know exactly what is going to happen in the Middle East and what part he will have under the leading of the Holy Spirit of God. So, it's a tremendous time to be alive." Jeannette Walls, "Is Bush Getting Apocalyptic Advice?" no pages. Van Impe is an ardent dispensationalist providing daily prophecy updates on his "Bible Prophecy Portal of the Internet" website: http://www.jvim.com.

The Late Great Planet Earth in 1970.[12] Both Presidents Jimmy Carter and Ronald Reagan were pro-Israel and opened the way for dispensational consultation.[13] "In the last forty years, three Christian leaders, each given a White House platform by Reagan, have probably achieved more than any others in ensuring American foreign policy remains resolutely pro-Zionist. They are Jerry Falwell, Pat Robertson, and Hal Lindsey."[14]

During the latter part of the 1800s William E. Blackstone, an enthusiastic disciple of John Darby (the father of dispensational thought) had a significant influence on American politics. Sizer notes that

> In March 1891, Blackstone lobbied the US President, Benjamin Harrison with a petition signed by no less than 413 prominent Jewish and Christian leaders including John and William Rockefeller. The petition called for an international conference on the restoration of the Jews to Palestine. The petition, which became known as the Blackstone Memorial, offered this solution:
> 'Why not give Palestine back to them [the Jews] again? According to God's distribution of nations it is their home, an inalienable possession from which they were expelled by force'[15]

President Bill Clinton in a 1994 speech affirmed the ongoing influence of dispensational thought in America's political position when he echoed Blackstone's sentiments, saying, "If you abandon Israel, God will never forgive you. . . . it is God's will that Israel, the biblical home of the people of Israel, continue forever and ever," and "your [Israel's] journey is our journey, and America will stand with you now and always."[16]

Important aspects of the world political scene have been and continue to be very much influenced by how such advisors and politicians understand God's purposes for Israel. The past and present track record of significant political and world-impacting events, the financial cost reaching into many billions of dollars, and the price paid in human suffering and loss of life is real; the future appears set to maintain this reality.[17]

---

12. Sizer, "Christian Zionism: True Friends of Israel?" no pages.

13. Ibid.

14. Sizer, *Christian Zionism*, 89.

15. Sizer, "Christian Zionism: Misguided Millennialism," no pages.

16. Robertson, *Israel of God*, 1.

17. Burge, *Whose Land?* 161. Burge states that America supplies Israel with $3.5 billion per year in aid and has sold them over $7.4 billion in arms.

Britain, like America, has also been significantly influenced by the dispensational understanding of Israel and its future. Sizer notes with regard to Lord Shaftesbury (1801–1885) that

> Zionism would probably have remained simply a religious ideal were it not for the intervention of a handful of influential aristocratic British politicians who came to share the theological convictions of Darby and his colleagues and translated them into political reality. One in particular, Lord Shaftesbury . . . *single-handedly translated the theological positions of Henry Finch, and John Nelson Darby into a political strategy.*[18]

While other political motivations may well have influenced the writing of this declaration, David Fromkin writes that "Biblical prophecy was the first and most enduring of the many motives that led Britons to want to restore the Jews to Zion."[19]

It is, therefore, imperative that Christians give careful thought to the Israel-church issue and seek to come to a biblical understanding of this key tenet of dispensationalism.[20] The influence of dispensationalism that permeates individual, church, and political thought through both written and electronic media continues to be substantial while the view presented is often uncritically accepted as biblical truth. That this understanding influences the thought and manner of life of many Christians is frequently evidenced by strong, and at times fanatical, support for present-day Israel and sadly with little thought given to its corollary of oppression and injustice toward Palestinians who are equally loved by God, many of whom are our brothers and sisters in Christ. The forcefulness by which many Christians are pro-Israel—and, by implication, anti-Palestinian—can be heard in the following statement by John Hagee, founder of Christians United for Israel; "For twenty-five, almost twenty-six years now, I have been pounding the evangelical community over television. The Bible is a very pro-Israel book. And if a Christian admits, 'I believe the Bible,' I can make him a pro-Israel supporter or *they will have to denounce their faith.* So I have the Christians over a barrel you might say."[21] Ironically, fellow

18. Sizer, "Christian Zionism: Misguided Millennialism," no pages.

19. Fromkin, *Peace to End All Peace*, 298.

20. Robertson, *Israel of God*, 2.

21. One Jerusalem conference call with John Hagee, January 25, 2007; cited April 19, 2010, online: http://www.onejerusalem.org/2007/01/audio-bloggers-conference-call-8.php located at 14:13–14:40 minutes on file (emphasis added).

American John J. Mearsheimer, an internationally renowned professor of political science, made this statement in a speech delivered on April 30, 2010, at The Palestine Center in Washington, DC, "the Israel lobby is effectively helping Israel commit national suicide. Israel, after all, is turning itself into an apartheid state, which, as Ehud Olmert has pointed out, is not sustainable in the modern era."[22] Fervor such as heard in Hagee's words, along with the amount of publicity through various forms of media and the widespread acceptance of a dispensational view concerning Israel, however, does not necessarily imply correctness. This chapter seeks to present in a descriptive manner the normative dispensational viewpoint, to critically assess it, and as a consequence, to form some conclusions as to the validity of the dispensational perspective regarding their answer to the Who is Israel? question.[23]

THE PEOPLE OF GOD: THE NORMATIVE
OR CLASSIC DISPENSATIONAL VIEW

As a result of utilizing the literal principle of interpretation, the normal or classic dispensational view[24] concludes that in biblical usage "Israel means Israel."[25] That is, when the word *Israel* is used in Scripture, it is always, without exception, a reference to the literal physical nation of Jewish people. With this statement John Walvoord specifically upholds the validity of the literal interpretive principle and affirms that there is by no means any correlation or continuation of Israel as the people of God revealed in the Old Testament with the church as a people of God

22. Mearsheimer, "Future of Palestine," no pages.

23. I will not be addressing the "British-Israel" theory which understands that the Anglo-Saxons stemmed from the ten tribes of the Assyrian-induced exile and that the British monarchy is the continuation of the throne of David. This theory, while still held to by some, is generally considered to be without any reliable evidence. An early edition of the *Encyclopedia Britannica* notes, "The theory [of British-Israelism] . . . rests on premises which are deemed by scholars—both theological and anthropological—to be utterly unsound." (*Encyclopaedia Britannica*, 11th ed. [1910] 2:31); cited in Greer, "British-Israelism," no pages.

24. The terms "normative" and "classic" are borrowed from Ryrie. These are his terms by which he labels dispensationalism as understood and presented by him in his book *Dispensationalism*.

25. Cited in Crenshaw and Gunn, *Dispensationalism Today*, 235, quoting Walvoord, *Millennial Kingdom*, 129–30. See also Allis, *Prophecy and the Church*, 19. "This literalistic emphasis has shown itself most plainly in their insistence that Israel means Israel: it does not mean or typify the Church."

in the New Testament. For Walvoord when the Bible mentions Israel it always refers to natural Jews, the physical Israelite nation, and never to the church of believers in Jesus Christ, the Messiah of Israelite hopes. From such literalism dispensationalists have, as we have noted, a fervent interest in the future of the modern-day state of Israel—the land and the people.[26]

Such a national focus may perhaps be warranted if a literal hermeneutic is, as Ryrie argues, "the logical, obvious and only valid method of interpretation,"[27] though only by disregarding the many other factors that contribute to the interpretive process. The previous chapter, however, has already refuted the validity of this claim. If we were to concede for a moment that literalism is the only valid interpretive method, as claimed by dispensationalists, then God certainly has yet to fulfill many things he has promised to natural Israel through the Old Testament prophets. On the basis of a literalistic interpretive principle, the church could in no way fulfill anything spoken by them as prophecies of the Old Testament era spoken to Israel the nation; rather, they must be fulfilled in that nation. Ryrie has written,

> The church is not fulfilling in any sense the promises to Israel. . . . The church age is not seen in God's program for Israel. It is an intercalation. . . . The church is a mystery in the sense that it was completely unrevealed in the Old Testament and now revealed in the New Testament.[28]

---

26. Sizer, *Christian Zionism*, 107. "Christian Zionism is founded first of all upon a literal and futurist interpretation of the Bible which leads proponents to distinguish between references to Israel and the Church. Injunctions and promises concerning the ancient Jews are applied to the contemporary State of Israel rather than to the Church. From this hermeneutic flows the conviction that the Jews remain God's 'chosen people', distinct from the Church. . . . The destiny of the Jewish people is to return to the land of Israel and reclaim the inheritance promised to Abraham and his descendants forever. . . . Within their land, Jerusalem is recognised to be their exclusive, undivided and eternal capital, and therefore it cannot be shared or divided. At the heart of Jerusalem will be the rebuilt Jewish Temple to which all the nations will come to worship God. Just prior to the return of Jesus, there will be seven years of calamities and war known as the tribulation, which will culminate in a great battle called Armageddon, during which the godless forces opposed to both God and Israel will be defeated. Jesus will then return as the Jewish Messiah and king to reign in Jerusalem for a thousand years and the Jewish people will enjoy a privileged status and role in the world."

27. Ryrie, *Dispensationalism*, 20.

28. Cited in Crenshaw and Gunn, *Dispensationalism Today*, 135.

From this general understanding, many dispensationalists believe that "the restoration of Israel in 1948 is positive proof that we are living in the end times, and that the return of the Lord is at hand."[29] Thus they speculate as to when this return might occur, often followed by less specific revisions when the speculated day passes without Christ appearing.[30] Tim LaHaye and Thomas Ice in *Charting the End Times* write,

> As with the church and the nations, God is moving his chosen people—Israel—into place for the future fulfillment of His prophecies relating to the nation. He has already brought the Jewish people back to their land (1948) and has given them Jerusalem (1967).[31]

They further write, "If you want to know where history is headed, simply keep your eye on what God is doing in Israel," and, "Israel, God's 'super-sign' of the end times, is a clear indicator that time is growing shorter with each passing hour."[32] Such is the significance of the Israel-church distinction within dispensationalism. The present state of Israel established in 1948 is the super-sign that God is bringing things to an end.

29. Cited in Preston, *Israel: 1948 Countdown*, 2, quoting Jack Van Impe. However, Preston proceeds to refute this claim and concludes that due to the covenant's containing no concept of God returning Israel to the land while in unbelief, the events of 1948 are "totally insignificant prophetically." 25. This unbelief is acknowledged by dispensationalist Arnold Fruchtenbaum when he states that the majority of Jews who returned since 1948 are either atheist or agnostic. See his *Footsteps of the Messiah*, 65.

30. Sizer, *Christian Zionism*, 125–26. "Lindsey's difficulty with finding an accurate and lasting interpretation is nowhere more evident than in his attempts to date the Second Advent. In Matthew 24:34, Jesus said, 'I tell you the truth, this generation will certainly not pass away until all these things have happened.' In 1970 Lindsey raised the question: 'What generation?' Logically, he suggested, it would be the generation that had seen the signs Jesus had described, but added, 'chief among them the rebirth of Israel'. He then suggested a biblical generation was around 40 years: 'If this is a correct deduction, then within forty years or so of 1948, all these things could take place. Many scholars who have studied Bible prophecy all their lives believe that this is so.' Lindsey was not the only writer to suggest that the Messiah would return in 1988. When Jesus did not return that year, however, Lindsey revised his timescale by suggesting that a biblical generation could be anything from 40 to 100 years and that perhaps Daniel's prophetic clock had only started ticking again not in 1948 but in 1967 when Israel captured Jerusalem. Undaunted, in 1988 Grant Jeffrey calculated that Daniel's last 'week' would begin in 1993, the Tribulation would occur in 1997 and the cleansing of the temple and millennium would begin in the autumn of 2000. Like Lindsey, his subsequent books have avoided being so specific."

31. LaHaye and Ice, *Charting the End Times*, 84.

32. Ibid., 86–87.

This radical distinction of Israel and the church is, nevertheless, a radical departure from historic Christian belief. The premillennialism of the early centuries after Christ acknowledged a continuation of Israel in the church. Justin Martyr (second century) in his *Dialogue with Trypho the Jew* asserted frequently that Christians "are the true Israelite race," thus, anachronistically speaking, firmly distancing himself from the much-later dispensational form of premillennialism.[33] The amillennial and postmillennial views that dominated Christian thought through the fourth to nineteenth centuries have likewise held to a continuation of Israel in the church. Keith A. Mathison, a postmillennialist, writes, "As Christians we have no choice but to reject it [the dispensational Israel-church distinction] and affirm the oneness of the true church and the true Israel."[34] Kim Riddlebarger, writing as an amillennialist, states,

> The Bible everywhere supports the idea of an organic unity of the people of God, despite the fact that these people are citizens of national Israel in the Old Testament and members of Christ's church in the New. . . . the organic unity of God's redemptive purpose is clearly evident. . . . Therefore it is quite wrong-headed to interpret a distinction made in the Scriptures between the church and Israel. . . . In Christ, God takes the two peoples and makes them one.[35]

The historicity in Christian thought of the unity of Israel and church as opposed to a distinction between the two raises the question of when this dispensational peculiarity came to be a part of the theological landscape. Crenshaw and Gunn provide an answer:

> The consistent dispensationalist is a theologian in the grip of an idea—the idea that there is a strong dichotomy between Israel and the church. This idea is a relatively modern theory in the history of doctrine that was initially developed and popularized by J. N. Darby (1800–1882), the father of dispensational thought. During a period of convalescence in 1827, Darby meditated on the fact that the true Christian through the baptizing work of the Spirit is in union with Christ and therefore is seated with Christ in the heavenlies (Ephesians 2:4–7). With this in mind, Darby read Isaiah 32:15–20 about a prophesied outpouring of the Spirit on Israel that would bring earthly blessings on the people of God.

33. Grier, *Momentous Event*, 25; Waldron, *End Times*, 137.

34. Mathison, *Dispensationalism: Rightly Dividing*, 42.

35. Riddlebarger, *Case for Amillennialism*, 119–20.

Darby took this Scriptural data and concluded that the passages implied a strong contrast between earthly blessings prophesied for Israel and heavenly blessings promised to the Christian in the New Testament. From this Darby developed his theory that God has two peoples, an earthly people and a heavenly people.[36]

The dispensational bifurcation of Israel and the church as two separate peoples of God—whereby the church is considered a parenthesis (or intercalation) interrupting God's plan for Israel[37]—is therefore a relatively recent novelty in theological thought. This distinction appears to be based on Darby's commitment to a literalistic interpretive principle and the ensuing understanding of the nature of the promises to Israel being earthly, as seen in the Isaiah reference, and those of the church being heavenly, as in the Ephesians reference.[38] Such differences must, according to Darby, indicate two different recipients and therefore the conclusion was reached that God has two peoples—an earthly people (Israel) and a heavenly people (the church)—each with differing destinies and promises.

Clarence Bass confirms however,

> Such a concept is singularly missing from historic Christian theology. . . . Darby is pointedly correct in stating that this came to him as a new truth, since it is not to be found in theological literature prior to his proclamation of it. It is not that exegetes prior to his time did not see a covenant between God and Israel, or a future relation of Israel to the millennial reign, but they always viewed the church as the continuation of God's single program of redemption begun in Israel.[39]

James Barr states this point more tersely when he writes that premillennial dispensationalism was "individually invented by J. N. Darby . . . concocted in complete contradiction to all main Christian tradition."[40]

---

36. Crenshaw and Gunn, *Dispensationalism Today*, 142.

37. Ibid., 133–36.

38. Sizer, "Biblical Interpretation," no pages. "Based on his commitment to literalism, Darby formulated the doctrine of Dispensationalism and the rigid distinction between Israel and the Church which forms the basis of much contemporary Christian Zionism."

39. Bass, *Backgrounds to Dispensationalism*, 26–27.

40. Barr, *Escaping from Fundamentalism*, 6.

It must, however, be acknowledged that Darby's conclusion regarding the Isaiah and Ephesians passages has the appearance of being quite reasonable. This would be so *if*, and *only if*, strict literalism alone was *the* single governing principle by which to interpret Scripture. However, if other interpretive principles can legitimately be taken into account, as demonstrated in the previous chapter, then perhaps there are other ways to understand the nature of the earthly and heavenly blessings brought about by the outpouring of the Spirit—and in turn to understand the nature of the fulfillment of Old Testament prophecy regarding Israel and who it is that participates in that fulfillment.

A number of points are worth reiterating at this stage. First, there is a general acknowledgment of the recentness of the Israel-church dichotomy in Christian thought. Second, and related to the first, is that there have been eighteen centuries of historical interpretation prior to Darby during which a contrasting view was the norm. The third is the doubtfulness of the literalistic interpretive methodology adopted by dispensationalist interpreters, and fourth, the considerable impact this tenet of dispensationalism has in world affairs. These points strongly suggest that a consideration of how non-dispensational scholars throughout history, both before and after Darby, have understood "Israel" as it unfolds in the biblical narrative of redemptive history is very much warranted.

THE PEOPLE OF GOD: A NON-DISPENSATIONAL VIEW

Non-dispensational interpreters, whether historic-premillennial, amillennial, postmillennial, partial or full preterist in their understanding of God's working in history, commonly consider the church to be the continuation of God's redemptive plan—a plan that began to be actualized with the call of Abraham and the promises given to him (Gen 12:1–3), and continued through the creation of Israel the nation. That is, the church of Christian believers is a continuation of faithful Israel as recipient of God's redemptive promises rather than a distinct people with whom God deals differently. If this is so, then Samuel Waldron is entirely accurate when he comments that prophetic speculations and emphasis on the Middle East and the nation of Israel, as noted earlier within dispensationalism, is "simply groundless speculation."[41]

---

41. Waldron, *End Times*, 136.

Non-dispensational interpreters base their understanding regarding the unity of Israel and the church on a number of factors. They take seriously New Testament terminology and statements based within their own contexts and how they present a united view of the people of God. They take into account the continuity inherent within the progressive development of salvation history and covenant, and the use of the Old Testament in the New Testament—both its quotations and historical connectedness. They regard the person and work of Christ as *the* central key event of redemption history *and* as fulfillment of the Old Testament shadows, hopes, and promises—that is, a Christological (or Christotelic) hermeneutic is foremost in non-dispensational interpretation of the Old Testament. Before considering these elements of non-dispensational hermeneutics it is appropriate at this point to consider the Who is Israel? question in regard to natural descent or bloodline.

Thoughts Concerning Natural Descent

BIOLOGICAL OR PARENTAL CONSIDERATIONS

The question being asked at this point is this: Is it appropriate to define "Israel" as those who are bloodline descendants of Abraham and as such are heirs of the promises made to Abraham?

David Holwerda attends to this question in his book *Jesus and Israel: One Covenant or Two?*[42] In this work, Holwerda reveals some of the difficulties inherent within contemporary Judaism as they seek to answer this question. Some, he notes, have suggested that "a Jew is one who is born a Jew"—a notion that would allow for even Jewish-by-birth atheists to remain Jews and heirs of God's promises.[43] Others assert that "no one can be born a Jew because being a Jew is a matter of decision."[44] This preference in understanding would apply equally to those who consider themselves to be of biological descent from Abraham. The issue of parentage is, however, only one facet to be considered as Judaism has throughout its history allowed for non-Jewish people to convert to Judaism and to live according to the Torah.[45] Jewish commentator Benno Jacobs writes,

42. Holwerda, *Jesus and Israel*, 27–47.
43. Ibid., 28.
44. Ibid.
45. The writer is aware that by utilizing the term "non-Jewish" assumptions have

> Indeed, differences of race have never been an obstacle to joining Israel. . . . Circumcision turned a man of foreign origin into an Israelite.[46]

Apostasy, however, would not negate one's identity as Jewish. Unbelief would not cause one to cease being a Jew.[47] Burge notes that in the present time, "Atheism does not invalidate one's Judaism."[48] In fact, some Jews who have been allowed to return to the land are practicing Christians and Moslems.[49] In 1992 an Israeli leader estimated that "fewer that thirty percent of Israelis are actually practicing their religion."[50] Being Israel is clearly hard to define, and many conflicting ideas present themselves.[51]

Further, and adding to the confusion, Messianic Jews maintain that their belief in Jesus as the Messiah completes their Jewishness, despite this being contrary to traditional rabbinic Judaism. These Jews assert that "the true definition of what it means to be a Jew can be found in

---

been made as to who is a Jew and who is not, thus highlighting the difficulty of the issue being discussed. For the sake of clarity the term in this instance is being used to denote any persons who are not generally considered to be Jewish by locale, parentage, or conversion and are generally recognized to be of other ethnicity.

46. Cited in Robertson, *Israel of God*, 35.

47. Holwerda, *Jesus and Israel*, 29. Burge, *Whose Land?* 162.

48. Burge, *Whose Land?* 163.

49. "Israeli newspapers reported at the end of December 1994 that churches in Nazareth were full to overflowing due to the large influx of olim [migrants to Israel] from the former Soviet Union, many of whom are believing and practicing Christians. If this were not enough, it has been disclosed that hundreds of new olim have been coming in from Iraqi Kurdistan, a Moslem area under UN control. Reportedly, up to 80 percent of these olim are believing and practicing Moslems, and yet they qualify to enter Israel under the Law of Return. . . . However, over the years questions arose about exactly who is a Jew. Perhaps the most celebrated and notorious case was that of Brother Daniel. Brother Daniel, born a Polish Jew named Daniel Rufeisen, came to Israel as a Carmelite monk and requested citizenship under the Law of Return. A landmark decision by Israel's Supreme Court determined that a Jew who had of his own free will adopted another faith was not eligible to enter Israel under the Law of Return. By this ruling the law of the land contradicted Jewish law, since according to rabbinic halakhah, a Jew remains a Jew even if he is converted to another faith." Clayman, "Law of Return," no pages.

50. Burge, *Whose Land?* 163.

51. "Judaism, Basic Jewish Beliefs," "The question of what determines Jewish identity was given new impetus when, in the 1950s, David ben Gurion requested opinions on mihu Yehudi ("who is a Jew") from Jewish religious authorities and intellectuals worldwide. The question is far from settled and is one of the recurrent tensions in Israeli politics and in the divide between Orthodox vs. Reform (or Conservative) Judaism."

Jesus only."[52] It appears that this group is in agreement with the Apostle Peter as recorded in the book of Acts. Here, in a reference to Jesus as Messiah, recalling the words of Moses, Peter says,

> The Lord your God will raise up for you from your own people a prophet like me. You must listen to whatever he tells you. And it will be that everyone who does not listen to that prophet will be utterly rooted out of [NIV: completely cut off from among] the people. (Acts 3:22–23)

The implication of this latter understanding is that non-Messianic Jews are therefore less Jewish and that traditional parentage or conversion criteria, while important to some, are nonetheless inadequate for defining who is truly Jewish. According to Peter's statement, by not acknowledging and listening to Christ, some are actually "cut off" from God's people. Restated conversely, to remain being part of the covenant people one must listen to the words of Jesus as the Messiah and fulfiller of Israel's hopes. This criterion alone would exclude the vast majority of present-day Jews from the people of God and from having any legitimate claim to or participation in the covenant blessings—not to mention the multitudes throughout history who have denied the Messianic status of Jesus.

It becomes evident that even those who might in the most general of terms be considered Jewish find it difficult within themselves to define what it is that makes a person a true Jew and, by extension, who it is that will inherit and participate in the fulfillment of the promises to Abraham. The Who is Israel? question under discussion can be restated: Who is the true seed of Abraham? And Who are the designated and rightful heirs of the covenant promises of God? This restatement is especially in order since bloodline or parentage appears to be inadequate as a conclusive factor.

It seems the answer to such questioning is to be found elsewhere than simply by tracing parentage back to Abraham. Given that the record of the creation of the Israelite race and their distinctive role in redemptive history is to be found in the biblical narrative, it seems most reasonable to seek answers from that source. "The entire Scripture, both Old and New Testaments, is a record of God's activity in creating and defining Israel and thereby answering our question."[53] What can be de-

---

52. Holwerda, *Jesus and Israel*, 30.
53. Ibid.

duced from that source is that from the earliest of days in the history of God's covenant people it is clear that incorporated within that people were people who were not descendant from Abraham.

> Throughout your generations every male among you shall be circumcised when he is eight days old, including the slave born in your house and the one bought with your money from *any foreigner who is not of your offspring*. Both the slave born in your house and the one bought with your money must be circumcised. So shall my covenant be in your flesh an everlasting covenant. (Gen 17:12–13, emphasis added)

Robertson notes,

> From the most ancient history of the Abrahamic covenant, the "ingrafting" of those not of natural Israelite birth was made a possibility (Gen 17:12, 13). Through the incorporation of the proselyte, peoples of any nation could become Israelites in the fullest sense.
>
> Any definition of the biblical significance of "Israel" must not fail to include this dimension. Israel must include the proselyte who does not belong to "Israel" according to the flesh, but is absorbed into Israel by the process of ingrafting. . . .
>
> By the process of "ingrafting," the Gentile becomes an "Israelite" in the fullest possible sense (cf. Gal 3:29). From the point of ingrafting, his subsequent seed becomes heir to the promises given to Abraham.[54]

Of particular relevance for this discussion is that foreigners were included in the covenant family through the rite of circumcision. This did not stop them from being biologically Gentile, but caused them as Gentiles to be integrated into the covenant people—the one people of God. This opens up the possibility that as time progressed there could well be a greater proportion of non-bloodline covenant people than those who were of direct descent from Abraham. In fact, at the time of the covenant promise, Abram was childless. Sarai was not of his seed and Lot was his brother's son. Abraham had no direct descendants yet he did have slaves not of his seed who became legitimately and equally covenant people through circumcision. This leads to the compelling likelihood that the great majority of what became Israel over time were non-seed of Abraham and Gentile in origin—indeed, as was Abraham himself (Josh 24:2).

---

54. Robertson, *Christ of the Covenants*, 39.

Much later in time John the Baptist is presented as saying to his Jewish audience, "Do not presume to say to yourselves, 'We have Abraham as our ancestor'; for I tell you, God is able from these stones to raise up children to Abraham" (Matt 3:9). By this he is making a clear statement that being children of Abraham, and as a consequence heirs of the blessing promised to him (i.e., Israel) is not a matter of claiming descent from Abraham—God could, if he chose, create descendants from rocks. Holwerda states that

> God's promises are for Israel, but [the identity of] Israel is not established simply by birthright. The blessings are not automatically guaranteed by preserving the purity of an Israelite gene pool or an impeccable family tree. Much more is involved.[55]

Having noted the inclusion of Tamar and Rahab the Canaanites, Ruth the Moabite, and Bathsheba the wife of a Hittite in Matthew's genealogy (Matt 1), Holwerda asserts that Matthew is saying that "the true descendants of Abraham are not preserved by their purity of descent."[56] He continues, "As the people of God Israel was always intended to be and to become a universal people, not limited by racial purity."[57] This aspect of universal inclusion is extremely important and in complete agreement with the biblical record of God's promise to Abraham as recorded in Genesis 12:1–3, which explicitly states that the creation of a people from Abraham was in order that through this people all peoples would be blessed. God's ultimate intent in that promise was not to create a physical nation who would forever remain distinct and special, but rather to create a physical nation who would mediate the restoration of people from all nations. The backdrop or historical context preceding the giving of the Genesis 12:1–3 covenant promise is the universal separation from God through Adam's sin. As the sin of Adam had a universal impact so the promise to Abraham is the beginning of a universal restoration and "lays the foundation for the entire ensuing history of redemption recorded in the Scriptures"[58]—even to a restoration of the cursed earth (Gen 3:17–18; Rom 8:19–23). This universal backdrop to the Abrahamic covenant and the universal scope of that covenant should caution the interpreter from undue emphasis on Israel as the primary focus of God's purposes.

55. Holwerda, *Jesus and Israel*, 34.

56. Ibid., 35.

57. Ibid.

58. Ibid., 32.

The futility of emphasizing bloodline descent is reiterated in considerably stronger terms by Jesus when responding to a group of natural Israelites claiming Abraham as their father, when he says to them,

> If you were Abraham's children, you would be doing what Abraham did. . . . You are from your father the devil, and you choose to do your father's desires. (John 8:39, 44)

It appears from these words of Jesus that evidence of descent from Abraham is to be discerned from an action; if the claimants were Abraham's children, they would be *doing what Abraham did*. Inclusion in the people of God (i.e., Abraham's offspring) is clearly to be found by that criterion rather than parentage. By his use of the word "if," Jesus is in effect denying the Jewish leaders' claim to Abrahamic descent;[59] indeed, in light of their actions—what they "choose to do"—he attributes their parentage to the devil. Yet the promises of God to Abraham were to him and his offspring. Taking this last statement at face value, or plain meaning, would exclude those included through circumcision. That foreigners were, however, not excluded but rather welcomed according to the covenant affirms further that to be of Abraham's offspring is to be defined by criteria other than by bloodline descent.

The Factor of Conditionality

Intrinsic to the covenant made by God with Abraham and the ensuing people of God was the element of condition. Holwerda notes that "the promises given to Israel were not like automatic guarantees to be received apart from faith and obedience."[60] Steve Wohlberg issues a reminder that Israel's continued status as God's people, though elected by God apart from obedience on their part, was "conditional upon their response to His goodness, upon their choices to obey."[61] The Sinai giving of the law (Exodus 20 and Leviticus) as well as the national recommitment at the covenant renewal ceremony just prior to entering the land as recorded in Deuteronomy (esp. chaps. 27–28) reveal emphatically this conditional basis for receiving God's ongoing and continued blessing. The consequence for disobedience would ultimately be judgment and removal from the land. Only by the people turning back to God with all

---

59. Wohlberg, *Exploding the Israel Deception*, 27.

60. Holwerda, *Jesus and Israel*, 27.

61. Wohlberg, *Exploding the Israel Deception*, 35–36.

their heart and soul evidenced in obedience to God's covenant would there be a return to the land:

> When all these things have happened to you, the blessings and the curses that I have set before you, if you call them to mind among all the nations where the Lord your God has driven you, and return to the Lord your God, and you and your children obey him with all your heart and with all your soul, just as I am commanding you today, then the Lord your God will restore your fortunes and have compassion on you, gathering you again from all the peoples among whom the Lord your God has scattered you. (Deut 30:1–3)

These covenant documents became the basis of the Old Testament prophets' message throughout their ministry. These prophets continually reminded the nation how they had disobeyed God through idolatry and injustice, and they were persistent in calling the nation to repent and turn back to God. If the people did repent, they would be restored to a place of blessing.

Consequently, Holwerda writes, "because of Israel's historical disobedience, the prophets announced that in the end it will be a remnant that is saved (Isaiah 10:20–23; Amos 9; Micah 7:18)."[62] Gary Burge echoes this element of conditionality when, referring to Romans 2:25–29, he states, "Unrighteous behavior can invalidate a person's claim to being God's people."[63] This verifies that descent from Abraham or being his offspring is, from a biblical viewpoint, determined by righteous actions based on faith rather than through claims of Abrahamic or Israelite parentage, or by conversion to Judaism.

If, as the book of Deuteronomy reveals, being the people of God and receiving covenant blessings, including land and prosperity, is conditional on loyalty to God and behavior that reflects covenant faithfulness, then the contemporary state of Israel would be disqualified due to its general state of unbelief and its apartheid-like policies and actions towards the Palestinian people.[64] Pastor Evan Albertyn, having grownup

---

62. Holwerda, *Jesus and Israel*, 27.

63. Burge, *Whose Land?* 135.

64. B. White, *Israeli Apartheid*, 10. "Increasingly, Israelis, Palestinians, South Africans and international observers are pointing out the parallels between apartheid South Africa and Israel. Several prominent South Africans have expressed their solidarity with the Palestinians, denouncing what they see as a similar (or worse) structure of oppression to the apartheid regime many of them fought against."

in apartheid South Africa, goes as far as to say that the situation in Palestine today is like "apartheid on steroids."[65] These policies intentionally discriminate against Palestinians and constitute what Ilan Pappe, an Israeli historian, has described as ethnic cleansing. He states that Israel's 1948 "Plan D . . . contains a repertoire of cleansing methods that one by one fit the means the UN describes in its definition of ethnic cleansing, and sets the background for the massacre that accompanied the massive expulsion" of Palestinians from their homes and land at that time.[66] Pappe's understanding is confirmed through the words of David Ben Gurion—perhaps the most significant leader in achieving Zionist ideology and the new state of Israel's first prime minister—who in a letter to his son in 1937 wrote, "We must expel the Arabs and take their places . . . to guarantee our own right to settle in those places—then we have force at our disposal."[67] This way of thinking was translated into reality in 1948 through Israel's depopulating and destruction of hundreds of Palestinian villages and thus creating roughly 700,000 refugees. A similar forceful expulsion following the six-day war in 1967 saw between 100,000 and 260,000 more refugees from the newly occupied West Bank.[68] This form of activity continues to the present time as evidenced by the Israeli built "security" wall that creeps deep into the Palestinian West Bank, thus accumulating more Palestinian land on Israel's side of the wall, and through the relentless building of Israeli settlements within

---

65. Albertyn, "With God on Our Side" DVD at 40:46 minutes.

66. Pappe, *Ethnic Cleansing of Palestine*, 2. Pappe lists methods such as "large-scale intimidation; laying siege to and bombarding villages and population centres; setting fire to homes, properties and goods; expulsion; demolition; and, finally, planting mines among the rubble to prevent any of the expelled inhabitants from returning," xii. He further writes "Plan D (*Dalet*) . . . sealed the fate of the Palestinians within the territory the Zionist Leaders had set their eyes on for their future Jewish State. . . . Plan Dalet called for their systematic and total expulsion from their homeland." 28. See also Haddad, "Palestinian Refugees," 265. Haddad writes, "The conscious and deliberate policy of 'emptying' the land is now well documented. Israeli politicians and decision-makers have admitted their plans to drive the Palestinians into an exodus from a time as early as the 1930s."

67. Shlaim, *Israel and Palestine*, 58.

68. Mearsheimer, "Future of Palestine," no pages. He continues, "Nevertheless, a Jewish apartheid state is not politically viable over the long term. In the end, it will become a democratic bi-national state, whose politics will be dominated by its Palestinian citizens. In other words, it will cease being a Jewish state, which will mean the end of the Zionist dream."

the West Bank on land that rightfully belongs to Palestinians. Speaking of the future, Mearsheimer states,

> Israel is not going to allow the Palestinians to have a viable state of their own in Gaza and the West Bank. Regrettably, the two-state solution is now a fantasy. Instead, those territories will be incorporated into a "Greater Israel," which will be an apartheid state bearing a marked resemblance to white-ruled South Africa.[69]

The United Nations, on November 10, 1975, stated that "Zionism should be considered racism—a political philosophy that excludes others based on race, history, and creed."[70] This kind of activity is the antithesis of Old Testament Israel's calling to be a blessing to the nations (Gen 12:1–3) and counter to the demands of God's covenant with them as revealed in the Old Testament. The nature of Israel's present-day governance would have seen the Old Testament prophets of God calling for the nation to repent, to welcome the aliens,[71] to love justice, and for them to turn back to God and to his ways in order to meet the covenant stipulations for receiving his blessing.

If the question Who is Israel? is reworded as, Who are the legitimate heirs of God's promises? then perhaps the answer is to be found, not by descent issues or in the modern state of Israel, but rather by asking, Who is meeting the covenant conditions? Burge echoes this concept when noting that in Matthew 2:6 Jesus redefines who qualifies to inherit the earth (*gē*, land)—"not people who are ethnically Jewish, who fight for land, or who claim ancestral right, but those who are humble."[72] He asks, "If [the modern state of] Israel qualifies prophetically [as claimed in dispensational thought], does Israel also qualify ethically and morally to be God's people in the land?"[73] By the nature of its oppressive and dehumanizing treatment of Palestinians—by placing over three million Palestinians under illegal military occupation,[74] apartheid-like dis-

---

69. Mearsheimer, "Future of Palestine," no pages.

70. Burge, *Whose Land?* 141.

71. It must be noted that "alien" is not an appropriate term for Palestinians who do not consider themselves to be foreigners or aliens in the land.

72. Burge, *Whose Land?* 174.

73. Ibid., 135.

74. The military occupation is in breach of UN Resolution 242 passed unanimously by the UN Security Council on November 22, 1967, which emphasizes "inadmissibility of the acquisition of territory by war" and calls for the "Withdrawal of Israel armed

crimination, home demolitions, theft of water and unreasonable water restrictions for Palestinians, land confiscation, and checkpoints limiting freedom of movement (even within designated Palestinian territory), and many other violations of human rights[75]—the modern-day state of Israel, as a political and secular nation, is without doubt being unfaithful to the covenant stipulations. Therefore, by Old Testament criteria, Israel's tyrannical activity forfeits any legitimate claim or right to dwell on the land. The Hebrew Scriptures are clear about this: any claim to the land based on the Old Testament must also give equal weight to that covenant's requirement of justice and righteousness. Being the people of God and dwelling in the land is contingent on faithfulness to God and to God's prescribed way of living; the two go hand in hand. Injustice through the ill-treatment of people (along with idolatry and pride) was the precise activity that saw Old Testament Israel exiled from the land in 722 BC by the Assyrians, and Judah in 586 BC at the hands of the Babylonians.

From the above observations, that is, the irrelevance of parentage, the historical inclusion of non-bloodline foreign people, and the conditional nature of the covenant stipulations, it appears we can assert at this point that one's belonging to Israel

- cannot be determined from natural descent;

- cannot be determined by conversion to Judaism;

- is not exclusive of those of Gentile origin; and

- is not without conditions, that is, obedience, faithfulness, justice, and an acknowledgement of Jesus as the Christ (Acts 3:22–23).

It remains now to establish what factors do determine inclusion in the people of God and to propose an answer to the Who is Israel? question. This evidence will be drawn primarily from the biblical record and will seek to represent a view counter to that of dispensational

---

forces from territories occupied in the recent conflict," and further, for the "right to live in peace within secure and recognized boundaries free from threats or acts of force." Cited April 26, 2010. Online: http://daccess-dds-ny.un.org/doc/RESOLUTION/GEN/NR0/240/94/IMG/NR024094.pdf?OpenElement.

75. On the assumption of being on "firm biblical soil," Malcolm Hedding of the International Christian Embassy Jerusalem says, "If there are political ramifications, OK, so what." In "With God on Our Side" DVD at 50:12 minutes.

understanding. My analysis thus far leads me to consider that the dispensational view is hermeneutically unsound and therefore inadequate, and that to a substantial degree it deprives Christians of a biblical understanding of who they are as God's people, places undue emphasis on the physical and secular state of Israel in God's future purposes, demonstrates a diminished view of the person and work of Christ as *telos* and fulfiller of the Old Testament Scriptures as a whole, misunderstands the implications of progressive revelation, and disregards the clear teaching of the New Testament in regard to this issue.

A Rationale for Oneness

JESUS: THE TRUE ISRAEL

Non-dispensational scholars commonly understand that Israel's identity is summed up in Jesus.[76] He is both the true Israelite and the essence of what it means to be Israel. Scripture attributes to both Israel and Jesus the title "Son of God," indicating at the very least the same identity and status. The New Testament begins with Matthew's Gospel recording the birth of Jesus, and immediately evident are parallels to the birthing of Israel as a nation.[77] Two Josephs have dreams and go to Egypt. Both Moses as deliverer of Israel's exodus from Egyptian bondage and Jesus as new deliverer are spared from death as infants by kings who feel threatened by their presence.[78] The Old Testament records Israel's exodus from Egypt, whereas the New Testament tells of Jesus going to Egypt. Of this Matthew writes that this was to fulfill what had been spoken by the Lord through the prophet: "Out of Egypt I have called my son" (2:15). His going made possible his being called out of Egypt, thereby anticipating a new exodus. This event in the life of Jesus is not something that merely happened; it fulfilled a lived prophetic event. The words from God as spoken by Hosea (11:1), in context, refer back to Israel's miraculous exodus from Egypt and forward to a new exodus from bondage; perhaps

---

76. Holwerda, *Jesus and Israel*, 27–47; N. T. Wright, *Jesus and the Victory of God*, 517; Walker, *Jesus and the Holy City*, 45; Mathison, *Postmillennialism*, 104–5; Chapman, *Whose Promised Land?* 159–60; Goldsworthy, *Gospel and Kingdom*, 92–93; Riddlebarger, *Case for Amillennialism*, 37; Snodgrass, "Use of the Old Testament in the New," in *Right Doctrine from the Wrong Texts?* 37; Strimple, "Amillennialism," 87; Strom, *Symphony*, 200; Dumbrell, *Search for Order*, 178–79; C. Wright, *Knowing Jesus*, 44.

77. Wohlberg, *Exploding the Israel Deception*, 21–22.

78. Holwerda, *Jesus and Israel*, 27.

partially fulfilled when the nation returned from the Babylonian exile, nevertheless, they were still experiencing exilic conditions.[79] Ultimately, however, the exodus event was fulfilled when Jesus returned from Egypt to bring about a new deliverance through the cross. The Old Testament exodus event, it seems, was not an end in itself but prophetically pointed forward to Jesus as a new Moses, a new deliverer of a new exodus.

As Israel went into the wilderness post-exodus, Jesus also went into the wilderness, where, like Israel, his obedience was tested according to covenant faithfulness.[80] Israel as Son of God (Exod 4:22) failed. Jesus, pronounced by God at his pre-temptation baptism as "Son of God" (Matt 3:17), did not fail—he did what Israel was not able to do.[81] He remained faithful to God and the covenant.[82] Of this Wohlberg writes,

> What does this mean? It means that in Matthew's book, Jesus is repeating the history of Israel, point by point, and is overcoming where they failed. He is becoming the new Israel.[83]

Non-dispensational thought regards Jesus as Israel and being what Israel was meant to be. If, as dispensational thought maintains, the promises made by God to Israel must be fulfilled in Israel, then Matthew's Gospel presents Jesus as being *the Israel* in which these promises find their fulfillment.

Holwerda notes a genealogical fulfillment of Jesus as Israel from Matthew 1. In this passage Jesus is declared to be Son of Abraham and Son of David as he brings to fulfillment Genesis 12 and 2 Samuel 7—that is, both the Abrahamic covenant of nationhood, land, and universal blessing and the Davidic covenant of eternal kingship. As Son of David, Jesus, as Israel's king, in his person corporately represents true Israel. He is "the representative embodiment of Israel through whom the nations

---

79. Ibid., 40. Walker, *Jesus and the Holy City*, 43–44; N. T. Wright, *New Testament and the People of God*, 268–70. Wright builds a theology extensively on this partial return concept, noting that despite being back home Israel was very much still in exilic conditions being under foreign domination and the failure to experience the glorious conditions foretold by the prophets.

80. Note that Jesus's response to his testing was to quote from Deuteronomy; the covenant document formed after Israel's wilderness wandering.

81. Strom, *Symphony*, 163. Strom writes, "Therefore, when the Father spoke at his Son's baptism, he affirmed that Jesus was both the Messiah and the true Israelite, the true covenant Son."

82. Ibid., 200.

83. Wohlberg, *Exploding the Israel Deception*, 20.

will be blessed,"[84] thus fulfilling the wider multinational intent of God's covenant with Abraham. Holwerda concludes, "Israel can never again be defined apart from Jesus Christ."[85]

Added to the above parallels and fulfillments are many other ways in which Jesus is portrayed as assuming in himself the life of Israel. Consider for example the metaphorical characterization of a vineyard. Old Testament prophets often spoke of Israel (as people and/or place) as God's vineyard.[86] Hosea added to this metaphor the concept of yielding fruit (10:1). Throughout their history as God's vineyard Israel had failed to yield the fruit required of them, resulting in their removal from the land according to covenant stipulations (Deut 28:63–64). Jesus, as "Son of God," the one who had come out of Egypt, having endured obediently a wilderness experience, said John 15:1, *ego eimi he ampelos he alethine*—lit. "I am the true vine"—a statement that implies the existence of a less real or less authentic vine. Otherwise the adjective "true" would be redundant. Raymond E. Brown comments,

> *Alethinos* implies exclusivity in the sense of 'the only real,' as compared with the putative or would-be. It is used in a contrast between the heavenly and the earthly, or between the NT reality and the OT type. . . . In [John] xv 1, Jesus, and not Israel is the real vine.[87]

Herman Ridderbos likewise says that

> "the true" emphasizes distinction from or even the contrast with persons or things that have received the same predicate. . . . The main thing, however, is that Jesus, by calling himself the true vine . . . applies to himself this redemptive-historical description of the people of God.[88]

This seems to be, as already seen in the exodus parallel, a reliving of Israel in the life of Christ—assuming both her identity and purpose.[89]

84. Holwerda, *Jesus and Israel*, 33.

85. Ibid., 36.

86. See Isa 5:3–7; Jer 2:21; 12:10; Hos 10:1. See also Ps 80:8, 14. New Testament parables assume and further develop this metaphor, e.g., Matt 20:1–16; 21:28–32; 21:33–41; Mark 12:1–12 and its parallel in Luke 20:9–19.

87. Brown, *John*, 500–501.

88. Ridderbos, *John*, 515.

89. N. T. Wright, *Jesus and the Victory of God*, 531. "He [Jesus] believed that Israel's destiny was reaching its fulfilment in his life . . . that he should summon Israel to re-

However, in Jesus, the fruit expected of a vineyard was present. Jesus is in effect saying, "I am the true Israel."[90] By extension of the metaphor Jesus states that the vine has fruit-bearing branches representative of those who abide in him. "This implies that the disciple's belonging to Jesus as the branches of the vine (vs. 5) denotes not only a personal relationship but also their incorporation into the great community of the people of God."[91] The people of God, that is, Israel, are those who remain *in* Christ *the true Israel*. Those who are in Christ are children of God (Gal 3:26), and if they belong to Christ, they are Abraham's offspring and heirs according to the promise (Gal 3:29), at the middle point of which was the promise of land. To be *in Christ* is therefore to be *in Israel*. Burge writes, "God the Father is now cultivating a vineyard in which only one life-giving vine grows. Attachment to this vine and this vine alone gives the benefits of life once promised through The Land."[92] Thus, as with the people of Israel, Israel's land is caught up in this metaphor and also finds its fuller meaning in Christ and the kingdom of God. On December 11, 2009, a collective of leading Palestinian Christian leaders released their newly formulated Kairos Palestine document, "A Moment of Truth." In it they write,

> We believe that our land has a universal mission. In this universality, the meaning of the promises, of the land, of the election, of the people of God open up to include all of humanity, starting from all the peoples of this land. In light of the teachings of the Holy Bible, the promise of the land has never been a political programme, but rather the prelude to complete universal salvation. It was the initiation of the fulfilment of the Kingdom of God on earth.[93]

This Christological concept of Christ as Israel is a key link in the chain that is crucial for understanding the progressive development of the people of God. Christians "are the Israel of God, Abraham's seed, and

---

group, and find a new identity, around him."

90. Strom, *Symphony*, 200.

91. Ridderbos, *John*, 516. See also Beasley-Murray, *John*, 272. Here he writes, "That the Vine is *Jesus*, not the church, is intentional; the Lord is viewed in his representative capacity . . . that is in union with him a renewed people of God might come into being and bring forth fruit for God."

92. Burge, *Jesus and the Land*, 55. Davies, *Land and the Gospel*, 217. "To be 'in Christ' . . . has replaced being 'in the land' as the ideal life."

93. Kairos Palestine, "Moment of Truth," article 2.3.

heirs of the promises, only because by God's grace we are united to him who is alone the true Israel, Abraham's *one* seed."[94]

A further example of Jesus's assuming Israel's identity is seen in the metaphor of light. Old Testament Israel was called to be a light to the nations (Isa 42:6; 49:6; 60:1–3) yet her subsequent history failed to see this become a reality. Again, at his arrival, Jesus takes on Israel's purpose by declaring, *egō eimi to phōs tou kosmou*, "I am the light of the world" (John 8:12; see also 9:5; 12:46).[95] In the same manner that the vineyard metaphor was extended to include the people of Jesus—as fruitful branches of the true vine—so it is with the light metaphor. Jesus, as the light of the world also said to his disciples, "You are the light of the world" (Matt 5:14).

These two metaphorical word pictures show that Israel has been fully realized in Christ and by extension in those who are "in Christ," the church. The physical nation appears to share the same end in so many aspects of her way of life such as prophet, priest, king, tabernacle, temple, sacrifice, land, promise, covenant, and law. All these features of Israel find their greater meaning in Jesus Christ. The nation too, shares a greater reality in Jesus. Jesus is true Israel, along with those who are in Christ, and fulfills all she was meant to be.

Robert B. Strimple points out the ambiguous nature of the "servant" in Isaiah's prophecies (Isa 42, 44, 45, 48, 53).[96] In these passages the identity of the servant appears to vacillate between Israel as a nation and an individual.[97] Matthew 12:18–21 quotes Isaiah directly and applies this servant imagery to the ministry of Jesus. Again, this shows Jesus not only as fulfiller of Old Testament prophecy, but as Israel. Strimple writes,

---

94. Strimple, "Amillennialism," 89.

95. "The whole New Testament assumes that Israel was chosen to be the people through whom the creator God would address and save the world. Salvation is of the Jews. And the early Christians believed that the one true God had been faithful to that promise. He'd done it and he'd brought salvation through the king of the Jews, Jesus himself. Israel was called to be the light of the world and that history and vocation had now devolved onto Jesus—solo. He was the true Israel; he was the light of the world." N. T. Wright, "Jesus as the World's True Light," mp3 audio, time 7:29 to 10:58. See also Beale, *Revelation*, 988–89.

96. Strimple, "Amillennialism," 88.

97. Strom, *Symphony*, 241. Strom writes, "Ultimately, however, the two possibilities came together through Jesus acting on behalf of the people he was creating."

> Yes, Israel was called to be God's Servant, a light to enlighten the nations and to glorify God's name. But since Israel was unfaithful to her calling and failed to fulfill the purposes of her divine election, the Lord brought forth his Elect One, his Servant, his True Israel.[98]

Jesus is the true Israel to whom the Abrahamic promises were made. Paul the apostle says as much when he writes, "Now the promises were made to Abraham and to his offspring; it does not say, 'And to offsprings,' as of many; but it says, 'And to your offspring,' that is, to one person, who is Christ" (Gal 3:16). In 2 Corinthians 1:20 we read, "For no matter how many [*hosai*, as many as] promises God has made, they are 'Yes' in Christ" (NIV). No promise is excluded. Therefore, a Christian understanding should not circumvent this clear statement of Christ as fulfiller of *all* God's promises to Israel. The words of Luke, as Jesus spoke to two men who had hoped he was the one to redeem Israel, affirm this perspective, "Then beginning with Moses and *all the prophets*, he [Jesus] interpreted to them the things about himself in *all the scriptures*" (Luke 24:27, emphasis added). All the Scriptures, the story of Israel and her promises, are in fact the story of Jesus and point to him. This point is succinctly stated by Christopher J. H. Wright:

> the vitally important fact is that the New Testament presents him [Jesus] as the *Messiah*, Jesus the *Christ*. And the Messiah 'was' Israel. That is, the Messiah was Israel representatively and personified. The Messiah was the completion of all that Israel had been put in the world for—i.e. God's self-revelation and his work of human redemption. For this reason, Jesus shares in the uniqueness of Israel. What God had been doing through no other nation he now completed through no other person than the Messiah Jesus. The paradox is that precisely through the narrowing down of his redemptive work to the unique particularity of the single man, Jesus, God opened the way to the universalizing of his redemptive grace to all nations. Israel was unique because God had a universal goal through them. Jesus embodied that uniqueness and achieved that universal goal.[99]

This fulfillment of Israel, her promises and her calling, in the life of Christ must therefore radically affect how one interprets the Old

---

98. Strimple, "Amillennialism," 88.

99. C. Wright, *Knowing Jesus*, 44.

Testament prophecies concerning Israel. Burge notes, with particular reference to the writings of Hal Lindsey, that much of dispensational thought assumes that "modern day Israel has indeed resumed the life of Ancient Israel, that a direct line may be drawn between the biblical nation and the Israeli government in Jerusalem today."[100] This "direct line" in dispensational thought, however, bypasses the person and work of Jesus as the fulfiller of Israel's identity, promises, calling, and restoration. Peter Walker concisely presents the impact of a Christological interpretation of Israel:

> If Matthew defined the true people of 'Israel' in relation to Jesus, the same would apply to Israel's 'restoration'. There can be no restoration of Israel without Jesus. Indeed, if Jesus' own life encapsulates the history of Israel, then a whole new way of understanding restoration becomes possible. When this Jesus is 'restored' to life and raised by God from the dead, this event may itself be the 'restoration' of Israel, the true revelation of Israel's glory before the world. In light of the resurrection Jesus himself was 'the *restored* Son Israel'. In Matthew, therefore, the resurrection was not just a rebuilding of the temple (26:61), but also the moment when the 'true Israel' was 'restored'.[101]

Historical Continuity of the People of God

Jesus, as true Israel, fulfilled the Old Testament hopes. Simeon and Anna recognized him as the "hope of Israel," the "consolation of Jerusalem" (Luke 2), but the story didn't end there. His life, death, and resurrection usher in a new exodus from bondage; an exodus available to people of all nations. As the true and faithful seed of Abraham, Jesus makes possible the blessing for all nations inherent in Abraham's covenant. The New Testament story telling of the inclusion in God's people of Gentiles together with Jews is therefore not a brand-new story. It is a continuation of God's universal plan to restore what was lost through sin. Jesus is the center of that story as the one who completes and realizes this eternal

---

100. Burge, *Whose Land?* 134.

101. Walker, *Jesus and the Holy City,* 45. Chapman, *Whose Promised Land?* 223. See also Walker, "The Land and Jesus Himself," 107. "[T]he only clear prophecy which speaks about something happening on the third day is Hosea 6:2: 'on the third day he will restore us.' . . . a prediction which ostensibly concerned the restoration of *Israel* has now been applied by Jesus to his *own* resurrection . . . 'the resurrection of Christ *is* the restoration of Israel of which the prophets spoke.'"

purpose of God (Eph 3:11). Having accomplished this, those who come to faith in Christ enter into the newer expression of Israel, God's people, by being in Christ, who is the true Israel.

As this new expression of God's people emerges and expands throughout the book of Acts, those who tell the story of Jesus continually refer back to the Old Testament. This is seen in the speeches of Peter, Stephen, and Paul, and in Philip's explanation of Isaiah 53 to the Ethiopian eunuch. In order to understand what was happening in their time, as Gentiles come to share in the blessing of the Spirit being poured on all peoples (Jews, Acts 2; Samaritans, Acts 8; God-fearing Gentiles, Acts 10; and Gentiles, Acts 19), these men go back to Israel's history to show how these times come to be. Israel's story is traced through to Christ and seamlessly to what God is now doing among all peoples. Israel's history is the history of the emerging multinational people of God, the Christian church, not a distinct and separate program. The Messiah of Israel's hopes, the one destined to restore Israel as told by the prophets, had come and fulfilled God's purposes for the world through the cross. Israel's restoration is achieved through Christ's resurrection and is being achieved as people of all nations come to acknowledge Christ as Messiah and Savior.[102]

Peter, in his Acts 2 Pentecost address, informed his Jewish hearers that "the promise [originally spoken to Israel, Joel 2] is for you [Israel], for your children, *and for all who are far away*" (Acts 2:39, emphasis added). The church, far from being a separate people with a separate destiny, is a God-intended continuation and expansion of the believing Jewish remnant as Gentiles come in to share in the same promise. Believing Gentiles along with believing Jews together constitute true Israel by being in Christ.

Regarding the Apostle Paul, George Eldon Ladd points out that in support of his teaching Paul appealed to the Old Testament ninety-three times, and he notes,

---

102. Note Jesus's answer to the disciples' question in Acts 1:6. "Will you at this time restore the kingdom to Israel?" Jesus's answer is that they would receive power to be witnesses in Jerusalem, in all Judea and Samaria and to the end of the earth (1:8). Is this contextually how the restoration is realized? "For Ἰσραήλ can also be the name for the people of God to whom Christ will restore the βασιλεία, 1:6 (cf. also 28:20). Here the frontier of the people of God is not yet crossed, but there is an extension of the term to cover the new people of God." Gutbrod, Ἰσραήλ."

His primary concern is not to gain biblical authority for specific doctrines so much as to show that redemption in Christ stands in direct continuity with the revelation of the Old Testament and is in fact the fulfillment of that revelation . . . showing that the church is directly continuous with Israel. . . . Thus he can apply to the church quotations that in the Old Testament refer only to Israel . . . [illustrating] something essential in Paul's thought; . . . that the people of the Messiah are the true people of God, continuous with the Israel of the Old Testament. The church is in fact the true Israel of God.[103]

This historical record in Acts and elsewhere displays, not a radical discontinuity from Israel, but rather a progression in the development of God's redemptive purpose—a development that has moved forward from the shadows and types of the Old Testament to the reality of Christ's better ministry. Inherent in this progressive development there is both continuity and discontinuity. There is continuity in that the redemptive story progresses according to God's purpose, but discontinuity in that the nature of the people of God is of a greater nature than before, and the shadowy forms of Israel and her way of life have given way to the intended greater realities.

Specific New Testament Passages Presenting Continuity and Oneness

Paul, a once radical fighter for the cause of Judaism and exclusive national hopes for Israel,[104] now understands this multiracial dimension of the people of God. In Acts 13 Luke records Paul's first visit to Galatia. On this occasion Luke presents Paul as specifically including Gentiles in the promises made to Israel (vv. 16, 26, 32, 33, 48). He also marks a definitive turning toward Gentiles (v. 46) and quotes Isaiah 49:6, a prophecy for Israel, as his basis for doing so. Israel's calling to be a light to the Gentiles is now being put into action by a Jewish follower of Christ.

In Paul's subsequent letter to the Galatians, he is at pains to counter the narrow nationalism of Judaizers by explaining that being children of Abraham is a status shared by all who are in Christ—whether Jew or Gentile. He writes,

---

103. Ladd, *Theology of the New Testament*, 433.
104. Tom Wright, *What Saint Paul Really Said*, 29–30.

Just as Abraham "believed God, and it was reckoned to him as righteousness," so, you see, those who believe are the descendants of Abraham. And the scripture, foreseeing that God would justify the Gentiles by faith, declared the gospel beforehand to Abraham, saying, "All the Gentiles shall be blessed in you." For this reason, those who believe are blessed with Abraham who believed. (Gal 3:6–9)

And if you belong to Christ, then you are Abraham's offspring, heirs according to the promise. (Gal 3:29)

Paul is unambiguous. Christians, those who belong to Christ, are Abraham's offspring—not only that, but they are heirs according to the promise.[105] This raises a most crucial point; there are two Israels. From Abraham a physical nation of people emerged that is Israel the nation. Paul refers to these people of Israel as "*syngenōn mou kata sarka*" (my kindred according to the flesh, Rom 9:3) and again as "*Israēl kata sarka*" (Israel according to the flesh, 1 Cor 10:18). By using this descriptive definition Paul is distinguishing which Israel he is referring to and thus implying the existence of another Israel. He defines this other Israel elsewhere as the "*Israēl tou theou*" (Israel of God, Gal 6:16), Abraham's descendants by faith, who put no confidence in the flesh (i.e., their Jewishness[106]). Being of the former, that is, being of Israel according to the flesh is of no value in being of God's people. This point has already been noted, as when Jews claimed Abraham as their father, but now Paul adds his affirmation:

For neither circumcision nor uncircumcision is anything; but a new creation is everything! As for those who will follow this rule—peace be upon them, and mercy, and upon [NIV: even to] the Israel of God. (Gal 6:15–16)[107]

105. Ladd, "Holy Spirit," 215. "Paul affirms that the blessing of Abraham has already come upon the Gentiles, in the mission of Jesus Christ (Gal 3:8). This means that 'Israel' has received a new definition; all men of faith are the sons of Abraham (Gal 3:7). In light of this, it is probable that the 'Israel of God' in 6:16 refers to the church. The point is that this blessing of the Gentiles, from an OT perspective, is an eschatological blessing, which has been fulfilled, unexpectedly, in history."

106. See Phil 3:3–6 where he again uses the phrase "put no confidence in the flesh" while claiming to have more reason for confidence than any other. He then proceeds to clarify this by naming his Jewish identity credentials and prior commitment to Judaism.

107. The word "and" (Gk: *kai*) can be interpreted as "even"—allowing the phrase to function as a further description of all who see circumcision (Israelite) or uncircumcision (Gentile) as of no value in being part of God's people.

When later writing to the predominately Gentile church in Philippi, Paul writes, "For it is we who are the circumcision, who worship in the Spirit of God and boast in Christ Jesus and have no confidence in the flesh" (3:3). Of the emphatic "we" in this passage Gordon Fee notes:

> the primary issue is not the Philippians' salvation, but rather the identification of the people of God under the new covenant. . . . Paul . . . knows nothing of a 'new' Israel; for him there is only one people of God, newly constituted—quite in keeping with OT promises—on the basis of Christ and the Spirit; and it is by the Spirit in particular that Gentiles have entered into their inheritance of the blessings promised to Abraham. (Gal 3:14)[108]

As in Gal 6:15 above, Paul again uses "circumcision" as a metonym for Israel and claims that the defining identity markers of the "circumcision"—Israel—is that they worship in the Spirit of God and boast in Jesus as the Christ. These are the marks of true Israel. "The right to claim Abraham as father, and enjoy membership in Israel, is forfeited by Jews who refuse to believe."[109] True Israel *boasts in Christ*; this is certainly not a characteristic of the modern political state of Israel. Paul makes a similar point when writing to the believers in Rome:

> For a person is not a Jew who is one outwardly, nor is true circumcision something external and physical. Rather, a person is a Jew who is one inwardly, and real circumcision is a matter of the heart—it is spiritual and not literal. (Rom 2:28–29)

Paul maintains this theme of true Israel as made up of both Jewish and Gentile believers when writing to the Ephesians. In the early section of this letter Paul is outlining the purpose of Christ's cross. The first purpose noted is that of human reconciliation to God (1:1–2:10). A second purpose of the cross is the creation of one people of God, made up of both Jew and Gentile in Christ (2:11–22). This passage is worth including in full—with a few key phrases italicized for emphasis:

> So then, remember that at one time you Gentiles by birth, called "the uncircumcision" by those who are called "the circumcision"— a physical circumcision made in the flesh by human hands— remember that you were at that time without Christ, being aliens from the commonwealth of Israel, and strangers to the covenants

108. Fee, *Philippians*, 298–99.
109. Motyer, "Israel, The New," 572.

of promise, having no hope and without God in the world. *But now in Christ Jesus* you who once were far off have been brought near by the blood of Christ. For he is our peace; *in his flesh he has made both groups into one* and has broken down the dividing wall, that is, the hostility between us. He has abolished the law with its commandments and ordinances, that he might create in himself *one new* [*kainos*, new in nature[110]] *humanity in place of the two, thus making peace, and might reconcile both groups to God in one body* through the cross, thus putting to death that hostility through it. So he came and proclaimed peace to you who were far off and peace to those who were near; for through him both of us have access in one Spirit to the Father. So then you are *no longer strangers and aliens*, but you are citizens [*sympolitai*, co-citizens] with the saints and *also members of the household of God*, built upon the foundation of the apostles and prophets, with Christ Jesus himself as the cornerstone. In him the whole structure *is joined together* and grows into a [Gk: singular] holy temple in the Lord; in whom you also are built together spiritually into a [Gk: singular] dwelling place for God.

This section of Scripture offers strong evidence for the incorporation of believing Gentiles into the covenant people of God through the cross of Christ. Keith Mathison makes the following comparison followed by a summary of this passage:

Gentiles—Pre Christian (Without Christ)	Gentiles—Now Christian (With Christ)
1. Separate from Christ	1. In Christ
2. Excluded from the commonwealth of Israel	2. Included in the commonwealth of Israel
3. Strangers to the covenant of promise	3. Heirs of the covenant of promise
4. Without hope	4. With hope
5. Without God in the world	5. With God in the world

Dispensationalists grant that 1, 4, and 5 are true of Gentile Christians, but not 2 and 3. Paul however, argues that *everything* in verse 12 was formerly true of the Gentiles and that *everything* in verse 12 is no longer true of the Gentile Christians. If believing Gentiles are no longer separate from Christ, they are also

---

110. Behm, "καινός," as opposed to *neos*, new in time.

no longer separate from the commonwealth of Israel. If they are now with hope, they are also now heirs of the covenants of promise.[111]

In reference to this passage, F. F. Bruce once wrote that, "No privilege is bestowed on the people of God in which Gentiles do not enjoy an equal share."[112] Paul, in light of the Christ event in history, considered the church of both Jewish and Gentile believers to be the one body of people who are together the dwelling place of God and heirs of his covenant promises. He believed that Gentile Christians are incorporated in the commonwealth of Israel as co-citizens and co-heirs of the promises— not a distinct and separate people. They belong to the Israel of God in the same manner as do believing Jews and together they share the same hope. To deny this reality is to deny much of what Christ died to accomplish. Gentile believers being included in Israel and her promises parallels what Paul had earlier written in the form of an extended metaphor about an olive tree (Rom 11:17–24).

In this metaphor, natural Israel is pictured as an olive tree (another Old Testament metaphor for Israel, cf. Jer 11:16; 17:4–6) made up of believing and unbelieving Jews. From this tree the unbelieving Jews are said to be cut off, leaving only believing Jews[113]—the true Israel within Israel (cf. Rom 9:6, "not all Israelites truly belong to Israel"). From another tree, a "wild olive shoot," Gentiles who believe are grafted into the very same tree from which the unbelieving Jews were removed, and now together with believing Jews these believing Gentiles share in its richness. This single tree is not a different tree, a brand-new tree called the church. Rather, it is the same tree being Israel now composed of believers from both Jew and Gentile peoples. To share in the richness of its root is to share in that which sustains it, that is, the covenant promises of God to Israel's patriarchs, and the Messiah in whom these are fulfilled.[114]

111. Mathison, *Dispensationalism*, 34. Comparison in table form by this author.

112. Bruce, *Colossians, Philemon, and Ephesians*, 307.

113. Mathison, *Dispensationalism*, 33. Also cf. Acts 3:22–23 as noted earlier. Moses said, "The Lord your God will raise up for you from your own people a prophet like me. You must listen to whatever he tells you. And it will be that everyone who does not listen to that prophet will be utterly rooted out of [NIV: "cut off from among"] the people." Being cut off is a consequence of not listening to Christ as fulfiller of this prophetic statement.

114. N. T. Wright, "Romans," 684; Dunn, *Theology of Paul*, 524; Ladd, *Theology of the New Testament*, 583. "This makes it perfectly clear that the church of Jesus Christ lives

James D. G. Dunn, writing of this passage in Romans (9–11), states that the theme contained here is not "the church and Israel" as is often assumed, but is simply, "Israel" and how Israel is to be understood. He states that Paul's point in this passage is that, "Paul, himself an Israelite (11:1), seeks to understand his heritage as an Israelite and to claim a place for Gentiles within that heritage."[115]

Over and over again the New Testament shows this development whereby the church made up of Jew and Gentile believers assumes the identity of true Israel through being in Christ, and is therefore the beneficiary of God's promises to Abraham. Not only is this so, but there are many times where the church is attributed with names or characteristics once held by Israel of old.

The Suggestion from Common Identity Markers

As one scans the whole of Scripture and identifies terms and concepts that identify God's people, one can quickly observe that characteristics and privileges of Israel from the Old Testament are attributed to the church in the New Testament. Waldron has succinctly summarized these similarities in the following table.[116]

Old Israel or Church	New Israel or Church
1. Saints (Num 16:3; Deut 33:3)	1. Saints (Eph 1:1; Rom 1:7)
2. Elect (Deut 7:6, 7; 14:2)	2. Elect (Col 3:12; Tit 1:1)
3. Beloved (Deut 7:7; 4:37)	3. Beloved (Col 3:12; 1 Thess 1:4)

---

from the root and the trunk of Old Testament Israel." Moo, *Romans*, 702. "As Gentiles, they have no 'natural' relationship to the patriarchs and the promises given to them. Only by God's grace and their faith have they been able to become 'fellow participants' (with Jewish Christians) of the rich root of the olive tree."

115. Dunn, *Theology of Paul*, 507–8.

116. Waldron, *End Times*, 143. This writer would prefer terms other than Old Israel and New Israel. While recognizing two Israels, such terms may imply two different peoples of God rather than a continuation of a people due to ingrafting of believing Gentiles with believing Jews (Rom 11). Perhaps the distinction is better expressed simply by "Israel" and "True Israel" or "Natural [or Empirical, see Ladd, *Theology of the New Testament*, 583] Israel" and "Spiritual Israel." The latter of the comparative terms allows for true believers to be present whether they are part of God's people pre or post the Christ event or whether Jewish or non-Jewish. There has always been a true Israel within natural Israel.

4. Called (Isa 41:9; 43:1)	4. Called (Rom 1:6,7; 1 Cor 1:2)
5. Church (Ps 89:5; Mic 2:5 LXX; Acts 7:38; Heb 2:12)	5. Church (Eph 1:1; Acts 20:28)
6. Flock (Ezek 34; Ps 77:20)	6. Flock (Luke 12:32; 1 Pet 5:2)
7. Holy Nation (Exod 19:5, 6)	7. Holy Nation (1 Pet 2:9)
8. Kingdom of Priests (Exod 19:5, 6)	8. Kingdom of Priests (1 Pet 2:9)
9. Peculiar Treasure (Exod 19:5, 6)	9. Peculiar Treasure (1 Pet 2:9)
10. God's People (Hos 1:9, 10)	10. God's People (1 Pet 2:10)
11. Holy People (Deut 7:6)	11. Holy People (1 Pet 1:15,16)
12. People of Inheritance (Deut 4:20)	12. People of Inheritance (Eph 1:18)
13. God's Tabernacle in Israel (Lev 26:11)	13. God's Tabernacle in Church (John 1:14)
14. God walks among them (Lev 26:12)	14. God walks among them (2 Cor 6:16–18)
15. Twelve Patriarchs	15. Twelve Apostles
16. *Christ married to them* (Isa 54:5; Jer 3:14; Hos 2:19; Jer 6:2; 31:32)	16. Christ married to them (Eph 5:22, 23; 2 Cor 11:2)

While I would question the specific use of numbers 5 and 16, the many similarities between Old Testament Israel and the New Testament church are unmistakably clear.[117] This is strong biblical evidence for the proposition that these common identity markers reveal that the two are in fact one and the same group—believing Gentiles are incorporated into the same people as believing Jews and together constitute true Israel. Terms that Old Testament writers by the inspiration of God applied to Israel, New Testament writers under the same inspiration have then applied to the Christian church.

117. Though Waldron adopts the word "church" for "Old" Israel, this is perhaps anachronistic. However, in support of his inclusion of this parallel, it is true that the Septuagint (LXX) translates the Old Testament Hebrew *qahal* as *ekklēsia*, the Greek word used for the church throughout the New Testament. By doing this there is at least some connection made between early and later expressions of the people of God. See Riddlebarger, *Case for Amillennialism*, 121; Hoekema, *Bible and the Future*, 215; Strom, *Symphony*, 241.

CHAPTER CONCLUSION

N. T. Wright, nearing the end of a chapter titled "Jesus and Israel: The Meaning of Messiahship," asks the question, "Who did Jesus think he was?" To this he responds, "The first answer must be: Israel-in-person, Israel's representative, the one in whom Israel's destiny was reaching its climax."[118] That is the proposal of this chapter: Jesus is true Israel, Israel-in-person. Further, the church, by being "in Christ" who is Israel-in-person, is incorporated into and assumes the identity and mission of true Israel. The church as the Israel of God is a continuation of the believing remnant of Old Testament Israel, having been grafted into her to share in her life source—the covenants of promise. If the proposition presented above along with the associated evidence is valid, then the opposing view of dispensationalism must by necessity be invalid. It does appear that the great weight of New Testament evidence supports the historical position of the church prior to Darby as represented in historic-premillennial, amillennial, and postmillennial views. The mid-nineteenth-century Israel-church distinction proposed by Darby is therefore questionable. The corollary of this understanding is that the church as the body of Christ for whom he died is not a parenthesis, a plan B in the purposes of God brought about solely due to ethnic Israel's rejection of Christ. Rather the church of Christian believers, both Jew and Gentile, *is* the focus of God's love and the focus of God's redeeming plan through the ages. This should in turn cause the church to respond by living up to God's calling for his people in the present, by being a light to the nations of our world.

The contemporary focus on the present state of Israel as a key feature of "end time" speculations is unwarranted and costly in many ways, including both in financial misappropriation and by diverting attention away from the church's purpose of proclaiming the present reality of the kingdom of God—the gospel of forgiveness and peace, a diversion that is at this time perhaps most felt by Palestinians. The Zionist cause has initiated political policies of both the United States and Britain to favor Israel, while the enactment of these has seen many injustices toward the Palestinian people in the last sixty years. Dispensationalism, with its emphasis on a restored political Israel and temple is considered by some Jewish Christians in Israel as a "dangerous heresy," an "unwelcome and

---

118. N. T. Wright, *Jesus and the Victory of God*, 538.

alien intrusion . . . undermining the genuine ministry of justice, peace and reconciliation in the Middle East."[119] The Kairos Palestine 2009 document, written by Palestinian Christian leaders expresses similar concern,

> we know that certain theologians in the West try to attach a biblical and theological legitimacy to the infringement of our rights. Thus, the promises, according to their interpretation, have become a menace to our very existence. The "good news" in the Gospel itself has become "a harbinger of death" for us. We call on these theologians to deepen their reflection on the Word of God and to rectify their interpretations so that they might see in the Word of God a source of life for all peoples.
>
> . . . We suffer from the occupation of our land because we are Palestinians. And as Christian Palestinians we suffer from the wrong interpretation of some theologians. Faced with this, our task is to safeguard the Word of God as a source of life and not of death, so that "the good news" remains what it is, "good news" for us and for all. In face of those who use the Bible to threaten our existence as Christian and Muslim Palestinians, we renew our faith in God because we know that the word of God can not be the source of our destruction.[120]

The Middle East Council of Churches has stated:

> The Christian Zionist programme, with its elevation of modern political Zionism, provides the Christian with a worldview where the gospel is identified with the ideology of success and militarism. It places its emphasis on events leading up to the end of history rather than living Christ's love and justice today.[121]

It is without doubt a very unsatisfactory outcome when one seemingly erroneous theological idea is so easily accepted while theologies of justice and mercy to the oppressed and displaced people of Palestine are either ignored or seen to be of little importance.

---

119. Sizer, "Dispensational Approaches," 167.

120. Kairos Palestine, "Moment of Truth," 2009, articles 2.3.3 and 2.3.4.

121. Cited by Chapman, *Whose Promised Land?* 265.

3

The Kingdom of God

THE PREVIOUS CHAPTERS SUBJECTED to critique the two foremost indispensable criteria of dispensationalism. Both the literal principle of interpretation as the sole guiding rule for the interpretation of Scripture and the absolute distinction between Israel and the church were found to be claims that cannot be sustained when placed under scrutiny. On the other hand, dispensationalism needs these two indispensable and foundational claims to be true in order to undergird the entire system of thought. This raises doubts as to the correctness of the many other tenets of the dispensational system. One such tenet is its understanding of the kingdom of God.

THE DISPENSATIONAL PERSPECTIVE ON THE KINGDOM OF GOD: A POSTPONED POLITICAL JEWISH KINGDOM

According to dispensational thinking, Jesus at his first advent made a genuine offer of a political earthly Davidic kingdom to Israel.[1] Further, according to Chafer, this kingdom offer "was a bona fide offer and, had they received him as their king, the nation's hopes would have been realized."[2] This offer, however, was rejected by Israel. As a result of this rejection of Jesus as their king the realization of Israel's kingdom was postponed until the second coming of Christ and the subsequent millennial dispensation—the kingdom dispensation.

The implications of this understanding with reference to the person and work of Christ are immediately apparent and important to consider. Had Israel accepted Jesus's "bona fide" kingdom offer and thereby receiving the full realization of the nation's hopes, it follows that Jesus

1. Ladd, *Crucial Questions*, 50.
2. Cox, *Examination of Dispensationalism*, 34.

would have been crowned as their king; they would not have had him crucified. The question becomes: What then of the gospel upon which Christians base their faith? What then of the cross by which Christ died in order to reconcile all things to God? Allis rightly poses the question, "If the sequence could have been, first the kingdom, then the Cross, and if the kingdom is to be 'without end,' where can the Cross come in?"[3] S. D. Gordon, being at least consistent with the ramifications of such an understanding, stated, "It can be said at once that His [Christ's] dying was not God's own plan. It was a plan conceived somewhere else and yielded to by God . . . God did not intend the death of Christ."[4] William Cox notes a statement by Clarence Larkin to the same effect: referring to the ministry of John the Baptist, Larkin wrote, "Prepare the way of the Lord for what? Not for the cross but for the Kingdom."[5] Such statements, while no doubt unthinkable to many contemporary dispensationalists, are nonetheless entirely appropriate in light of the dispensational kingdom offer and postponement theory. These statements reflect a deficient Christology in the dispensational system by failing to acknowledge the full extent of the fulfillment motif in the person, life, death, and resurrection of Jesus Christ. They reveal a decidedly literalistic and non-Christological interpretive approach to the Old Testament.

It is essential at this point to note that in dispensational thought the kingdom referred to above is the kingdom of heaven, not the kingdom of God; these two New Testament terms are not understood as referring to the same thing. Drawing on the *Scofield Reference Bible*, O. T. Allis clarifies the dispensational understanding of these two kingdom terms.

> According to Scofield the kingdom of heaven is Jewish, Messianic, Davidic. It is the kingdom promised to David, which promise he tells us enters the New Testament "absolutely unchanged." It was announced as "at hand" from the beginning of the ministry of John the Baptist to "the virtual rejection of the king." Then it was "postponed"; and the prophetic, i.e., future form of this kingdom will be Messianic and millennial: "the kingdom to be set up after the return of the King in glory.

3. Allis, *Prophecy and the Church*, 75.

4. Cited in Ibid., 76.

5. Cox, *Examination of Dispensationalism*, 31.

> The kingdom of God, on the other hand, Scofield defines as "universal, including all moral intelligences willingly subject to the will of God, whether angels, the Church, or saints of past or future dispensations.". . . The present church age is, therefore, a dispensation of the kingdom of God; but it is not a dispensation of the kingdom of heaven.[6]

The kingdom of God, by Scofield's definition, is therefore a present reality; the kingdom of heaven is entirely for a future time (a one-thousand-year period after Christ returns) and will constitute the fulfillment of Old Testament promises to Israel. Due to Christ's rejection and the consequent postponement of the Davidic "kingdom of heaven," the church age was introduced. The church, however, is not in any way related to the yet-to-come kingdom of heaven; this is the same as saying the church has no relationship to the Old Testament promises given to national Israel. Dispensationalists therefore continue to look for a future Davidic earthly kingdom (ironically called the kingdom of heaven) to be established subsequent to Christ's second advent. This theory is in every respect wholly reliant upon the dispensational insistence that God has distinct redemptive purposes for Israel and the church—a distinction refuted in the previous chapter and thereby presenting a considerable challenge to Scofield's two-kingdom view. A rudimentary survey of the Synoptic Gospels where the terms "kingdom of God" and "kingdom of heaven" are employed (the latter found only in Matthew's Gospel[7] will reveal that the two terms are in fact synonymous; they are equivalent and entirely transposable terms referring to one and the same kingdom. The synonymy of the terminology is clearly seen in Matthew 19:23–34 by Jesus's employment of a form of communication similar to that of a parallelism, a device unique to Hebrew poetry whereby a thought is repeated by the use of different wording. Verses 23–24 read as follows:

> 23 Then Jesus said to his disciples, "Truly I tell you, it will be hard for a rich person to enter the kingdom of heaven. 24 Again [*palin de*] I tell you, it is easier for a camel to go through the eye of a needle than for someone who is rich to enter the kingdom of God.

6. Allis, *Prophecy and the Church*, 68; see also Ladd, *Crucial Questions*, 102.

7. It is frequently acknowledged that Matthew (a Jew) is writing to a Jewish audience. As such he is sensitive to Jewish concerns regarding the use of and potential mispronunciation of God's name and employs a known substitute, i.e., heaven. For example, Cox, *Examination of Dispensationalism*, 35; Hoekema, *Bible and the Future*, 44.

The emphatic position of *palin de* in the Greek text of verse 24 stresses the fact that despite the different wording Jesus is repeating again the same point of his first statement in which he spoke of entry into the *kingdom of heaven* being hard for the rich. In the second statement, the term *kingdom of God* is parallel to *kingdom of heaven* in the first, affirming that these two terms refer to only one kingdom. Further, the twice-stated references to the kingdom appear to have been understood by the disciples as referring to a singular concept—that is, salvation.[8] They responded to Jesus with only one question: "Then who can be saved" (v. 25). Furthermore, a comparison of Matthew 10:7 and Luke 9:2—both a record of Jesus's sending the twelve disciples on a mission—demonstrates the same point. In Matthew they are to proclaim the kingdom of heaven, whereas in the Lukan parallel account they are to proclaim the kingdom of God. Parallel passages, same contexts, and Jesus's use of an emphatic parallel to express a single point each affirm that the terms *kingdom of God* and *kingdom of heaven* are both references to one and the same thing.[9]

The dispensational bifurcation of the kingdom, despite appearing erroneous, is nonetheless of paramount importance in the overall dispensational belief system. It parallels the equally misguided bifurcation of the people of God; one bifurcation makes necessary the other. There is, however, only one people of God; there is only one kingdom of God. This truth further undermines the validity of the dispensational hermeneutic and the belief system as a whole; dispensationalism relies entirely on a two-people, two-kingdom understanding—both of which are seen to be untenable claims.

It should be noted that the kingdom(s) as understood by dispensationalists can lead to confusion in how one makes use of the two terms. Immediately subsequent to accurately noting and defining the dispensational two-kingdom view, Riddlebarger proceeds to refer to the kingdom of God as that which will not come until the millennium after Christ's return.[10] This is not the case according to Scofield's definition of the terms. The proposed post–second advent millennial era is the time of the kingdom of heaven—the time of the earthly realization of the Old Testament promises to Israel. If, however, as has been shown, the two

8. Ladd, *Presence of the Future*, 126.

9. Cox, *Examination of Dispensationalism*, 34–37; Ladd, *Crucial Questions*, 172.

10. Riddlebarger, *Case for Amillennialism*, 101.

terms refer to the same kingdom, then, according to Scofield's definition, the kingdom of heaven/God is a present reality. Yet for dispensationalists this kingdom (of heaven) is considered to be the future earthly
reign of Jesus Christ in Jerusalem. This point has been labored in order
to ensure understanding of the use of the two different kingdom terms
within dispensationalism.

For the sake of clarity, this discussion will proceed on the basis that
in dispensational thought the kingdom, as it relates to Old Testament
promises, is now a post–second advent expectation. Having established
the fact of there being only one kingdom, it remains now to put forward
a non-dispensational understanding of this crucial tenet of eschatology.

THE KINGDOM OF GOD:
A NON-DISPENSATIONAL PERSPECTIVE

Establishing a Hermeneutical Framework

It was noted at the outset of this book that for any discussion between
dispensationalists and non-dispensationalists to be of value one must
first deal with the all-important issue of hermeneutics as it relates to
eschatological thought. Based on the discussion thus far, the following
interpretive criteria will now serve to form a non-dispensational understanding of the kingdom:

- The Old and New Testaments present one unified story of God's
  redeeming work that is accomplished in Christ (Eph 3:11). That
  purpose extends beyond Jewish nationalistic and political hopes to
  achieve redemption for humanity and all creation to the complete
  reversal of sin's effects.

- The progressive development of that overall biblical story demands a rereading of the Old Testament in light of the New
  Testament and the forward movement in the development of that
  story. New Testament writers consistently model the validity of this
  approach.[11]

- The New Testament often presents fulfillment of the Old Testament
  promises and prophecies in a surprisingly nonliteral manner. A
  strict literalist interpretation is insufficient to accurately interpret

11. Strom, "Walking into One Conversation," 6.

Scripture. "For the New Testament the interpretation of the Old Testament is not 'literal' but 'Christological.' That is to say that the coming of the Christ transforms all the Kingdom terms of the Old Testament into gospel reality."[12] In addition to good grammatical-historical interpretation of the Old Testament, there needs to be a readiness to see meaning as nuanced by the later revelation, development, and fulfillments in the New Testament, in particular in the life, death, and resurrection of Christ.

- Christ is the center and *telos* of Scripture.[13] The prophecies and promises of the Old Testament given to Israel find their fulfillment in Jesus.

- The church, by being in Christ, is a continuation of true Israel as recipient of God's redemptive promises rather than a distinct people with whom God deals differently. "Israel can never again be defined apart from Jesus Christ."[14] The church is now incorporated into and assumes the identity, hopes, destiny, and mission of true Israel.

The above-stated truths must come to bear on one's view of the kingdom of God. Without doubt, however, the foremost interpretive principle of Scripture is Jesus Christ himself. Noted earlier were Jesus's own words pertaining to his understanding of himself in relation to the Jewish Scriptures—how in their entirety they told of him and thereby how he declared himself to be the "hermeneutical key to all of scripture."[15] "Interpretation today must work from this same conviction."[16]

> Oh, how foolish you are, and how slow of heart to believe *all* that the prophets have declared! Was it not necessary that the Messiah should suffer these things and then enter into his glory?" Then beginning with *Moses* and *all the prophets*, he interpreted to them the things about himself in *all the scriptures*. (Luke 24:25–27, emphasis added)

---

12. Goldsworthy, *Gospel and Kingdom*, 91.
13. Strom, "Walking into One Conversation," 6.
14. Holwerda, *Jesus and Israel*, 36.
15. Strom, "Walking into One Conversation," 6.
16. Ibid.

Paul, when writing to the church at Corinth, appears to have understood this: "For no matter how many (*hosai gar*, lit: For as many as) promises God has made, they are 'yes' in Christ" (2 Cor 1:20 TNIV). As we noted in the previous chapter, the importance of these words should not be understated; all God's promises are included. This principle has been clearly seen as applied to Israel being redefined in Jesus, and likewise it equally has implications for understanding God's promises to Israel concerning the kingdom; kingdom promises must be included in the *hosai*. For Paul's claim to be true, fulfillment of Israel's promises of a kingdom must be found at work in Jesus Christ and by extension in his newly constituted "in Christ" Israel (the church), rather than being relegated to a future time. How else could Jesus say to his Father, "I glorified you on earth by finishing [*teleiōsas*, having completed] the work that you gave me to do"? (John 17:4)—a claim made by Jesus that is particularly damaging to the dispensationalist kingdom postponement view—one that could not be made had he failed to fulfill the kingdom promises. Jesus completed what he was sent to do; he was and is God's "yes" to all that he had promised Israel, including those promises related to their kingdom hopes.

Defining the Kingdom

The term "kingdom of God" is neither used nor specifically defined in Old Testament Scripture. The Gospels simply, and again without definition, declare its arrival. It is evident that writers of the Synoptic Gospels each have distinctive theological emphases and purposes that shape their witness to the ministry of Christ, yet they seem remarkably consistent in their documenting the historical reality that the kingdom of God had come: "The time is fulfilled, and the kingdom of God has come near; repent, and believe in the good news" (Mark 1:15; see also Luke 4:43; Matt 3:2, 4:17, 23). These verses present significant details that need to be identified. First, the seemingly sudden biblical use of the term and the lack of its explanation imply that the first (Jewish) hearers understood what was meant.[17] "Jewish writers after the Old Testament had used it

---

17. In time Jesus did teach about the kingdom as seen in passages such as Mark 4:26, "the kingdom of God is like . . . ," and Matt 13:47, "the kingdom of heaven is like . . ."; however, the notion of the kingdom and the term itself seems to come as no surprise to the original hearers in Jewish contexts.

frequently to describe the coming time of salvation associated with the appearance of the Messiah."[18]

Second, this kingdom announcement was one of fulfillment, thereby referring its hearers back to something previously promised and therefore expected. Third, the arrival of the kingdom was good news, that is, "gospel" (*euangelion* in LXX), a word associated in Isaiah 52:7 with God's reign by means of poetic parallelism:

> How beautiful upon the mountains
> are the feet of the messenger who announces peace,
> who brings good news, [*euangelion*]
> who announces salvation,
> who says to Zion, "Your God reigns."

This association of *euangelion* and kingdom is affirmed by N. T. Wright, who has shown that in both first-century Jewish and non-Jewish contexts *euangelion* was used for the announcing of a king.[19] The gospel is the gospel of the kingdom.

Fourth, this kingdom message becomes *the* dominant theme of Jesus's ministry.[20] It is something he must preach (Luke 4:43) and is spoken of by him frequently from the beginning of his ministry through to being the topic of his teaching to the disciples during the time between his resurrection and ascension (Acts 1:3). The theme of the kingdom continues to be the dominant theme in the mission and message of the church as recorded in the book of Acts (8:12; 17:7; 19:8; 20:25; 28:23, 31),[21] and still there is no explicit statement defining the term. Language of fulfillment, however, directs interpreters back to the Old Testament; there the concept of kingship is extensive.

A major emphasis throughout the Old Testament is that God is king. He was king of Israel (Deut 9:26). The psalmist writes that he is "enthroned as king forever" (Ps 29:10) and his rule or authority is "over the nations" (Ps 22:28). The extent of his kingship is seen in Isaiah 66:1: "Heaven is my throne, and the earth is my footstool." Riddlebarger

---

18. Strom, *Symphony*, 157.

19. Tom Wright, *What Saint Paul Really Said*, 41–44.

20. Ladd, *Theology of the New Testament*, 54; Hoekema, *Bible and the Future*, 41.

21. Though the term "kingdom of God" is used less frequently throughout the remaining New Testament books, Hoekema, quoting Karl Ludwig Schmidt, asserts that the concept is implicit in *Kurios Iēsous Cristos* language. Hoekema, *Bible and the Future*, 43. See also N. T. Wright, *Resurrection of the Son of God*, 563–66.

writes, "Clearly, the picture of a throne is meant to convey regal authority and rule."[22] Isaiah, however, by his use of *heaven* and *earth*, portrays the cosmic scope of that rule—all of creation is God's palace, "the throne room of the King of kings."[23]

Hoekema writes,

> The kingdom of God . . . is to be understood as the reign of God dynamically active in human history through Jesus Christ, the purpose of which is redemption of God's people from sin and from demonic powers, and the final establishment of the new heavens and the new earth. . . . The kingdom must not be understood as merely the salvation of certain individuals or even as the reign of God in the hearts of his people; it means nothing less than the reign of God over his entire created universe. "The Kingdom of God means that God is King and acts in history to bring history to a divinely directed goal."[24]

While scholarship frequently discusses whether "kingdom" refers to the concept of rule rather than a territory, Hoekema rightly brings the two together: "the reign of God over his entire created universe."[25] Rule, despite being the primary emphasis throughout the Old Testament's use of king/kingship language, nonetheless requires a place in which to be administered.[26] Ladd writes concerning this, "there should therefore be no philological or logical reason why the Kingdom of God may not be conceived of both as the reign of God and as the realm in which his reign is experienced."[27] Hoekema points readers to the final establishment of the kingdom/rule of God in the new heavens and new earth. Clearly God's kingdom is much greater than the idea that it is restricted to one race of people located on an extremely small block of land known as Israel/Palestine and limited to one thousand years; rather, it extends to the redemption of creation (Rom 8:23).

> When Yahweh comes to bring his kingdom, it is to this world that he comes and in this world that he establishes his reign. The

22. Riddlebarger, *Case for Amillennialism*, 104–5.

23. Kline, *Kingdom Prologue*, 27.

24. Hoekema, *Bible and the Future*, 45, quoting Ladd.

25. BDAG, "βασιλεία," 168–69. Glosses include "the act of ruling" and "territory ruled by a king."

26. C. Marshall, *Kingdom Come*, 43.

27. Ladd, *Presence of the Future*, 195.

hope of Israel is not for a home in heaven but for the revelation
of the glory of God in this world, when 'the earth shall be full
of the glory of the Lord as the waters fill the sea' (Hab 2:14). . . .
In the person of the Messiah God's purpose in history finds its
embodiment.[28]

Israel's prophetic voice provided the nation with grounds to hope
for restoration and to look for the coming of a messianic king; however,
the Gospels assert that the realization of that hope did come to them
in the Messiah, Jesus Christ. The opening chapters of Luke's Gospel are
unambiguous in declaring Jesus as the "consolation of Israel" and the
"redemption of Jerusalem" (Luke 2:25, 38). He was recognized to be that
redeeming Messiah of restoration hope by Simeon, whose words are
expressions of fulfillment and of hope realized:

Master, now you are dismissing your servant in peace,
according to your word;
for my eyes have seen your salvation,
which you have prepared in the presence of all peoples,
a light for revelation to the Gentiles
and for glory to your people Israel. (Luke 2:29–32)

Mary was told that her as yet unborn son was to be called Jesus,
that he was the one to whom God would give the throne of his ancestor David (Luke 1:32). He would reign over the house of Jacob forever,
and of his kingdom there would be no end (Luke 1:33). In Mary's
prayer of response she associated these kingdom fulfillments with God
remembering his promises to Abraham (Luke 1:55)—thereby is seen
Christ's kingdom as fulfillment of the Abrahamic covenant whereby
blessing would be universal. It has already been shown that believers,
by belonging to Christ, are heirs of the Abrahamic covenant and thus
incorporated into the covenant people and beneficiaries of the kingdom.
When the Gospels announced that "the kingdom of God was at hand,
this meant that God had come to his people to bring them salvation."[29]
Non-dispensationalists are in agreement with dispensationalists in recognizing that Israel collectively as a nation did reject Christ as Messiah
(despite the fact that his first followers were Jewish) but rather than result
in a postponement of the kingdom, the biblical story reveals it was to be

---

28. Beasley-Murray, *Jesus and the Kingdom*, 25.

29. Riddlebarger, *Case for Amillennialism*, 106.

"given to others"—"to a people that produces the fruit of the kingdom" as portrayed in the parable of the tenants (Matt 21:33–43; Mark 12:1–12; Luke 20:9–19). Redemption would be accomplished in a manner not expected and would extend beyond the nation of Israel. "For God so loved the world [*kosmos*] that he gave his only Son, so that everyone who believes in him may not perish but may have eternal life" (John 3:16). As well as being Israel's salvation, Jesus was at the same time salvation for the whole *kosmos*.

Kingdom of God, Salvation, Eternal Life, and the Age to Come

In stark contrast to the Synoptic Gospels, John's Gospel refers to the kingdom only four times. Only twice does he make use of the term "kingdom of God." On both occasions he regards *seeing it* and *entry into it* in ways that depict its nonnationalistic nature. Seeing the kingdom is by being "born from above" (John 3:3) and entry by being "born of water and Spirit" (John 3:5). Salvation is the sole requirement for belonging to the kingdom of God. This appears in keeping with his other two kingdom references, in which he records Jesus as saying,

> My kingdom is not from this world. If my kingdom were from this world, my followers would be fighting to keep me from being handed over to the Jews. But as it is, my kingdom is not from here. (John 18:36)

It should be noted that God's kingdom is one that is from God—its origin is not a human construct and is therefore entirely compatible with both the nature and timing of the kingdom predicted in Daniel 2:44–45. Humanity enters this kingdom by means of a work from above by the Spirit. John, it seems, has no notion of a Jewish political kingdom achieved by warfare and defeat of national enemies, a thought common to Jewish nationalistic hopes from their Messiah.[30] Instead he prefers to speak of "eternal life." Ladd writes that the place of the Synoptics' "kingdom of God" "has been taken by the concept of eternal life as Jesus' central message."[31] Leon Morris notes also that "John frequently speaks of eternal life, and for him the possession of eternal life appears to mean

---

30. N. T. Wright, *Jesus and the Victory of God*, 203; 223.

31. Ladd, *Theology of the New Testament*, 251.

very much the same as entering the kingdom of God as the Synoptists picture it."[32]

Jesus also associated eternal life with the kingdom of God, as seen in Matthew 19:23–24, previously referred to in order to establish the synonymy of "kingdom of heaven" and "kingdom of God." Of particular interest at this point, however, is that Jesus's words, speaking as he did regarding entry into the kingdom, were spoken in the context of the rich young ruler's question regarding what good thing he must do to have eternal life (19:16). Clearly Jesus regarded eternal life and kingdom of God as closely associated. Salvation, eternal life, and the kingdom therefore appear to be to a large extent, if not entirely, corresponding concepts. As noted earlier, the disciples, as a consequence of this conversation, asked Jesus what needed to be done in order to be saved. In the Lukan account of this conversation Jesus replied,

> Truly I tell you, there is no one who has left house or wife or brothers or parents or children, for the sake of the kingdom of God, who will not get back very much more in this age, and in the age to come eternal life. (Luke 18:29–30)[33]

Eternal life is now associated with "the age to come," thus introducing another term into the discussion. There are now a number of concepts that are correlated: salvation, eternal life, kingdom of God, and the age to come. Tom Wright suggests that *eternal life* may be appropriately understood as "the life of the age to come" rather than simply "existence without end"[34]—indicating that *eternal life* implies a quality of life. We are to hear the rich young man's question in verse 23 as, "How can I experience the blessings of the life of the age to come (or the kingdom of God), now?"[35] Ladd has noted this also and writes,

> In the Gospels the eschatological salvation is described as entrance into the kingdom of God (Mark 9:47; 10:24), into the age

---

32. Morris, *John*, 190.

33. The Lukan "age to come" is paralleled by Matthew's "at the renewal of all things" (Luke 18:30; Matt 19:28).

34. Tom Wright, *Acts for Everyone*, 205.

35. Marshall, *New Testament Theology*, 194–95, 205. N. T. Wright, *Surprised by Hope*, 205, comments, "Heaven's rule, God's rule, is thus to be put into practice in the world, resulting in salvation in both the present and the future."

to come (Mark 10:30), and into eternal life (Mark 9:45; 10:17, 30; Matt 25:46). These three idioms are interchangeable.[36]

F. F. Bruce concurs:

> Sometimes Jesus uses "life" or "eternal life" (the life of the age to come) as a synonym for "the kingdom of God"; to enter the kingdom is to enter life. This links the kingdom with the new age, when the righteous are brought back from death to enjoy resurrection life.[37]

Ascertaining the connectedness of these biblical terms is crucial to forming an overall understanding of the kingdom of God. Each term, being directly related to the others, will serve to inform this discussion.

This Age, the Age to Come, and the Now-Not Yet

The terms "this age" and "age to come" appear frequently throughout the New Testament.[38] The repeated use of this terminology in the Gospels and many of the epistles call for a close analysis of their usage in order gain the significance of their contribution to eschatological understanding and in particular to understanding the kingdom of God. Samuel Waldron has completed such a study and brought attention to important details concerning the use of these terms. In so doing he provides a helpful framework for understanding the kingdom in relation to a biblical view of time.[39] He suggests that "there is no more basic or formative issue for our understanding of the structure of biblical eschatology . . . than the teaching of the Bible with regard to . . . the two ages." His study develops through three successive and logically dependant discussions: the biblical terminology of the two ages, the basic scheme of the two ages, and the modified scheme of the two ages. From his study he presents the following, albeit abridged conclusions.

First, he concludes that "this age and the age to come are qualitatively different states of human existence and qualitatively different periods in the history of the world." Characteristics of this age include marriage, death, natural human existence, and the coexistence of both the righteous and the wicked. It is an evil age (Gal 1:4). Riddlebarger

---

36. Ladd, "Kingdom of God, Christ, Heaven," 610.

37. Bruce, "Eschatology," 364.

38. Other related terms are the "coming age" and "that age." All speak of the same age.

39. Waldron, *End Times*, 30–44.

writes, "The qualities assigned by the biblical writers to 'this age' were always temporal in nature and represented the fallen world. . . . the 'age to come' is an age of eternal life and immortality . . . characterized by the realization of all the blessings of the resurrection and consummation."[40] The age to come is characterized by no marriage, no death, resurrected human existence, and only the righteous are present (Luke 20:27–40). Second, together this age and the age to come "exhaust all of time including the endless time of the eternal state." Last, "The great realities of the age to come have broken into and are already operative in this age," thus creating an overlap of the ages. Riddlebarger concurs when he writes,

> Throughout the New Testament *this age* refers to the present course of human history, while the *age to come* refers to the age of redemption realized with the coming of Jesus Christ, his bodily resurrection, and his exaltation.[41]

Cornelis P. Venema writes in agreement, "the first and most fundamental dimension of the New Testament's outlook upon the future is, ironically, that the future is now."[42] The age to come is therefore a present in-part reality in this age, the fullness of which awaits the second coming of Christ. Figure 2 represents this framework in diagrammatic form.

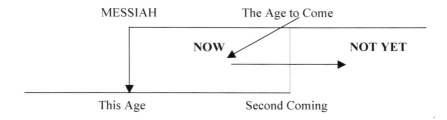

Figure 2: The Now, Not Yet of the Kingdom

This New Testament structure is a modification of the Jewish understanding that saw reality as comprised of two periods of time: this age and the age to come. The former period, the present time, is affected by sin and suffering and would be replaced by the in-breaking of the king-

40. Riddlebarger, *Case for Amillennialism*, 83.

41. Ibid., 81.

42. Venema, *Promise of the Future*, 24.

dom of God, the coming age of righteousness and peace. The age to come was thought to be subsequent to this age and would be fully introduced by the appearance of the Messiah.[43] Fee notes, however, that early Christianity believed that the age to come had arrived in the person of Christ through his death, resurrection, and giving of the Spirit. As such God had brought the future into the present to be consummated by a second coming of Christ. There is therefore a degree of continuity linking the present and future experience of the kingdom on earth.[44] Fee writes,

> Already God had secured their salvation; already they were the people of the future, living the life of the future in the present age—and enjoying its benefits. But they still awaited the glorious consummation of this salvation. Thus they lived in an essential tension between the "already" and the "not yet."[45]

Numerous biblical passages exist to support this two-age framework and the in-breaking of the age to come into the present. One example can be found in Paul's letter to Titus:

> For the grace of God has appeared, bringing salvation to all, training us to renounce impiety and worldly passions, and in the present age to live lives that are self-controlled, upright, and godly, while we wait for the blessed hope and the manifestation of the glory of our great God and Savior, Jesus Christ. (Tit 2:11–13)

Paul clearly teaches that that which brought salvation has appeared to change life in the present age while waiting for the return of Christ. Salvation, as has been seen before, is equated with the kingdom and the age to come, yet it has appeared in the present—a future reality has invaded the present. Eternal life, despite its being a future hope characteristic of the age to come and the kingdom of God, is emphatically declared by Jesus to be a present possession of believers; they now have the life of the age to come. "Very truly, I tell you, anyone who hears my word and believes him who sent me *has* eternal life" (John 5:24, emphasis added). William Dumbrell echoes this as he writes, "in [the Gospel of] John eternal life is not endless life, but the life of the age to come, life in the presence of God experienced now (17:3), the eschatological life drawn with anticipation into the present age (3:15–16; 5:40; 6:40, 47, 53; 68; 10:10)."[46] Waldron also notes,

---

43. Pate, *End of the Age*, 12–13.
44. Kusmič, "History and Eschatology," 151.
45. Fee, *1 and 2 Timothy, Titus*, 19.
46. Dumbrell, *Search for Order*, 247.

Everywhere the Bible assumes the two-stage nature of salvation: *Justification* (Romans 5:1; Matthew 12:37), *adoption* (Romans 8:14–16 with verse 23 of the same chapter and also Galatians 4:4–6 with Eph 4:30), and *redemption* (Ephesians 1:7 with 4:30), *eternal life* (John 3:36; Matthew 25:46), *rest* (Matt 11:29; Hebrews 4:9–11).[47]

Each of these aspects of salvation include a present experience yet also that which is yet to be. This reveals that the kingdom realities of the age to come are both now and not yet. The very close association of salvation terminology in relation to the kingdom of God and the clear present but two-phase dimension attributed to them supports a now but not-yet realization of that kingdom. To relegate the kingdom to only a future reality denies the strong biblical evidence for its present manifestation.

Resurrection has also been identified as a key characteristic of the age to come/kingdom of God. Peter's Pentecost address explicitly proclaims to his Jewish hearers that the resurrection of Jesus is the fulfillment of the Davidic kingdom promises; thus in Jesus's resurrection the age to come, the kingdom, has become a present experience.

Fellow Israelites, I may say to you confidently of our ancestor David that he both died and was buried, and his tomb is with us to this day. Since he was a prophet, he knew that God had sworn with an oath to him that he would put *one of his descendants on his throne.* Foreseeing this, David *spoke of the resurrection of the Messiah.* . . . Therefore let the entire house of Israel know with certainty that God has made him both Lord and Messiah, this Jesus whom you crucified. (Acts 2:29–31, 36, emphasis added)

Paul similarly associated the resurrection of Jesus with the fulfillment of kingdom promises made to David, saying,

And we bring you the good news that what God promised to our ancestors he has fulfilled for us, their children, *by raising Jesus;* as also it is written in the second psalm, "You are my Son; today I have begotten you." As to his raising him from the dead, no more to return to corruption, he has spoken in this way, "I will give you the *holy promises made to David.*" (Acts 13:32–34, emphasis added)

47. Waldron, *End Times,* 51.

Further support for the present presence of the future can be found in the language of *first fruits* as applied to resurrection and the giving of the Spirit. The Apostle Paul in his lengthy treatment regarding resurrection in 1 Corinthian 15 applies to Christ's resurrection from the dead this language of first fruits:

> But in fact Christ has been raised from the dead, the first fruits of those who have died. For since death came through a human being, the resurrection of the dead has also come through a human being; for as all die in Adam, so all will be made alive in Christ. But each in his own order: Christ the first fruits, then at his coming those who belong to Christ. (1 Cor 15:20–23)

Gordon Fee writes concerning the significance of Paul's thinking in this passage:

> Paul's thinking is thoroughly eschatological. He understood both the death and resurrection of Christ and the subsequent gift of the Spirit as eschatological realities. . . . The absolutely crucial matter in this view is the resurrection of Jesus from the dead. In Paul's Jewish eschatological heritage resurrection belonged to the final events of the End. The fact that *the* resurrection had already taken place within history meant that the End had been set inexorably in motion; the resurrection of Christ absolutely guaranteed for Paul the resurrection of all who are "in Christ."[48]

The use of the agricultural first fruits metaphor calls to mind images of a harvest whereby a first portion of a whole crop would be consecrated to God. Key to this is that first fruits were representative and part of the whole crop, not a distinct and separate entity. James Dunn writes, "The gift of the Spirit then is the first phase of the harvest which consists in the resurrection of the body. . . . The Spirit is the power of God's final purpose already beginning to reclaim the whole person for God."[49]

Resurrection, being of the age to come but yet experienced in Christ as first fruits (*aparchē*), and the gift of the Spirit both affirm that the age to come/kingdom of God has broken into the present as God's guarantee of its full arrival. Fee continues,

> In his usage, therefore, the [first fruits] metaphor functions similarly to that of the "down payment" or "earnest money" of the Spirit in 2 Cor 1:22 and 5:5 (cf. Eph 1:14); both serve as a present

48. Fee, *First Corinthians*, 746.

49. Dunn, *Theology of Paul*, 469.

pledge on the part of God for the final eschatological harvest or payment. . . . Paul is asserting by way of metaphor that the resurrection of the believing dead is absolutely inevitable; it has been guaranteed by God himself.[50]

The gift of the Spirit, "the promised gift of the new age for Israel (Joel 2:28)"[51] is mentioned here by Fee as a "down payment" (*arrabōn*). Its use in the above-mentioned references is affirming that the age to come is in part realized in the present. By borrowing a metaphor from the world of commerce, Paul's use of *arrabōn* firmly establishes the now in-part realization of what is still future. BDAG defines *arrabōn* as a "*first instalment, deposit, down payment, pledge,* that pays a part of the purchase price in advance, and so secures a legal claim to the article in question, or makes a contract valid."[52] Paul's usage, particularly in writing to a Greek context,[53] confirms the Spirit as an "in advance" part of the future inheritance as God's guarantee that the balance of that future, that is, the age to come, will indeed come. Dunn notes concerning *arrabōn*,

> This is what the Spirit is for Paul, the first instalment of the wholeness of salvation. By linking the Spirit as *arrabōn* with the thought of inheritance, Eph. 1.13–14 simply makes explicit what was implicit in the earlier inheritance references: the Spirit is the first instalment of the kingdom of God.[54]

Perhaps the most clearly stated affirmation of the future age to come being a partially present reality for believers is found in Hebrews 6:4–5,

> For it is impossible to restore again to repentance those who have once been enlightened, and have tasted the heavenly gift, and have shared in the Holy Spirit, and have tasted the goodness of the word of God and the powers of the age to come.

The writer of these words clearly states that those who have shared in the Holy Spirit have in some way "tasted" not only the goodness of the word of God, but also the powers of the age to come. That is, according to BAGD, they partake, enjoy, and (figuratively) have come to know and

---

50. Fee, *First Corinthians*, 749.

51. Dumbrell, *Search for Order*, 188.

52. BDAG, "ἀρραβών," 134. Present-day usage continues to regard a deposit as part of the whole purchase price rather than an amount distinct and separate.

53. Williams, *Paul's Metaphors*, 180.

54. Dunn, *Theology of Paul*, 469; see also N. T. Wright, *Paul*, 146.

experience something of the age to come.[55] This seems to be the thought in Paul's mind when he writes in 1 Cor 13:12, "Now I know only in part; then I will know fully."

It seems then that the New Testament consistently presents a clear structure of two overlapping ages for understanding time. Humanity continues to experience a temporal state of existence and yet many possess eternal life and have entered the kingdom. The overlapping period of the ages is "now"; the full realization of that age (of the kingdom) is "not yet."

> Jesus proclaimed *both* that the kingdom had already come *and* that it was still to come in its entirety. His kingdom message (and indeed the whole of New Testament theology) is pervaded by this distinctive 'already . . . not yet' tension.[56]

This view, according to Christopher Marshall, is the "interpretation that has won the scholarly consensus."[57] Consideration has been given to the parallel terminology of eternal life, salvation, age to come, and kingdom of God, and their synonymous and interchangeable nature shows that each of these is a present reality; it remains now to consider specific references to the kingdom in particular. It will be shown that there are both present and future aspects of the kingdom of God parallel to the now and not-yet structure.

The Kingdom of God as a Now-Present Reality

A survey of the New Testament kingdom of God/kingdom of heaven passages reveals that Jesus and the New Testament writers regarded the kingdom as a present reality. The frequent use of *estin*, a present-tense verb, in combination with kingdom language indicates that the kingdom is indeed present; for example, "Blessed are the poor in spirit for theirs *is* the kingdom of heaven" (Matt 5:3). Jesus, in so many of his parabolic teachings, said the kingdom God or heaven "*is* like . . ." John the Baptist declared that "the time *is* fulfilled, and the kingdom of God *has* come near" (e.g., Mark 1:15). The fact that this now-arrived kingdom was to be announced with accompanying healings, and so on (Matt 10:7–8) and that people are to respond and believe the good news implies it was pres-

---

55. BAGD, "γεύομαι," 157.

56. C. Marshall, *Kingdom Come*, 48.

57. Ibid.

ent and to be experienced in tangible ways. The announcement of the present kingdom is an activity that continued many years after Christ, as seen when Philip proclaimed the good news about the kingdom to the Samaritan people (Acts 8:12), and again as the Apostle Paul spoke out boldly and argued persuasively about the kingdom in Ephesus (Acts 19:8) and in Rome (Acts 28:23, 31). It is significant that so many years after the rejection and crucifixion of Christ that these witnesses do not speak of the kingdom as postponed, but rather they continue to proclaim it as a present reality. In fact, nowhere in the New Testament is there any teaching of a postponed kingdom.

Forgiveness of sin was a significant part of Jewish expectations for the coming age of Messiah's reign. Jeremiah, in speaking of the coming days of the new covenant that God would make with Israel and Judah, said, "I will forgive their iniquity, and remember their sin no more" (Jer 31:34; see also Zech 13:1). Jesus came causing a stir because he announced the forgiveness of sin (Matt 9:2; Mark 2:5, 10; Luke 1:77; 5:20, 24; 7:48). Forgiveness of sins is like many other terms closely paralleled to the kingdom, and like the kingdom, forgiveness is something to be proclaimed to all nations (Luke 24:47). Forgiveness of sins is a further sign that the kingdom of God has come in the person of Christ.

The miracles of Jesus likewise testify about the kingdom as a present experience. In his sending the seventy, Jesus told these disciples to "cure the sick . . . and say to them, 'The kingdom of God has come near to you'" (Luke 10:9). The experience of their healing appears to be an experience of the kingdom present with them. In the same context, Jesus tells his disciples to say to those who do not welcome them, "Even the dust of your town that clings to our feet, we wipe off in protest against you. Yet know this: the kingdom of God has come near" (v. 11). To reject this message of the presence of the kingdom was to have devastating consequences (v. 12). The rejection of some did not, however, result in a postponement of the kingdom; despite the rejection by such people, they were to "know" that the kingdom of God had indeed invaded the present age. In Luke 11:20, the association of the kingdom's presence with miraculous activity is again seen in the exorcising of demons. Having just expelled a demon, Jesus said to his antagonists, "But if it is by the finger of God that I cast out the demons, then the kingdom of God has come to you." When asked about the timing of the arrival of the kingdom, Jesus replied, "the kingdom of God *is* among you" (Luke 17:20–21). It was present in the person and restorative ministry of Jesus. This is entirely consistent with the claim earlier made that the Old Testament hopes and promises of a kingdom find their fulfillment in Christ. Hoekema writes,

> We may say, therefore, that Jesus himself ushered in the kingdom of God whose coming had been foretold by the Old Testament prophets. We must therefore always see the kingdom of God as indissolubly connected with the person and work of Jesus Christ. In Jesus' words and deeds, miracles and parables, teaching and preaching, the kingdom was dynamically active and present among men.[58]

It was to his miracles that Jesus referred John the Baptist when he became unsure if Jesus really was the expected Messiah. Preaching and healing functioned as Jesus's evidence, the proof that he was the one bringing in God's kingdom rule. Jesus told John's disciples,

> Go and tell John what you hear and see: the blind receive their sight, the lame walk, the lepers are cleansed, the deaf hear, the dead are raised, and the poor have good news brought to them. (Matt 11:4–5)

Of this event Ben Witherington III writes,

> Though it does not involve the phrase *basileia tou theou*, Q material like Matthew 11:2–19/Luke 7:18–35 further supports the conclusion that Jesus understood the in-breaking of the *basileia* in and through his ministry to mean God's saving and healing activity in the present. Thus G. Theissen is likely right when he says, "Jesus is unique in religious history. He combines two conceptual worlds which had never been combined this way before, the apocalyptic expectation of universal salvation in the future and the episodic realisation of salvation in the present through miracles."[59]

The Kingdom of God as a Not-Yet Future Hope

Equally common as the present-tense "is" in the New Testament is the recurring use of the future "will" in combination with kingdom language;

---

58. Hoekema, *Bible and the Future*, 43.

59. Witherington, *Jesus, Paul and the End of the World*, 69, quoting Theissen, *Miracle Stories*, 278–80.

Jesus said, "Then people will come from east and west, from north and south, and will eat in the kingdom of God" (Luke 13:29), and again, "I tell you that from now on I will not drink of the fruit of the vine until the kingdom of God comes" (Luke 22:18) This language presents a future aspect of the kingdom. Both the present *is* and the future *will* is biblical affirmation that "there is both a realized *and* a future eschatology in the New Testament teaching."[60] Jesus spoke of the kingdom as both a present experience and a future hope. In fact, Jesus, the one by whom the kingdom was present in the world, taught his disciples to pray, "Your kingdom come. Your will be done, on earth as it is in heaven" (Matt 6:10).[61] While present in the person of Christ, the kingdom was also something yet coming and to be prayed for.

It has previously been noted that Paul's use of *arrabōn* (deposit) and *aparchē* (first fruits) affirm a present, partial realization of the kingdom by way of the presence of the Spirit and by Christ's bodily resurrection. But it is equally true that they, by their meaning, imply a still-future consummation or completion; a deposit, being part of a greater whole, is a guarantee that the remainder is still to come. While some may regard the idea of a present and future kingdom to be an incongruity, D. C. Allison writes that

> the seeming contradiction between the presence of the kingdom and its futurity is dissolved when one realizes that Jewish thinking could envision the final events—the judgment of evil and the arrival of the kingdom of God—as extending over time, and as a process or series of events that could involve the present (compare Jubilee 23; 1 Enoch 91:12–17; 93).[62]

Such a progression, as regards the kingdom, can be found in Daniel's retelling of Nebuchadnezzar's dream (Dan 2:34–35 and 44–45):

> As you looked on, a stone was cut out, not by human hands, and it struck the statue on its feet of iron and clay and broke them in pieces. Then the iron, the clay, the bronze, the silver, and the

60. Kusmič, "History and Eschatology," 136–37.

61. The parallelism of "Your kingdom come" and "Your will be done" indicates in some way the presence of the kingdom where the will of God is being done (see also Matt 7:21, noting the present active ποιέω). Robert Lindsay notes that "The phrases are synonymous: people come into the kingdom when they accept God's authority and begin to do his will." Lindsay, "The Kingdom of God," no pages.

62. Cited in Witherington, *Jesus, Paul and the End of the World*, 64.

> gold, were all broken in pieces and became like the chaff of the summer threshing floors; and the wind carried them away, so that not a trace of them could be found. But the stone that struck the statue became a great mountain and filled the whole earth. (vv. 34–35)

> And in the days of those kings the God of heaven will set up a kingdom that shall never be destroyed, nor shall this kingdom be left to another people. It shall crush all these kingdoms and bring them to an end, and it shall stand forever; just as you saw that a stone was cut from the mountain not by hands, and that it crushed the iron, the bronze, the clay, the silver, and the gold. The great God has informed the king what shall be hereafter. The dream is certain, and its interpretation trustworthy. (vv. 44–45)

Daniel understands the stone (an image applied to Christ in the New Testament in Mark 12:10; Luke 20:17; Rom 9:33; and 1 Pet 2:4–8) as a symbolic representation of the in-breaking kingdom. The stone, as an initial in-breaking of the kingdom, becomes a great mountain filling the earth, thus implying a period of expansion. There is a partial realization as Christ, the rejected stone, inaugurates the kingdom. But it is to *become* much greater still. Jesus's well-known kingdom parables in Matthew 13 echo this phase of kingdom growth. In speaking of the kingdom as seed that is planted, Jesus said to let it grow until the harvest and while the sower of the kingdom seed was away (13:24–30). The harvest, with its associated separation of weeds from the wheat (i.e., judgment) is at "the end of the age" (vv. 40–42)—thus affirming that a period of time (age) continues for a season. The kingdom is also likened to a mustard seed (13:31–32) that grows (again implying time) to become the greatest of shrubs; the point being that "despite unimpressive beginnings, the messianic kingdom will grow until it is huge."[63] In the words of Ladd,

> [T]he kingdom of God is the redemptive reign of God dynamically active to establish his rule among men, and . . . this kingdom . . . has already come into human history in the person and mission of Jesus to overcome evil, to deliver men from its power and to bring them into the blessings of God's reign. The Kingdom of God involves two great moments; fulfilment within history, and consummation at the end of history.[64]

63. Mathison, *Postmillennialism*, 108.
64. Ladd, *Presence of the Future*, 218.

It was noted in chapter 1 that dispensationalism understands the prophecy of Amos (chap. 9) speaking of a rebuilding of the booth of David to be the "full kingdom blessing of restored Israel" in a millennium subsequent to Christ's return.[65] It was also noted that James in Acts 15 understood Amos's words as being fulfilled as Gentiles came to believe the gospel. Here it is seen that a full establishment of the kingdom is neither nationalistic nor sudden. Many years after Christ the Davidic hopes continue to be realized over time—even to our time.

CHAPTER CONCLUSION

The dispensational view of the kingdom as a political national kingdom for Israel, offered but rejected, and subsequently postponed until a proposed post–second advent millennium is not supported by the great weight of biblical evidence. Nowhere within the text of Scripture is there any clear statement nor any implied teaching that supports these claims, claims essential to the overall dispensational system. Instead, as has been shown, the consistent witness of the New Testament testifies to a historical coming of the kingdom in the person of Jesus the Messiah. The dispensational kingdom understanding is wholly reliant on the appropriateness of a literal hermeneutical principle and the validity of a radical distinction of Israel and the church. Both of these claims are indispensable for the formation of a kingdom understanding such as proposed by dispensationalists. Both of these, however, have been shown to be erroneous, and as such a kingdom understanding that is built on these claims cannot be considered reliable.

It appears to be true also that dispensationalism, specifically by its proposition that the mission and purpose of Jesus Christ at his first advent was to offer a political kingdom to Israel, implies a devaluing of the cross of Christ and the redemptive message of hope to all nations. It is simply incorrect to assert that Jesus failed to accomplish the purpose for which he was sent. Jesus himself claimed to have completed the task given him by God. The establishment of a national Jewish kingdom was not the intent of his arrival on earth; the cross was the purpose for which he came and the manner by which to achieve the redemption of a fallen creation. Dispensationalism reduces the gospel to simply forgiveness of

65. *Scofield Reference Bible*, Amos 9:11–15.

sin, whereas the biblical witness testifies to the gospel of the kingdom (of which forgiveness of sin is an indispensable part).

The literalism by which dispensationalists interpret Old Testament kingdom promises prevents them from acknowledging Jesus Christ as the fulfiller of those promises—despite the claims of both Jesus and Paul. This present study has shown that not only does Jesus claim to be the one in whom Israel's promises are fulfilled, but also in his preaching, healing, forgiving of sins, his death, resurrection, and giving of the Spirit, Jesus actually did fulfill what was promised concerning the kingdom. These actions of Jesus were testimony in praxis concurrent with his announcing that the kingdom had come. Jesus as Messiah was in his person the kingdom come. To not acknowledge this reality once again reflects a diminished understanding of the person and work of Christ within dispensationalism.

An additional weakness of the dispensational interpretive method and the resultant understanding of the kingdom is revealed in the apparent unwillingness to acknowledge the language of *this age* and *the age to come*, the distinctive characteristics attributed to them, and the contribution these terms bring to a biblical understanding of the timing and nature of the kingdom. This weakness is magnified by the observable synonymous nature of the terms age to come, kingdom of God, eternal life, and salvation, whereby if a person has one of these (e.g., eternal life), one by necessity possess the others (e.g., the kingdom). There also seems to be a failure to recognize the very frequent use of present-tense language that surrounds so much of the salvation/kingdom/eternal life language of the Bible. And further, the clear now and not-yet kingdom teaching conveyed in the use of the *arrabōn* and *aparchē* metaphors seems not to be understood.

It is now significant that the dispensational literalistic hermeneutic, Israel-church distinction, and understanding of the kingdom are seen to be inconsistent with the biblical witness.

The view of historic premillennialism, postmillennialism, and amillennialism are, despite other differences, united in this: The kingdom of God is present and future; it is both now and not yet. This in-breaking kingdom is present and active by the indwelling Spirit of Christ empowering and effecting redemption.

> From now on we are living in the new age; the already begun new world. The light is shining in the darkness and the dark-

ness has not overcome it. And this means that we who follow
Jesus live in the bright interval between Easter and the final great
consummation. . . . The reason the early Christians were so joyful
was because they knew themselves to be living, not so much in
the last days—though that was true in a sense as well—but more
in the first days; the opening days of God's new springtime. . . .
The whole point of New Testament Christianity is that the end
came rushing forward into the present in Jesus of Nazareth. . . .
There is still a final great consummation still to come . . . the
time when creation itself will receive its liberation, its exodus.
The time when death itself will be defeated and God will be all in
all. . . . We live therefore between Easter and the consummation.
We are following Jesus Christ in the power of the Spirit and are
commissioned to be for the world what He was for Israel, bringing God's redemptive reshaping to our world.[66]

These truths are not insignificant for Christian life in the present. It
is crucial for the church's understanding of Christian mission, Christian
praxis, and the manner in which the gospel is proclaimed. As people of
the kingdom, Christians need to come to terms with what it means to
be God's people living between the times of the kingdom now and the
kingdom as yet to be fully realized.

Instead of waiting passively around for God to beam us up to
glory, to rescue us from this godforsaken world, we come to see
our role as *active participants* in extending and expressing God's
kingdom here in this (far from God-forsaken!) world.[67]

66. N. T. Wright, "Jesus as the World's True Light," mp3 audio, time 7:29 to 10:58.
67. C. Marshall, *Kingdom Come*, 103.

4

The Rapture and the Tribulation

I T IS HIGHLY PROBABLE that when one mentions the "end-times" the first thought of many Christians will be of the so-called rapture. The Left Behind series of novels by LaHaye and Jenkins have once again popularized this word and with it the seven-year tribulation that is understood to follow. The pretribulation rapture portrayed in these books is believed by many Christians to be the next expected event on the end-time calendar. Christ could come at any moment, silently and secretly; the church will be snatched out of the world, leaving those who remain mystified at the sudden disappearance of millions of people while they are "left behind" to endure the terrifying horrors of a seven-year tribulation before Christ's return in glory.

There exists some difference of opinion regarding the origin of this two-stage return of Christ; first, for the church (the rapture) and second with the church seven years later. The rapture is frequently considered to have been first revealed in the form of a prophetic revelation by a young Scottish girl named Margaret MacDonald in 1830 and subsequently woven by J. N. Darby into his then very newly formed dispensational eschatological system, particularly in view of his two people of God hypothesis.[1] The concept of the rapture as part one of a two-phased return of Christ is, therefore, a relatively recent novelty in theology, its emergence coinciding with the nineteenth-century rise of dispensationalism. The premillennialism prior to Darby knew nothing of a two-stage coming of Christ with a seven-year tribulation period in between. Ladd, as a non-dispensational premillennialist, writes,

---

1. Clouse, "Rapture of the Church," 908–9. Paul Thigpen notes earlier rapture-type concepts from the early eighteenth century, but these are not in the form of a two-stage return. Thigpen, *Rapture Trap*, 143–48.

> If the Blessed Hope is in fact a pretribulation rapture, then the
> church has never known that hope through most of its history,
> for the idea of a pretribulation rapture did not appear in pro-
> phetic interpretation until the nineteenth century.[2]

Dispensational perspectives as to the timing of the rapture are mul-
tiple. In addition to those espousing the pretribulation view, some hold
to either a mid-tribulation or a post-tribulation understanding, that
is, the rapture will take place either midway through or after a future
seven-year tribulation. As portrayed in the Left Behind books, it is the
pretribulation view that is without doubt the most common view and
that which shapes much of the popular contemporary understanding.
For this reason, this chapter will be restricted to consideration of the
dispensational premillennial understanding of a pretribulation rapture
of the church and the subsequent seven-year period known as "the
tribulation." This concept of the rapture is absent from historic Christian
thought and unique to dispensationalism.

THE DISPENSATIONAL PRETRIBULATION RAPTURE
OF THE CHURCH

The events of the rapture and the subsequent tribulation are particularly
significant events in the dispensational system. The return of Christ is
understood to occur in two distinct stages. The first phase will see Jesus
coming part way to the earth for his church who will meet him in the air
(the rapture) to return with him to heaven. This secret and silent event
will signal the end of the "parenthesis" church age and the commence-
ment of Daniel's seventieth week, the seven-year tribulation (Dan 9:27).
LaHaye and Ice suggest that

> The church is unique in the plan of God and separate from His
> plan for Israel. While the church partakes of the spiritual prom-
> ises of the Abrahamic Covenant as fulfilled through Christ,
> Israel, and not the church, will fulfill her national destiny as a
> separate entity after the Rapture and Tribulation and during the
> Millennium. The New Testament teaches that the church was an
> unrevealed mystery in the Old Testament . . . which is why she
> began suddenly, without warning, in Acts 2, and why this age will
> end suddenly and mysteriously, without warning, at the Rapture.
> Therefore, the church has no earthly prophetic destiny beyond
> the Rapture.[3]

2. Ladd, *Blessed Hope*, 19.

3. LaHaye and Ice, *Charting the End Times*, 48.

Seven years after the rapture, on completion of the tribulation, Jesus will return again[4]—this time he will descend all the way to earth for the establishment of Israel's national kingdom—the millennial reign of Christ on earth. Dispensationalism, in its normative and popular forms, believes that the removal of the church from earth is necessary in order for God's Old Testament prophetic purposes for Israel to resume.[5] H. A. Ironside writes,

> The moment the Messiah died on the cross, the prophetic clock stopped. There has not been a tick upon that clock for nineteen centuries. It will not begin to go again until the entire present age has come to an end, and Israel will once again be taken up by God.[6]

Dwight Pentecost proposes this same idea on the basis that the church is a "mystery program" not "revealed until after the rejection of Christ by Israel." He writes,

> The church is manifestly an interruption of God's program for Israel, which was not brought into being until Israel's rejection of the offer of the kingdom. It must logically follow that this mystery program must itself be brought to a conclusion before God can resume His dealing with the nation Israel. . . . This mystery concept of the church makes a pretribulation rapture a necessity.[7]

It becomes evident that the idea of a pretribulation rapture as understood by most dispensationalists rests on three a priori criteria: (a) the literal interpretation of Scripture,[8] (b) the distinction of Israel and the church, without which J. F. Strombeck, in his book *First the Rapture*, says it is "impossible to interpret properly many passages,"[9] and (c) the assertion that the promised Davidic kingdom was postponed due to the rejection of Christ's kingdom offer. Such kingdom promises are not

4. Ibid., 118 (refer to the chart "Setting the Stage").

5. Ibid., 90 (refer to the chart "The 70 Weeks of Daniel," noting the post-rapture seventieth week and the caption, "Prophetic time clock resumes for fulfillment for Jewish nation").

6. Cited in Young, *Daniel*, 194.

7. Pentecost, *Things to Come*, 201.

8. Ibid., 194. "The literal method of interpretation, consistently employed, can lead to no other conclusion than that the church will be raptured before the seventieth week."

9. Strombeck, *First the Rapture*, 14.

understood as already fulfilled in Christ, and neither is the church to have any part in their fulfillment. As we just read from Pentecost in the quote above, dispensationalism regards God's program for Israel to be his primary purpose, while the church—the body of Christ, the fullness of him (Eph 1:23), loved by him and for whom he gave his life (Eph 5:24–25), and for whom God has placed all things under Christ's feet (Eph 1:22)—is considered "manifestly an interruption" that needs to be removed (i.e., raptured) in order for God to carry out his primary objective: the kingdom for Israel.

In Titus 2:13 Paul, in the form of a hendiadys, refers to Christ's return as the "blessed hope" and the "glorious appearing" (NIV). Strombeck correctly regards the two terms as one event, yet mistakenly understands them as referring to the rapture[10] and as something believers should be looking for.[11] "Nothing should be allowed to distract attention from this glorious prospect," and due to the reestablishment of Israel in 1948, he writes, "the promise [of Jesus] to come again must be very near at hand."[12]

Strombeck works with a number of passages to show a difference between Christ's coming for the church at the rapture and his second coming to save Israel and fulfill her kingdom promises seven years later.[13] In doing so he teaches that from the time of the rapture the church will be with the Lord in heaven "there to dwell with Him forever."[14] This is concluded from John 14:1–3 and the principal rapture passage, 1 Thessalonians 4:15–17:

---

10. LaHaye and Ice regard the "glorious appearing" as being Christ's coming after the rapture and the seven-year tribulation. LaHaye and Ice, *Charting the End Times*, 65. "The term 'the glorious appearing' is not found in the book of Revelation, but in Titus 2:13. There it describes the physical, visible return of Christ to Earth in distinction from that 'blessed hope' . . . which is the Rapture of the church, or the coming of Christ for His believers prior to the tribulation."

11. Most scholars understand these two terms as speaking of a single event (a hendiadys) but as a reference to the actual return of Christ, not a rapture of the church seven years earlier. See Rossing, *Rapture Exposed*, 30–31.

12. Strombeck, *First the Rapture*, 11–12.

13. Ibid., 24–30.

14. The author acknowledges that this is a view not held to by some dispensationalists, particularly those of the progressive dispensational understanding. Such scholars have come to hold that the eternal destiny is on a new earth and not distinct from Israel's destiny.

> Do not let your hearts be troubled. Believe in God, believe also in me. In my Father's house there are many dwelling places. If it were not so, would I have told you that I go to prepare a place for you? And if I go and prepare a place for you, I will come again and will take you to myself, so that where I am, there you may be also. (John 14:1–3)

> For this we declare to you by the word of the Lord, that we who are alive, who are left until the coming of the Lord, will by no means precede those who have died. For the Lord himself, with a cry of command, with the archangel's call and with the sound of God's trumpet, will descend from heaven, and the dead in Christ will rise first. Then we who are alive, who are left, will be caught up in the clouds together with them to meet the Lord in the air; and so we will be with the Lord forever. (1 Thess 4:15–17)

He further implies, by his use and interpretation of Matthew 24, that this rapture of the church to heaven occurs prior to the coming seven-year tribulation, of which he says, "World Wars I and II pale into insignificance compared with the carnage of that time"; it will be worse than the effects of the atomic bomb on Hiroshima.[15] For Strombeck, Matthew 24 is understood as being for the most part—that is, from verse 9 onwards—referring to events yet to occur, and it constitutes Jesus's teaching of a seven-year tribulation subsequent to the rapture, his coming for the church. The rapture—claimed to initiate this tribulation period—though not mentioned in the passage, is simply assumed to have already occurred subsequent to verse 8, but prior to verse 9.[16]

It appears then that in dispensational thought Matthew 24:9–28 is referring to the same proposed period of tribulation that is alleged to be the subject matter of Revelation 4–19 and Daniel 9:27 (in both of which, like Matthew 24, the idea of a rapture is assumed but not stated). The latter passage from Daniel 9 requires an interpretation that, in addition to an assumed rapture, also assumes an unmentioned gap of over two-thousand-years (the church age) between the sixty-ninth and seventieth weeks of Daniel's prophecy. It becomes apparent then that a few verses in 1 Thessalonians 4:15–17 are understood to be speaking of a crucial event—the rapture—that is never mentioned in any other pas-

---

15. Strombeck, *First the Rapture*, 39 and 45.

16. LaHaye and Ice, *Charting the End Times*, 36. This is evident from the chart "The Olivet Discourse (Matthew 24–25)."

sage of Scripture. This presumption is achieved only by piecing together verses from Scripture that would be better understood if left to speak for themselves rather than have meaning imposed on them. It is extraordinary that none of these key tribulation passages (as understood within dispensational eschatology) make any mention of *the* most significant event in the future of the church, which is alleged to initiate this dreadful time, that is, the "blessed hope"—the rapture. The remainder of this chapter will proceed in order to propose a counter view by means of a consideration of some selected relevant texts, thereby testing the validity of the dispensational view of both rapture and tribulation.[17]

THE NON-DISPENSATIONAL RAPTURE OF THE CHURCH

The traditional and historic view of the Christian church is that the return of Christ occurs as a single event at the end of the age. At this time the full realization of God's redeeming work will become the experience of all God's people. It will be shown that the dispensational belief in a future two-stage return of Christ with an intervening seven-year period of intense tribulation is not in any way supported by the biblical passages most commonly cited by proponents of this view. Before consideration of these passages two preliminary points should be noted.

Lack of Explicit Biblical Evidence Acknowledged

In the previous chapters three indispensable criteria for the formation of a pretribulational understanding of the rapture have been refuted: the validity of a strictly literal hermeneutic, the distinction of the people of God into two differing peoples, Israel and the church, and the suggestion of a postponed national kingdom for Israel. This discussion will proceed on the basis of what has already been concluded thus far: in Jesus Christ is found the ultimate definition and meaning of Israel and of the Old Testament as a whole. Thus, a nonliteralistic interpretation of its story and promises is permitted. Further, Christ's first coming redefined the meaning of who it is that constitutes Israel as the people of God, and he brought with him in his person the kingdom as both prophesied and promised. Each of these realities in and of themselves negates the need for a rapture and tribulation according to dispensational reasoning (i.e., to fulfill Israel's promises: these are fulfilled in Israel's Messiah Jesus).

---

17. Space available will by necessity limit this discussion to a few selected texts. Related texts not discussed, though important, are less crucial at the doctrine's foundational level.

The second issue just cited, that of Israel and the church, is essentially an issue of ecclesiology, that is, who it is that makes up the people of God and are heirs of his redemptive work. Understanding passages attributed by dispensationalists to the rapture must by necessity be influenced by a prior understanding of a definition of the church for which Christ comes again and in whom the Old Testament promises are fulfilled. This has been defended already as those who are "in Christ," the Israel of God, joined together as one people whether Jew or Gentile, that is, the church. There is, therefore, no need for the church to be taken away in order for Israel's promises to be fulfilled; the church is the Israel of God (Gal 6:16), and these promises are declared in Scripture to be "Yes," that is, fulfilled, in Christ Jesus and therefore in those who belong to him (2 Cor 1:20). The issue of ecclesiology (and Christology) is therefore foundational for the formation of a biblical understanding of so-called rapture and tribulation passages. Catholic writer David Currie (a former pretribulation rapturist), in his book *Rapture: The End-Times Error that Leaves the Bible Behind*, notes the following:

> In the first edition of his 1957 book, *The Rapture Question*, Walvoord wrote, "The rapture question is determined more by ecclesiology [theology of the church] than eschatology [theology of future events, specifically the last things]. *Neither postribulationism nor pretribulationism is an explicit teaching of Scripture. The Bible does not state it in so many words.*"[18]

This is a significant concession from of one of dispensationalism's most competent proponents—and one that concurs with this writer's conclusion regarding the significance of ecclesiology in the rapture debate—yet at the same time an acknowledgment of the lack of explicit biblical support for the church's rapture that his book seeks to defend. Currie continues,

> This admission—that the believer's rapture is not a clear and concise teaching of the Bible—was so explosive that in all future editions of this book it was deleted. . . . But there it is: nowhere does one passage of the Bible speak of both the rapture and the second coming. Nowhere does one passage of the Bible lay out the time scheme that rapturists must justify by piecing one verse here with another verse there.[19]

18. Currie, *Rapture*, 25–26 (emphasis original).
19. Ibid., 26.

The Question of the Church's Post-Rapture Destiny

Consistent with Chafer and Ryrie's assertion that Christianity constitutes God's "heavenly people" with "heavenly objectives involved,"[20] it was noted above that Strombeck advocates a pretribulation rapture followed by a subsequent and permanent heavenly destiny for the church. In support of this he cites John 14:1–3 and 1 Thessalonians 4:15–17, both of which speak of Christ coming for his church. However, it is significant to observe that neither of these supposed rapture references mention a tribulation to follow nor a location in which the redeemed are to be forever with Christ.[21] It is also significant to note that there is not one text anywhere in Scripture teaching heaven as being the eternal destiny of believers.[22] This notion about heaven is in fact inconsistent with the overall goal of an all-creation-inclusive redemption as portrayed in Scripture.

> Jesus speaks of the goal of eschatology as "the regeneration" (Matt 19:28). Peter speaks of it as "the restoration of all things" (Acts 3:21). Paul speaks of it as "the creation . . . set free from its slavery" (Romans 8:21). Eschatology has to do with the bringing of creation and mankind to its original God-intended destination.[23]

There is no place in Christian thinking for a destroyed and replaced earth. Redemption is to be seen in terms of restoration, reconciliation, renewal, and the regeneration of all things—this earth included, in which the redeemed will ultimately enjoy life as God intended it to be. After surveying a number of texts (Acts 3:19–21; Eph 1:9–10; Col 1:19–20; 2 Pet 3:10–13; Rom 8:19–23) J. Richard Middleton concludes two things:

> First, salvation is conceived, not as God doing something completely new, but rather as re-doing something, fixing or repairing what went wrong. . . . Second, this restorative work is applied as holistically and comprehensively as possible to all things in heaven and earth . . . the final salvific state envisioned in these

---

20. See chapter 1 above.

21. It is important to note that this discussion has now shown that there is no passage of Scripture claimed to be teaching of the rapture that mentions the tribulation and no passage claimed to refer to the tribulation that makes mention of the rapture; the two are never brought together in Scripture.

22. Middleton, "New Heaven and New Earth," no pages.

23. Waldron, *End Times*, 11.

texts clearly contradicts an understanding of "heaven" as the ultimate dwelling of the redeemed.[24]

Consistent with Jesus's prayer, "Your kingdom come, Your will be done *on earth* as it is in heaven," Revelation 5 records a vision of Jesus who is worshipped and praised for his redeeming work by means of an angelic song that clearly locates the redeemed on earth:

> You are worthy to take the scroll and to open its seals, for you were slaughtered and by your blood you ransomed for God saints from every tribe and language and people and nation; you have made them to be a kingdom and priests serving our God, and they will reign on earth. (Rev 5:9–10)

Further, the new Jerusalem envisioned in Revelation 21, an image of the redeemed bride, the people of God, is seen to be "coming down out of heaven from God" toward earth (21:2, 10) so that "God's dwelling place is now among the people" (21:3 TNIV).

It would appear inconsistent with the biblical narrative to envision a future whereby God's redeemed creation and his redeemed humanity are forever alienated from each other. A redeemed world uninhabited by the redeemed people is biblically inconceivable. Middleton concludes,

> "Heaven" in Scripture is certainly portrayed as the throne of God (with earth as God's footstool), the place where salvation is being prepared for the faithful, and the realm . . . where God's will is perfectly accomplished prior to the eschaton. Nevertheless, it does *not* describe the Christian eschatological hope. Not only is the term "heaven" never used in Scripture for the eternal destiny of the redeemed, but continued use of the term distorts the legitimate biblical expectation for the present transformation of our earthly life to confirm to God's purposes.[25]

The idea of a rapture that removes the church to heaven is therefore in complete contradiction to the central biblical theme of salvation—God's all-encompassing goal for the redemption of all things. The words of the old hymn by J. R. Baxter, "This world is not my home, I'm just a-passing through," appear to be not only tragically misguided, but sadly, are a reflection of the widespread nature of an inadequate view of redemption and the essential meaning of the kingdom of God.

24. Middleton, "New Heaven and New Earth," no pages.
25. Ibid.

The ideas of an "at any moment" rapture, followed immediately by the carnage of a proposed tribulation, along with a view of a heavenly eternal destiny for the church have contributed to a disengagement from the world and at times failure to participate in positive social transformation as portrayed in the Gospels by the presence of the kingdom in Christ's person and work. Pretribulationalism is well known for the cliché, Why polish brass on a sinking ship? And thus it promotes evangelism or mission aimed solely at getting people "saved" so as get them off the ship before it goes down (i.e., to be ready for the rapture and to escape the tribulation and the end of the world). The issue is, therefore, of greater significance than its purely academic value; the historical (and no doubt future) effect from these beliefs have had a negative influence on how Christians understand and participate in the commission given by Christ to preach the gospel and to make disciples of all nations. This gospel has been shown in the preceding chapter to be the "gospel of the kingdom" as a transforming redemptive presence in this age—the life of the future experienced in part now and on earth.

> Our salvation is not simply for the next life. It is our rebirth as new creatures, our restoration as citizens in His present and everlasting Kingdom. Greek dualism saw man's salvation as an escape into the spiritual and away from this world. But we are called to be salt and light to this world. As salt we are to preserve the world from decay and the death to which it naturally moves. . . . Our duty is more than "spiritual" as a dualist views spirituality; it is to witness to God in every area of life and thought.[26]

Pretribulational rapturism with its heavenly eternal destiny for the church, therefore, has more compatibility with Greek dualism than it does with the biblical portrayal of a comprehensive and earthly redemption. It is critical therefore to examine the teaching of a pretribulational rapture and the texts cited in support of this doctrine. Do these texts really teach what is claimed? If not, what do they speak of?

A Brief Consideration of Selected Relevant Passages

David Currie writes, "The book of Daniel lays the foundation for the entire time framework of rapturist theology" and further notes the dispensationalist claim as recorded in Unger's *Bible Handbook*, that Daniel

---

26. Rushdoony, "The Christian and the Social Agenda," no pages.

is the key to all biblical prophecy. Apart from the great eschatological disclosures of this book, the entire prophetic portions
of the Word of God must remain sealed. Jesus' great Olivet
Discourse, as well as 2 Thess. 2 and the entire book of Revelation,
can be unlocked *only through an understanding of the prophecies
of Daniel.*[27]

It is therefore appropriate to consider the dispensational interpretation of
this prophetic source.[28] Daniel's interpretation of King Nebuchadnezzar's
dream (chap. 2) comes to its climactic conclusion by foretelling when the
unending kingdom of God would be powerfully inaugurated on earth.
After four successive kingdoms of Babylon, Medo-Persia, Greece, and
Rome, then,

in the days of those kings the God of heaven will set up a kingdom that shall never be destroyed, nor shall this kingdom be left
to another people. It shall crush all these kingdoms and bring
them to an end, and it shall stand forever. (Dan 2:44)

As detailed in the previous chapter, pretribulation rapturists believe
that this Messianic kingdom is still future and concerns national Israel.
The stone that becomes a great mountain filling the earth (Dan 2:34–35,
which 2:44 interprets), they agree refers to Christ and the kingdom of
God, but contrary to their stated claim of *literal* and *plain-meaning* interpretation, they bifurcate the fourth kingdom to refer also to a future
revived Roman Empire.[29] Between the Roman Empire of New Testament
times and the alleged future revived Roman Empire they impose a gap,
now spanning approximately two millennia. It is during the time of this
alleged still future revived Roman Empire that the kingdom of heaven,
in fulfillment of Daniel's stone imagery, is set up (the literal one-thousand-year millennium when Christ returns)[30]—despite there being no
mention of a gap in either the vision itself or in Daniel's interpretation of

---

27. Currie, *Rapture*, 79 and 83.

28. Differing opinions exist regarding the time of writing of Daniel (whether written
before or after the events spoken of) and the function of apocalyptic texts such found in
the parts of Daniel and Matthew to be hereafter discussed. It is not, however, within the
scope of this book to address such concerns. My intent is to assess the pretribulational
interpretation of these passages as they appear in Scripture.

29. LaHaye and Ice, *Charting the End Times*, 88.

30. Ibid.

it, and that its duration is said to "stand forever." This unmentioned gap is the so-called Great Parenthesis—the church age.

Nebuchadnezzar's dream of successive kingdoms is paralleled in greater detail in Daniel's personal vision as recorded in chapter 7. In Daniel's vision a little horn appears during the time of the fourth kingdom to make war with the saints (7:21). LaHaye and Ice consider this "little horn" to be the Antichrist of a future tribulation period—again inserting a gap where the text does not.[31] This pattern of inserting two millennia into these passages is repeated in Daniel 9:24–27, the primary passage upon which the dispensational idea of a rapture followed by a seven-year tribulation is developed.[32]

Daniel 9:24–27—Daniel's Vision of Seventy Sevens

> 24 Seventy weeks are decreed for your people and your holy city: to finish the transgression, to put an end to sin, and to atone for iniquity, to bring in everlasting righteousness, to seal both vision and prophet, and to anoint a most holy place. 25 Know therefore and understand: from the time that the word went out to restore and rebuild Jerusalem until the time of an anointed prince, there shall be seven weeks; and for sixty-two weeks it shall be built again with streets and moat, but in a troubled time. 26 After the sixty-two weeks, an anointed one shall be cut off and shall have nothing, and the troops of the prince who is to come shall destroy the city and the sanctuary. Its end shall come with a flood, and to the end there shall be war. Desolations are decreed. 27 He shall make a strong covenant with many for one week, and for half of the week he shall make sacrifice and offering cease; and in their place shall be an abomination that desolates, until the decreed end is poured out upon the desolator.

Walvoord, writing as a dispensational pretribulation rapturist, says,

> Based on a literal interpretation of Daniel's prophecy, it is held that there has been no fulfillment of Daniel 9:27 in history, and that therefore it prophesies a future period, familiarly called "the tribulation."[33]

---

31. Ibid., 89.
32. Grenz, *Millennial Maze*, 103.
33. Walvoord, *Rapture Question*, 51 (note: new edition).

Concerning this same passage, Pentecost writes,

> Since it [the church] had no part in the first sixty-nine weeks, which are related only to God's program for Israel, it can have no part in the seventieth week, which is again related to God's program for Israel after the mystery program for the church has been concluded.[34]

These statements from Walvoord and Pentecost reveal the dependence on both a literal hermeneutic and the dispensational distinction of Israel and the church as they interpret this passage. From these two a priori criteria the parenthesis period of the church is here imposed mid sentence in the middle of verse 26 after the sixty-ninth week when Messiah is cut off (crucified). The seventieth week (v. 26b) begins at least two millennia later and is deemed to be concerned with events of the seven-year post-rapture tribulation.

This is the only place in Scripture claimed to reveal the seven-year *duration* of the tribulation.[35] This theory, however, is not without serious implications; by placing the seventieth week after the still-to-come rapture, and in order for the blessing of verse 24 and events of verses 26b–27 to be fulfilled, Christ must have to come again to deal with sin,[36] the temple must be rebuilt in order to be destroyed, and the temple sacrifices reinstated in order to be made to cease. Currie rightly says,

> They [dispensationalists] had better be right. . . . Both Darby and present rapturists claim that this vision is *the basis for their entire time line.* Remember, that without a future seven-year Great Tribulation, the need for a rebuilt Jewish Temple and a secret rapture of believers disappears, and the entire rapturist system falls like a house of cards.[37]

---

34. Pentecost, *Things to Come*, 196.

35. This is based on the understanding that a prophetic week represents seven years. See LaHaye and Ice, *Charting the End Times*, 90. The word *years* does not appear in the original manuscripts and is a later insertion in some translations; the NIV correctly says simply 'Seventy sevens are decreed" (v. 24). Counter to LaHaye and Ice, Currie quotes Eusebius (approximately AD 260–341) as writing, "*Most authorities* extend the one [last] week of years to the sum of *seventy years* reckoning each year as a ten year period." Currie, *Rapture*, 118. This is entirely compatible with the genre and the flexible use of *shabua* (seven) in the Hebrew language. Ibid., 107. See also Young, *Daniel*, 195–96.

36. Butler, *Approaching the New Millennium*, 80.

37. Currie, *Rapture*, 108 (emphasis added)

The question arises: Is there any legitimate grounds for imposing a gap in these visions and so establishing the basis for a future rapture and tribulation? The church's historical interpretation prior to Darby would answer "No." The dispensationalist gap appears to be necessary, not by sound exegesis of the passage, but "because rapture enthusiasts need it to make their prophetic framework fit with Israel's history,"[38] by a prior belief in a postponed kingdom implying that Christ failed to bring the kingdom at his first coming and by the even more surprising implication that he failed to deal with sin.

The vision declares that it would take the *full* seventy sevens to achieve six things: (1) to finish the transgression, (2) to put an end to sin, (3) to atone for iniquity, (4) to bring in everlasting righteousness, (5) to seal both vision and prophet, and (6) to anoint a most holy place.[39] These must occur within the period of seventy sevens, up to and including the seventieth seven,[40] and so, according to the rapturist teaching, within the future tribulation period. All six, however, were believed by the early church to be "absolutely without exception" accomplished by Christ at his first advent.[41] They understood the blessings of the seventy weeks (v. 24) to be completed by Christ in his life, his sacrificial death, and in the events leading up to and including the destruction of the temple (vv. 26b–27)—ultimately achieved by the Roman armies in AD 70 (being Christ's instrument of judgment)[42]—and thus causing sacrifices to cease.[43] This close connection between the crucifixion of Christ and the destruction of the temple is clearly seen in Jesus's words spoken as he walked to his death:

> Daughters of Jerusalem, do not weep for me, but weep for yourselves and for your children. For the days are surely coming when

38. Rossing, *Rapture Exposed*, 27.

39. The original text does not make it clear that the anointed is a place. See Young, *Daniel*, 201.

40. Otherwise the text would need to read, for example, "sixty-nine sevens are decreed" to achieve the six blessings listed.

41. Currie, *Rapture*, 113.

42. It is possible in Scripture to find a judgment coming of God actually realized by human agents. For example, in Isa 19:1 God is said to come in judgment to Egypt, but this is fulfilled by the Assyrian army (Isa 20:1–6). The exiles of Israel and Judah as judgments for their unfaithfulness to the covenant stipulations are meted out by God's sending of the Assyrians (722 BC) and the Babylonians (586 BC).

43. The subsequent interpretation of the church continued to follow this traditional understanding. Grenz, *Millennial Maze*, 103.

they will say, "Blessed are the barren, and the wombs that never bore, and the breasts that never nursed." Then they will begin to say to the mountains, "Fall on us"; and to the hills, "Cover us." (Luke 23:28–30)

Earlier, Luke records Jesus predicting the destruction of the temple as a direct consequence of the fact that they "did not recognize the time of your [Israel's] visitation from God" (Luke 19:41–44), and further (again in the context of his speaking of the temple's coming destruction, associating its destruction with his redeeming work—the six blessings of Dan 9:24): "Now when *these things begin to take place*, stand up and raise your heads, because your *redemption* is drawing near" (Luke 21:28, emphasis added). As Peter Walker rightly states, "When deciding the fate of Jesus, Jerusalem was deciding her own."[44] It is not unusual, therefore, to find both of these closely associated events foretold and interlinked within one vision in Daniel 9:24–27.

The nature of the events surrounding Christ's life and death along with those concerning the fall of Jerusalem in AD 67–70 are completely harmonious with those said to occur within the period of the seventieth week. "The prophecy of Daniel 9:24–27 finds its fulfillment in the atoning sacrifice of Christ and the destruction of Jerusalem,"[45] thus being entirely consistent with Paul's declaration that all God's promises find their "Yes" in Christ (2 Cor 1:30).

Of the first three blessings concerning sin (Dan 9:24), Young writes,

44. Walker, *Jesus and the Holy City*, 74. The Jewish historian Josephus blames the Jewish people themselves for the fall of the city and temple. Without denying the contribution of the armies of Vespasian and Titus he records the severe internal warring of Jerusalem's inhabitants: "they made each other suffer" and "They overthrew the city themselves." Josephus, *Wars of the Jews* 6.6.1; 5.10.1. J. Marcellus Kik records the barbaric internal wickedness and cites Josephus, "Neither did any city ever suffer such miseries nor did any age ever breed a generation more fruitful in wickedness than this was, from the beginning of the world." Things were so bad Josephus tells of Titus the Roman General, "In going about his rounds along these valleys [where the Jews threw there many dead], and the thick putrefaction called God to witness that this was not his own doing; and such was the sad case of the city itself." Kik, *Eschatology of Victory*, 118–19. Currie therefore regards the "people of the prince who is to come" (v. 26) to be Christ's kinsmen, the Jewish people who by their action effectively destroy their own city. Currie, *Rapture*, 124. This passage therefore predicts without doubt a time of great tribulation for the Jewish people, but not after a rapture of the church over two millennia later as proposed by pretribulation rapturists; it was to be much nearer in time.

45. Kik, *Eschatology of Victory*, 109.

How is this accomplished? The text does not say, but who, in the light of the NT revelation, can read these words without coming face to face with that one perfect Sacrifice which offered by Him, who "appeared to put away sin by the sacrifice of himself" (Heb 9:26)?[46]

The wider context of the above passage clearly refutes any implication of the rapturist theory that Christ is yet to deal with sin.

But as it is, he *has* appeared once for all at the end of the age *to remove sin* by the sacrifice of himself . . . so Christ, having been offered once to bear the sins of many, will appear a second time, *not to deal with sin*, but to save those who are eagerly waiting for him. (Heb 9:26b, 28, emphasis added)

It must therefore be concluded that to arrive at an entire end-time timeline and eschatological system that absolutely demands there being a future rapture and tribulation based on this vision (in which the rapture is not mentioned) is a careless manner of interpretation.[47] The historical realities of Christ's work coupled with the destruction of Jerusalem's temple in AD 70 adequately fulfill this content of this vision. There is no legitimate interpretive reason for inserting a parenthesis and to base a future rapture or tribulation on this passage of Scripture. Gary De Mar agrees,

There is no biblical warrant for stopping Daniel's prophecy of the seventy weeks after the sixty-ninth week. The idea of separation and the placement of an indeterminable gap between the two sets of weeks is one of the most unnatural and nonliteral interpretations of Scripture found in any eschatological system. This interpretation is taught by those who insist on a literal hermeneutic.[48]

"To justify their rapture system, rapturists must contradict both the clear meaning of Scripture and the teaching of the early church"[49]—to which I would add the great majority of historical scholarly interpreta-

---

46. Young, *Daniel*, 199.

47. Rossing, speaking of the *Left Behind* novels as fiction, states, "The trouble is, the interpretation of the Bible on which these books are based is also fiction." Rossing, *Rapture Exposed*, xi.

48. DeMar, *Last Days Madness*, 95.

49. Currie, *Rapture*, 115.

tion to the present time.[50] The entire dispensational timeline, including a rapture and seven-year tribulation, is built on a presumptuous claim of a gap nowhere mentioned in Scripture, implies that sin was not dealt with sufficiently by the cross of Christ, and is in complete contradiction to the dispensationalists' demand of consistent literal interpretation. Dispensationalism is again seen to be contradictory and unconvincing. This conclusion will be reinforced by a few brief comments concerning other passages claimed by dispensationalists in support of the belief system.

MATTHEW 24—THE OLIVET DISCOURSE

Dispensationalists regard the majority of Matthew 24 as being Jesus's teaching on a still-to-come future tribulation after the rapture of the church; thus it is considered as referring to the same time period of Daniel 9:27. Briefly, according to LaHaye and Ice, the dispensational chronology of Matthew 24 is as follows: Destruction of the temple in AD 70 (vv. 1–3); a world war (esp. World War I); famines, pestilence, and earthquakes (vv. 7–8); rapture (no reference stated); seven-year tribulation (vv. 9–25)—including the desecration of the temple and persecution of the Jews (vv. 15–20) and the second half of the tribulation, the "great tribulation" of three and a half years (vv. 21–25)—then Christ's glorious appearing (second coming, vv. 26–31), followed by judgment and the millennium (no reference stated).[51]

To this timeline questions must be asked: On what basis does the time of fulfillment leap from AD 70 to approximately AD 1914 between verses 3 and 7? Why include an unmentioned rapture between verses 8 and 9? Why are the events of verses 9 through 25 attributed to a time after the church is said to not be on earth (the tribulation)? And why did Jesus not comfort the disciples with the good news of the rapture that would remove them before this terrible time begins? The reason is what Currie refers to as the "presumptuous parenthesis"[52] as developed from their interpretation of Daniel's seventy-sevens. DeMar is of the same opinion: "The [dispensational] key to the futurizing of Matthew 24 is

---

50. Despite some differences in the detail of interpretation there is general agreement with this messianic interpretation.

51. LaHaye and Ice, *Charting the End Times*, 36. From the chart "The Olivet Discourse (Matthew 24–25)."

52. Currie, *Rapture*, 80.

the belief that the seventieth week of Daniel 9:24–27 has been disconnected from the sixty-ninth week."[53] Again, as in Daniel, in Matthew 24
a gap is inserted and again a rapture is presumed (despite there being no
mention of these in the text) in order to fit the dispensational timeline
and without any reasonable interpretive principle being evident.

It is crucial to note that Matthew 24 begins with very specific questions asked by the disciples. Jesus had just moments before spoken of the
desolation of the temple (Matt 23). Understandably, they have questions:
When will this temple be destroyed? When would he come and what
sign would signal the end of the age (vv. 1–3)? In what follows, Jesus
responds to *them* concerning *those* questions.

J. Marcellus Kik suggests that the solution for understanding
Matthew 24 is to be found in Jesus's words, "*Truly*, I tell you, *this generation* will not pass away *until all these things have taken place*" (v. 34,
emphasis added).[54] The force of this statement is accentuated by the emphatic placement of *amēn* (truly) and the by the demonstrative pronoun
hautē (this). As if not emphasized enough already, Jesus adds greater
force to his emphasis by adding, "Heaven and earth will pass way, but my
words will not pass away" (v. 35). Of all that is said in this long discourse,
Jesus vigorously calls attention to his words "this generation."[55]

There is no sound hermeneutical reason to understand "generation"
to refer to anything other than people living at that time and as such to
understand the content of Jesus's teaching to this point as referring to
that which initiated the disciples' concerns—the predicted destruction
of Jerusalem's (then existing) temple.[56] It is, once again, a departure from
a literal interpretive principle to suggest as some do that "this generation" is a reference to either the human race,[57] the Jewish race and its

---

53. DeMar, *Last Days Madness*, 94.

54. Kik, *Eschatology of Victory*, 63.

55. N. T. Wright, *Jesus and the Victory of God*, 362. "As a prophet, Jesus staked his
reputation on his prediction of the Temple's fall within a generation; if and when it fell,
he would be vindicated." See also Chilton, *Days of Vengeance*, 114.

56. Kik, *Eschatology of Victory*, 61. "Whenever the word in question is used in
Matthew, it means a contemporary race, people living at the same time, the generation
then living." Also Bruner, *Churchbook*, 518.

57. F. W. Grosheide, cited in Hoekema, *Bible and the Future*, 115. This would have
Jesus answering the disciples' question of when the temple was to be destroyed by in
effect saying, "Sometime when there are humans."

preservation in spite of persecution until the Lord comes,[58] the generation that sees Israel returned to their land (1948), or the "generation that sees the events of the tribulation."[59] Such interpretations of "this generation," however, could never be applied to the "some standing here" of Matthew 16:27–28:

> For the Son of Man is to come with his angels in the glory of his Father, and then he will repay everyone for what has been done. Truly I tell you, there are *some standing here* who will not taste death before they see the Son of Man coming in his kingdom. (emphasis added)

Taking Jesus's teaching in Matthew 24, especially his words "this generation" at face value (i.e., literally, or by plain meaning) it would appear that everything Jesus has said up to verse 33 would occur within the time of the generation then living. As we saw with Daniel's seventieth week, this is entirely possible in light of the historical situation. Jesus has answered the disciple's questions regarding the timing of temple's destruction—it will occur in their generation.[60] Only from verse 36, signaled by "But about *that* day," does he begin to speak of another time.

It is significant that there are no textual indicators in verses 4–33, nor any hint from Matthew's theological outlook (i.e., the kingdom has come as fulfillment of Jewish hopes, 4:17; its being given to another, 21:43; and his recording of Jesus's announcement of judgment for that generation, 23:3) to show that Jesus is speaking of events two millennia future from the generation of his day.

Further, in answering his disciples he makes consistent use of the second-person pronoun "you." It is *the disciples to whom Jesus is speaking who* are not to be led astray (v. 4), *who* will hear rumors of war (v. 6), *who* will be delivered up to tribulation, put to death, and so forth (v. 9), and it is *they* who will see Jerusalem surrounded by armies (v. 15, compare parallel in Luke 21:20).[61] *They* are to recognize the signs (v. 32) and when

---

58. Pentecost, *Things to Come*, 281. Ryrie, *Ryrie Study Bible*. In this theory Jesus's answer is in effect, "Sometime when there are Jews."

59. LaHaye and Ice, *Charting the End Times*, 36.

60. Matthew 23:36 also records Jesus using the term "this generation" in a context of the destruction of the temple.

61. Whereas the Matthean and Markan accounts speak of a desolating sacrilege, Luke "specifically names Jerusalem and refers clearly to a siege.... These changes can be explained in terms of the rewriting of Mk. by Luke. He will have clarified the allusion to

they do they will *know* that the kingdom of God is near (v. 33, compare parallel, Luke 21:30–31).[62] There is no shift in time or in the people concerned; Jesus is speaking to his disciples about what they will experience leading up to the destruction of the temple. The mere occurrence of the word "tribulation" in verse 9 does not substantiate what is now over a two-thousand-year leap in time by applying it to what is claimed as still yet to occur.

It should be noted also that in speaking of events prior to verse 33 Jesus informs the disciples of coming events so that they would *know*; they would see the signs and *know* when to flee. "Take note, I have told *you* beforehand" (v. 25); "So also, when *you* see *all* these things, *you know* that he [Luke: kingdom of God] is near, at the very gates" (v. 33). All these things would be *known* and would occur during the time of "this generation" (v. 34). After this pivotal verse the subject changes and the timing of its content becomes *unknown* as indicated by the emphatic adversative in the sentence, *Peri de tēs hēmeras ekeinēs kai hōras* (But about that day and hour no one knows, v. 36). Kik describes the many other dramatic differences between these two different periods of time in Jesus's teaching:

> The careful reader cannot help but be impressed with the difference in content and emphasis between Matthew 24:1–35 and Matthew 24:36–25:46. The first Section gives impression of abnormal times: wars, famine, pestilences, earthquakes, persecution and great tribulation; the Second Section of normal times: eating and drinking, marrying and giving in marriage, peaceful

---

the events of AD 66–70 in the light of history. He has removed the apocalyptic language which might make the fall of Jerusalem seem so closely associated with the End, and he has replaced it by prophetic language, thereby bringing out more strongly the element of divine judgment upon the Jews." I. H. Marshall, *Luke*, 770. See also Wohlberg, *End Time Delusions*, 46.

62. Lit: *ginōskete hoti engys estin epi thyrais*, i.e., "Know that near *it* is at gates." There is no gender, "he," in the Greek text to suggest this refers to a person; it is simply third-person singular, i.e., he, she, or it. Whereas the Matthean and Markan accounts incorporate the subject within the verb ἐστιν, Luke names the kingdom of God as being near. "Luke has inserted ἡ βασιλεία τοῦ θεοῦ [*hē basileia tou theou*, "kingdom of God"], diff. Mk., to make the point clear. . . . in Mk. the reference may well have been to the coming Son of Man, who is to be equated with the master who appears *at the door* in the following parable. Luke has substituted the abstract concept here . . . and Luke's point is that its [the kingdom of God's] advent here is introduced by the coming of the Son of Man." I. H. Marshall, *Luke*, 779. See also N. T. Wright, *Jesus and the Victory of God*, 362.

enjoyment. The First Section relates specific signs in relation to judgment upon Jerusalem; in the Second such specific signs are absent in regard to final judgment. The First Section is concerned with "those days"; the Second with "that day." The First Section limits the judgment to Palestine; the Second, embraces all nations. Warnings in the First; no warnings, except a general admonition to be prepared, in the Second. In the First the saints were warned to flee to the mountains; in the Second, the saints are taken up. The First pictures a judgment upon earth; the Second, judgment in heaven. All this points to a vivid and clear contrast of content. The two sections have different subject matter.[63]

These significant differences lead me to suggest with Kik that the subject matter of verses 1–35 is concerned with events leading up to and including the AD 70 destruction of the temple and that verse 36 through chapter 25 concerns the second coming of Christ and final judgment.

Objections may be raised against this view by claiming that many things Jesus said have not occurred; however, these objections are answerable. Space permits only few examples:

Verse 14
And this good news of the kingdom will be proclaimed throughout the world, as a testimony to all the nations; and then the end will come.

Dispensationalists argue that the worldwide spread of the gospel is not yet complete. This may be true based on a simple reading of the text. It is, however, necessary to note that the word used by Jesus is not *kosmos*, meaning the world, but *oikoumenē*, meaning the inhabited world. This word was also used at the time in a more specific sense of the Roman Empire.[64]

Paul, in Colossians 1:5–6 writes (approx. AD 64), "You have heard of this hope before in the word of the truth, the gospel that has come to you. Just as it is bearing fruit and growing *in the whole world*." Later in the same chapter, Paul says that this gospel has been preached to "every creature under heaven" (Col 1:23). Kik writes of these statements that they "indicate beyond a doubt that the Gospel was preached by the

---

63. Kik, *Eschatology of Victory*, 164–65. It could, however, be contested that the saints are not taken up, but rather it is the unbelieving who are "taken" for judgment, while the saints are left behind to enjoy the new earth.

64. BDAG, "οἰκουμένη," 699; Michel, "οἰκουμένη."

apostles and their fellow laborers throughout the habitable world before the destruction of Jerusalem."[65] The subject of Jesus's teaching being the destruction of the temple, the contemporary specific use of *oikoumenē*, the very emphatic "this generation," and the historical realities of the time strongly suggest that the "end" spoken of here is a reference to the end of the temple at that time.

> Verse 29
> Immediately after the suffering of those days
> the sun will be darkened,
>   and the moon will not give its light,
> the stars will fall from heaven,
>   and the powers of heaven will be shaken.

Dispensationalists understand that this will literally occur as a cataclysmic end of the world when Christ returns. The literalism of their interpretive method and lack of consideration for the nature of the apocalyptic genre here employed prevents them from hearing the intent of this unusual language. Hermeneutically there is no warrant to disregard the literary form and simplistically attribute a contemporary literal meaning to the words. Interpretation must take into account the distinctive characteristics of a given genre. Walter Kaiser notes of the above language, "Usually these phrases represent national and worldwide calamities."[66] Concerning the text in question, Currie writes, "Apocalyptic literature uses dramatic imagery of cataclysmic disruptions to describe changes within the human political sphere."[67] Scripture affirms this.

Consider Isaiah 13:10, 13, 19, spoken within an oracle concerning God's judgment on Babylon:

> For the stars of the heavens and their constellations
>   will not give their light;
> the sun will be dark at its rising,
>   and the moon will not shed its light. (v. 10)
> Therefore I will make the heavens tremble,
>   and the earth will be shaken out of its place,

---

65. Kik, *Eschatology of Victory*, 100.

66. Kaiser and Silva, *Introduction to Biblical Hermeneutics*, 155. See also Sandy, *Plowshares*, 152, 167–68, 176–77. "It is more likely that these celestial horrors are metaphoric. . . . Everything will be topsy-turvy, and one way to suggest that is to describe the heavens as completely disoriented (cf. Acts 2:19–20)."

67. Currie, *Rapture*, 64.

> at the wrath of the Lord of hosts
>   in the day of his fierce anger. (v. 13)
> And Babylon, the glory of kingdoms,
>   the splendor and pride of the Chaldeans,
> will be like Sodom and Gomorrah
>   when God overthrew them. (v. 19)

These dramatic words of cosmic commotion signified the end of Babylon. Ironically, the end of the Babylonian Empire came in quite a nondramatic manner as the Medo-Persian army (not God overthrowing them in a literalistic sense) dried up the river that ran through Babylon, walked under the city walls, brought an end to the empire, and were welcomed by its inhabitants as liberators. The stars did not fall, the earth did not shake out of place and there is no record of heavenly lights of day and night failing.

This same language is found again Isaiah 34:4–5 concerning Edom:

> All the host of heaven shall rot away, and the skies roll up like a scroll. All their host shall wither like a leaf withering on a vine, or fruit withering on a fig tree. When my sword has drunk its fill in the heavens, lo, it will descend upon Edom, upon the people I have doomed to judgment.

Of this Kik writes,

> Surely, no one will maintain that when the judgment of God came upon Idumea [Edom], the hosts of heaven were literally dissolved and the heavens actually rolled together as a scroll with all the stars falling down like leaves from a vine.[68]

In Ezekiel 32:7–8 this same apocalyptic genre is voiced by the prophet concerning God's judgment on Egypt. This biblical association of cataclysmic language, used to describe God's acting in judgment on nations, contributes to understanding Jesus's use of this language in Matthew 24:29. Wright notes,

> These verses . . . are not 'flat and literal prose'. They do not speak of the collapse or end of the space-time universe. They are . . . typical Jewish imagery for events within the present order that

---

68. Kik, *Eschatology of Victory*, 130.

are felt and perceived as 'cosmic' or, as we should say, as 'earth-shattering'.[69]

The context of Matthew 24:4–33 concerns God's judgment on Jerusalem. This is abundantly clear from the preceding context of chapter 23, which records Jesus's scathing condemnation of her way of life and from his concluding words, "See, your house is left to you desolate (23:38)." In a reference to the Markan parallel (Mark 13:24–25), Dumbrell writes,

> Though verses 24–27 are often treated as referring to the parousia, the organization of the entire chapter and the use of Old Testament theophanic language, particularly in verses 24–25, indicate that these verses also refer to the fall of Jerusalem.[70]

Considering the judgment context of Matthew 23 and 24 and the Old Testament use of this language in similar contexts, it is entirely reasonable to understand Jesus as speaking figuratively of Jerusalem's downfall. To interpret in a woodenly literalistic manner of actual cosmic fallout at Christ's return is inconsistent with the clear pattern established in Scripture.[71]

> Verse 30
> Then the sign of the Son of Man will appear in heaven, and then all the tribes of the earth will mourn, and they will see "the Son of Man coming on the clouds of heaven" with power and great glory.

LaHaye and Ice's timeline (above) considers these words to be a reference to the visible second coming of Christ after the tribulation. Its placement in the text, however, places it among the "all things" that "this generation" will see, that is, the generation then living. If the plain-sense meaning of Jesus's words is applied, then the things spoken here must

---

69. N. T. Wright, *Jesus and the Victory of God*, 362.

70. Dumbrell, *Search for Order*, 202.

71. This cataclysmic language is found also in Acts 2 in Peter's Pentecost speech (Acts 2:17–21). Here he announces the gift of the Spirit as being the fulfillment of Joel's prophecy (Joel 2:28–32). It is enormously significant that he includes Joel's cataclysmic language as part of what was fulfilled on that day. No biblical account records such events as literally occurring at that time. The presence of the Spirit being a sign that the kingdom of God had come into the world, however, meant a radical shift in human affairs, and the beginning of the end of human kingdoms (cf. Dan 2:44). See Sandy, *Plowshares*, 152.

have already occurred. The topic of Jesus's discourse at this juncture is still his coming in judgment on Jerusalem in AD 70. Can these words of Jesus fit that context?

"Son of Man" is a term Jesus applies to himself (e.g., Matt 20:28; 26:2). It should be understood that this passage of Scripture reveals that it is a *sign* of the Son of Man that will appear—not the Son of Man himself. People will see a *sign* indicating that the Son of Man is located "in heaven." There is no indication in this verse that the Son of Man is envisioned as making a physical descent to earth. In the genre of an apocalyptic vision, Daniel (7:13–14) sees one like a Son of Man "coming with the clouds of heaven," not earthward, but toward the Ancient of Days, whose throne *is* heaven, and he is given "authority, glory and sovereign power" of an everlasting kingdom. The kingdom of God is inherent in "Son of Man" language. This is also seen when Jesus, speaking to the High Priest at his trial, says, "But I tell you, from now on you will see the Son of Man seated at the right hand of power and coming on the clouds of heaven" (Matt 26:64). It must not be forgotten that Jesus is here drawing on the apocalyptic genre of Daniel's vision, therefore, it is expected to find figurative language being used to portray earthly realities. The High Priest, Jesus says, will see "from now on" Jesus as being in a kingly role and coming on clouds of heaven. How? Caiaphas is not in heaven to see this, and did he "from now on" actually see Jesus coming on the clouds? No, the language must be understood on the terms of its genre. Jesus is speaking of his kingdom, and of himself as seated at the right hand of God—in heaven.[72]

The closely associated term "coming on the clouds" should also be understood in light of its genre[73] and as found in Old Testament usage: this is figurative language portraying the earthly manifestation of God coming in judgment.[74] In Isaiah 19:1 this language, like cataclysmic language, is also used in a context of God coming in judgment—this time on Egypt.

72. Beasley-Murray, *Coming of God*, 52.

73. "Clouds," 157.

74. Dumbrell, *Search for Order*, 176. Of the Markan parallel Dumbrell writes that the terms "the sign of the Son of Man . . . in heaven" and the "coming of the Son of Man on the clouds of heaven," indicate that "the advent is not a physical one of the Son of Man but a witness to the Son of Man, who is in heaven. That is, the coming is to occur through historical events."

An oracle concerning Egypt. See, the Lord is riding on a swift cloud and comes to Egypt; the idols of Egypt will tremble at his presence, and the heart of the Egyptians will melt within them.

Of this Kik writes,

Although this passage speaks of the Lord riding upon a cloud and of his presence, nevertheless we know that the Egyptians did not see the Lord in a personal, visible way. The Lord riding upon a swift cloud indicated a coming judgment against the Egyptians.[75]

What Egypt did see was its earthly reality: judgment being carried out by human agents in the form of the Assyrian army (Isa 20).

Jesus, in Matthew 26:64 referred to above, associated his being given the kingdom with this judgment language: Caiaphas would see the earthly realities figuratively portrayed in this apocalyptic language; "you will see the Son of Man seated at the right hand of Power [kingdom] and coming on the clouds of heaven [judgement]."[76]

Matthew 24:30 can, due to both context and genre, be understood as a reference to the destruction of Jerusalem in AD 70.[77] Further, the destruction of Jerusalem is associated with redemption and the coming kingdom.[78] The "sign of the Son of Man in heaven" that would be "seen" can therefore be understood to be the destruction of Jerusalem, his judgment "coming on the clouds" realized through the use of human agents[79]—the Romans army. This is the sign the people of the day would definitely "see."

75. Kik, *Eschatology of Victory*, 141.

76. N. T. Wright, *Jesus and the Victory of God*, 341, quoting Caird. "Here, as in the book of Daniel . . . the coming of the Son of Man on the clouds of heaven was never conceived as a primitive form of space travel, but as a symbol for a mighty reversal of fortunes within history and at the national level." See Caird, *Jesus and the Jewish Nation*, 20.

77. Dumbrell, *Search for Order*, 202. "Using theophanic language of judgement . . . verse 26 [Markan parallel to Matt 24:30] describes the theological significance of the destruction of Jerusalem."

78. N. T. Wright, *Jesus and the Victory of God*, 362. "The 'coming of the son of man' is thus good first-century metaphorical language for two things: the defeat of the enemies of the true people of God, and the vindication of the true people themselves. Thus, the *form* that this vindication will take, as envisaged within Mark 13 and its parallels, will be precisely the destruction of Jerusalem and the Temple. This is what the whole chapter has been about from the start."

79. Dumbrell, *Search for Order*, 176.

The dispensationalists' assumed parenthesis between verses 4 and 7, the assumed rapture between verses 8 and 9, the attributing of Matthew 24:9–25 to a future tribulation, and their rejecting the plain normal-sense meaning of "this generation" requires them to radically abandon their strongly insisted upon requirement of a literal hermeneutic. All this is made necessary by their a priori belief in a postponed kingdom and a bifurcated people of God, and it requires (a) a failure to observe the consistent use of "you" throughout verses 4–34 and so a failure to apply its message to the time of the disciples then living, (b) a failure to recognize past historical fulfillment of Jesus's words to verse 33, (c) a failure to consider historical and biblical uses of the genre adopted by Jesus concerning judgment and kingdom, and (d) a failure to note the only dramatic shift in time at verse 36. There is no need to propose that Matthew 24:9–33 is speaking of a yet-to-be seven-year, post-rapture tribulation. Historical and literary consideration shows that this passage of Scripture is more suited to events long ago fulfilled.

1 Thessalonians 4:13–18—Meeting Christ

> But we do not want you to be uninformed, brothers and sisters, about those who have died, so that you may not grieve as others do who have no hope. For since we believe that Jesus died and rose again, even so, through Jesus, God will bring with him those who have died. For this we declare to you by the word of the Lord, that we who are alive, who are left until the coming of the Lord, will by no means precede those who have died. For the Lord himself, with a cry of command, with the archangel's call and with the sound of God's trumpet, will descend from heaven, and the dead in Christ will rise first. Then we who are alive, who are left, will be caught up in the clouds together with them to meet the Lord in the air; and so we will be with the Lord forever. Therefore encourage one another with these words. (1 Thess 4:13–18)

This popular passage likewise requires investigation. Dispensationalists often, if not always, refer to these verses to support the idea of saints being taken up off the earth to be with the Lord while unbelievers are "left behind" to endure the tribulation—despite there being no mention of a tribulation in this text. At this time, they believe, Christ comes only part way, the saints meet him in the air, after which they go back to where Jesus came from to be with him forever in heaven. I contend that these words do not teach this, but instead speak of the resurrection at the time of Christ's actual return, and that they do not teach that Christ executes a U-turn to take the saints back with him to heaven. It is the return of Christ that it teaches, not an event allegedly seven years before.

From verse 13 it is clear that the Thessalonian recipients have concerns about those who have already died and what happens to them when Christ returns. Paul seeks to give them words of hope by which they may comfort one another (v. 18). Their hope, Paul teaches, lies in the assurance that Christ was physically resurrected from the dead. As Christ was bodily resurrected, "in like manner" (*houtōs*) their believing dead will be bodily resurrected. Resurrection throughout Scripture is associated with Christ's second coming, therefore contextually this passage is not about an event seven years earlier. "This event is the long-anticipated redemptive historical climax, not a secret rapture which is but a prelude to the 'real' second coming."[80] It is in this second advent resurrection context that Paul speaks of being caught up (raptured) to meet Christ in the air.

The proposition from dispensationalists that Christ comes part way and then returns to heaven with the resurrected and transformed believers fails to comprehend the meaning and historical use of the Greek word translated "meet." This word, *apantēsin*, had a specific technical usage that is directionally opposite to the dispensational understanding of the rapture: that of a civic custom of welcoming important visitors.[81] Ben Witherington explains that in the first-century world when a visiting dignitary was due to arrive (*parousia*, meaning "arrival" or "presence") at a city, some of the citizens would travel out of the city to meet (*apantēsin*) his as a welcoming committee in order to escort the dignitary on the final leg of the journey. In the Thessalonians passage, *apantēsin* is employed concerning Christ's *parousia*, his arrival. Witherington writes,

> It is probable that Paul is drawing on secular parousia imagery, for when a king went to visit a city his herald would go before him to the city walls to announce with a trumpet blast and audible words the coming of the king. It might even include the "cry of command" to open up the city gates so as to let the visiting monarch in.[82]

80. Riddlebarger, *Case for Amillennialism*, 133.

81. Peterson, "ἀπάντησις."

82. Witherington, *Jesus, Paul and the End of the World*, 157–58. See also Bruce, *1 & 2 Thessalonians*, 102–3; G. Green, *Thessalonians*, 226–27; Stott, *Gospel and the End of*

Used of Christ's *parousia* in conjunction with the royal language of a *cry of command* and the *sound of a trumpet*, there is "little doubt that this custom formed the background of this teaching" by Paul.[83] It is entirely reasonable to conclude that 1 Thessalonians 4:17 portrays believers rising (context of resurrection) to meet Christ in order to accompany him as he completes his royal descent.[84] This public celebratory event has no hint of secrecy, silence, or that the descending Christ is visible only to believers. Neither is there any indication that this event has the express purposes of delivering the saints from a tribulation (*thlipsis* in Matt 24) to follow—on the contrary, Paul had just written a few verses before (3:4), "In fact, when we were with you, we told you beforehand that we were to suffer persecution (*thlipsis*); so it turned out, as you know"—nor are there any indicators that this event initiates the resumption of Israel's prophetic timetable.

This concept of welcoming is affirmed elsewhere in Scripture. As Paul is journeying to Rome from Puteoli, "The believers from there [Rome], when they heard of us, came as far as the Forum of Appius and Three Taverns to meet (*apantēsin*) us" (Acts 28:15). We know from what follows that Paul did not turn around and take the welcoming committee back to Puteoli; he continued in the same direction he was going—to Rome. Likewise in Matthew 25:6, the virgins who were ready for the arrival of the bridegroom go out to meet (*apantēsin*) him and walk with him to the wedding banquet—the place where he was going.

Time, 104; Hoekema, *Bible and the Future*, 168–69; Waldron, *End Times*, 189–90; N. T. Wright, *Resurrection of the Son of God*, 569; McClain, "Pretribulation Rapture," 243–44; Hill, *In God's Time*, 204; Dumbrell, *Search for Order*, 312.

83. G. Green, *Thessalonians*, 226; N. T. Wright, *Jesus and the Victory of God*, 341.

84. Witherington, *Jesus, Paul and the End of the World*, 158. "This suggestion becomes more than a conjecture when we point out that in 1 Thessalonians 4:17 Paul refers to the *apantēsin*. Cicero, in the course of his description of Julius Caesar's tour through Italy in 49 B.C., says, 'Just imagine what *apentēseis* he is receiving from the towns, what honours are paid to him' (*Ad. Att.* 8.16.2; compare 16.11.6 of Octavian). This word refers to the action of the greeting committee that goes out to meet the king or dignitary at his parousia who is paying an official visit to the town, and escort him back into the town on the final leg of his journey. 'These analogies (especially in association with the term *parousia*) suggest the possibility that the Lord is pictured here as escorted the remainder of his journey to earth by his people—both those newly raised from the dead and those who have remained alive.' Thessalonica, a Hellenistic town founded by the Macedonian king Cassander, was a free city within the Roman Empire from 42 B.C. The recipients of 1 Thessalonians would surely have been familiar with what Paul was implying by the use of the secular Hellenistic language of a parousia."

What may be understood by contemporary dispensationalists as the plain, literal, or normal meaning of this passage is therefore very different from what would have been the plain, literal, or normal meaning as understood by its original readers. These original readers would understand the language of *apantēsin* juxtaposed with *parousia* to be that of welcoming and escorting their king to their dwelling place. Of this Green writes,

> The picture presented here is of the royal coming of Jesus Christ. The church, as the official delegation, goes out to meet him, with the dead [now resurrected] heading up the procession as those most honored. One coming is envisioned, which will unite the coming King with his subjects. What a glorious hope![85]

It has been demonstrated through the above analysis that a priori beliefs in a postponed nationalistic kingdom and a future tribulation in which the church does not participate appear to dictate the pretribulational interpretation of this passage; it is not the result of sound grammatical-historical interpretation.

CHAPTER CONCLUSION

The ideas of the church being taken off the earth and a subsequent future seven-year tribulation, as understood by pretribulation rapturists, are not found in Scripture but rather are imposed on Scripture as a consequence of prior assumptions within a system of thought that is itself already an imposition on the text of Scripture. Based on the dispensational principle of "absolute" and "consistent" literalism, dispensationalists insist on the absolute distinction of Israel and the church. This in turn leads to their belief that the kingdom promised to Israel was postponed and will be resumed at a time still future. In order for this to happen for Israel, God must bring his plan for the church to an end by rapturing her to heaven. Ironically, this progression of beliefs now turns full circle to challenge the dispensationalists' starting point—that of "absolute" and "consistent" literalism.

The key tenets of the system, in order to be sustained, now require the imposition of a gap into various texts—a gap of what is now approximately two thousand years. It also requires an assumed rapture in alleged future tribulation texts, and an assumed tribulation in texts understood

---

85. G. Green, *Thessalonians*, 229.

as the rapture—for no single text speaks of both together. It is a highly inconsistent literalism to impose things literally unsaid on the text in this manner. By such inconsistencies dispensationalists radically betray their own required hermeneutic and the basic principle upon which the entire system of thought is built. This betrayal of literalism is perhaps most evidenced by their interpretation of Jesus's words, "this generation" (Matt 24:34). This departure is made worse in that Jesus vigorously emphasizes these words in a manner that suggests they mean exactly what they say. To then attribute their meaning to a time two thousand years later is overtly contradictory to a claimed "absolute" and "consistent" literalism.

At other points absolute literalism prevents dispensationalists from perceiving the literary intent of those passages where the genre of apocalyptic language is employed. To interpret such passages without any consideration for the form and context in which they are given must fail to perceive their intended meaning and result in the forming of erroneous beliefs. On these occasions there appears also to be a complete disregard for the testimony of how such passages are used in other places of Scripture. Craig Hill writes,

> Ironically, in their effort to interpret literally and consistently, proponents of the Rapture have mangled the biblical witness almost beyond recognition. . . . it is the Bible itself, this wonderfully diverse and complex witness to God and Christ, that has been left behind.[86]

Further, it would seem most strange that the event of the rapture as the climactic goal for the church, the "blessed hope," is—according to one of dispensationalism's most capable theologians (Walvoord)—not explicitly taught in Scripture. The goal of the church it seems is only implied, and then only by collapsing contexts to piece together a theology to fit the dispensational scheme.

The plain witness of Scripture, one that requires no imposing gaps in the text and history, is that dispensationalism's future tribulation texts are in fact speaking of events concerning the redeeming work of Christ and the destruction of Jerusalem and her temple. Texts applied to the rapture are to be understood as related to Christ's actual *parousia*, his royal descent to fully establish that which was initiated at his first com-

---

86. Hill, *In God's Time*, 207.

ing. The dispensational beliefs of literal interpretation, the distinction of Israel and the church, and a postponed kingdom have been shown to be incorrect. There is therefore no biblical need for a rapture of the church or a future tribulation. These ideas are simply the offshoots of an erroneous belief system.

Perhaps the most unfortunate consequence of such beliefs is the hugely diminished understanding of God's redemptive purposes for his creation. The idea that the church's mission is understood as being to "save souls" so they will be raptured off this soon-to-be-destroyed earth is tragically and utterly counter to the heart of God and his love for his creation. It encourages disengagement from seeking to redemptively transform this world, which would only delay the rapture. Rather than Christian people functioning according to the biblical metaphors of salt and light, pretribulationalism implies a metaphor of a travelling consultant issuing one-way tickets for a journey off the planet. Writing of the rapture, Barbara Rossing states,

> this theology distorts God's vision for the world. In place of healing the Rapture proclaims escape. In place of Jesus' blessing of peacemakers, the Rapture voyeuristically glorifies violence and war. . . . This theology is not biblical.[87]

The doctrine of a future seven-year tribulation preceded by rapture of the church at the first of a two-stage return of Christ is not found in Scripture. Through careful, contextual, and literary considerations, we find yet another essential component of dispensational premillennialism to be unsupported by Scripture.

87. Rossing, *The Rapture Exposed*, 2.

5

The Millennium

DISPENSATIONAL PREMILLENNIALISM, AS THE term suggests, antici-
pates that after the alleged seven-year tribulation Jesus Christ will
return to earth to establish a literal one-thousand-year period of time
when, according to Pentecost, "the purposes of God are fully realized on
earth,"[1] that is, the millennium. This millennium is, according to Ryrie,
"the climax of history and the great goal of God's program for the ages."[2]
For the duration of this millennium, Jesus will reign as king over all
the earth and will exercise his Davidic rule from a throne in the city
of Jerusalem, which will be the center of world government. Israel as a
nation will be exalted at this time and will have the Gentile nations as
their servants.[3] The temple will be rebuilt and the Old Testament sacrificial system reinstated in fulfillment of Ezekiel 40–48. In this millennial temple, "all that was prescribed and initiated in the Old Testament
ceremonial and ritual activities *will come to completion and find their
fullest meaning*."[4] This will be the time when the Abrahamic and Davidic
covenants and Israel's Old Testament prophecies are fulfilled and when
Israel will fulfill her national destiny as a blessing to the nations.[5]

---

1. Pentecost, *Things to Come*, 201.

2. Ryrie, *Dispensationalism*, 95.

3. Crenshaw and Gunn, *Dispensationalism Today*, 132–33.

4. Cited in Preston, *Israel: 1948 Countdown*, 9 (emphasis added), quoting Ice and
Demy, *Prophecy Watch*, 256. Note: This will be a fourth temple; a yet-to-be-built third
temple is to be destroyed by the Antichrist during the tribulation period. This implies
that the sacrificial system will also need to be restored twice in the future. Further, this
statement suggests counter to Scripture that the "fullest meaning" of Old Testament
ceremonial and ritual activities is not found in Jesus Christ (see Matt 5:17; Luke 24:27;
John 5:39, 46; Heb 7:22–8:6; 9:11–14, 23–28; 10:8–22).

5. LaHaye and Ice, *Charting the End Times*, 48.

It is immediately apparent that these expectations are, like the notions of rapture and tribulation discussed in the previous chapter, wholly reliant on the dispensational literal hermeneutic, the distinction between Israel and the church, and a postponed kingdom. These three indispensable tenets of the dispensational system have previously been demonstrated to be biblically unconvincing. It logically follows that if the foundational beliefs upon which dispensationalists formulate (and indeed require) a future millennium as the time of fulfillment for Israel are unconvincing, then the prospect of a future millennium must also be problematic. Due to Christ, in his life and ministry, being the fulfiller of Israel's Old Testament institutions, ceremonies, promises, and prophecies, and the one in whom the kingdom has already come, there is simply no biblically justifiable purpose or need for a future millennial kingdom such as expected by dispensationalists and as described above.

For this reason my discussion will be brief and will focus solely on the one-thousand-year period mentioned in Revelation 20:1–6, asking only one question: to when in time does this one thousand years refer?[6] Amillennialists and postmillennialists do not ignore this passage—it means something.[7] But neither do they take this one highly symbolic passage, nestled in the genre of an apocalyptic vision,[8] and in contradiction of the conventions of that genre invest it with such literalism so as to be the *only* place in all of Scripture that provides a time period in which

6. Many substantially more thorough works have been written on the subject of the millennium and the book of Revelation. I acknowledge that there is much more to be considered than is able to be covered in this chapter. I further acknowledge that when dealing with the text of Revelation a substantial degree of humility is needed and that a rabid and pedantic attitude is inappropriate. Many gifted scholars, even those of similar schools of thought, will understand the text in different ways. My goal is simple: to demonstrate the basic inadequacy of the dispensational view and to present a biblical basis for a non-premillennial understanding of the timing of the thousand years of Revelation chapter 20. In addition to the critique of the key tenets of dispensationalism in previous chapters, this present discussion will show that the popular view of a future millennium is in need of reconsideration.

7. Despite differences in the interpretation of Revelation 20:1–10 and the nature of the millennium, amillennialists and postmillennialists agree that the one thousand years refers to a time prior to the second advent. In this sense both are postmillennial as regards to the relationship of the second advent to the one thousand years.

8. Despite varied opinions it appears to be generally accepted that Revelation is, in addition to its epistolary and prophetic elements, a form of apocalyptic literature. For helpful discussions of this issue, see Beale, *Revelation*, 37–43; Witherington, *Revelation*, 32–40; Poythress, *Returning King*, 45–47.

a myriad of so-called unfulfilled Old Testament prophecies can finally be realized for Israel. Non-dispensational views, as previously defended, regard such promises to be fulfilled in Christ (e.g., Acts 13:32–34), and consider the church, through being "in Christ," to be Israel and heirs of the promises (e.g., Gal 3:7–9, 29; Eph 2:11–22; Phil 3:3). Non-dispensationalists believe that all that was prescribed and initiated in the Old Testament ceremonial and ritual activities *came to completion and have already found their fullest meaning* in the person of Christ (Heb 9:12, 24–28; 10:11–14)—not by a reinstated sacrificial system in a future millennial temple. They believe, in accordance with the testimony of Scripture, that Israel's promise of a Davidic king (thus, kingdom) has already been fulfilled by Christ's resurrection, not on a literal millennial throne. The resurrection of Jesus Christ was his enthronement as the eternal Davidic king.

> Since he was a prophet, he [David] knew that God had sworn with an oath to him that he would put one of his descendants on his throne. Foreseeing this, David spoke of the resurrection of the Messiah. (Acts 2:30–31)

Non-dispensationalists, therefore, approach Revelation 20:1–6 from a completely different biblical framework of redemption than that of dispensationalists. They are not looking to find *somewhere* in Scripture to locate a future fulfillment of Israel's prophecies; they have found *someone*—Jesus Christ—in whom their fulfillment is already realized.

THE THOUSAND YEARS OF REVELATION 20:1–6

As non-premillennialists interpret Revelation 20:1–6, they observe *prima facie* that this passage—the only passage in the entire Bible to mention a distinct one-thousand-year period—nowhere mentions prophecies being fulfilled, Israel as a location, Jews or their return to the land, a rebuilt temple, reinstated sacrifices, subordination of Gentiles, Jerusalem as the center of a world government, nor is there mention of many other ideas that dispensationalists attribute to this time. These concepts are collected from a multitude of Old Testament prophetic writings, brought together, and are simply assumed to find their literal fulfillment in this (proposed future and literal) one-thousand-year period of time, a time that is mentioned only once in all of Scripture within a literary genre that suggests it is to be understood symbolically rather than literally.

Interpreters seeking to understand the thousand years of Revelation 20:1–6 should in the first instance consider a meaning in a manner that acknowledges its relevance for those to whom it was historically written—its first hearers and readers. How would they most likely have understood this passage given their historical setting and propinquity to the use of the symbolism and genre of the text?[9]

Genre Considerations

Revelation declares from the start that it is a symbolic writing,[10] as indicated by the use of *sēmainō*, (signify)[11] in 1:1, and was communicated to its writer in the form of a vision mediated by an angel. It is, furthermore, important to acknowledge the nonchronological sequence of its visions. This can be seen, for example, from 11:15–19, a scene of judgment and reward at the end of the age,[12] and the immediately subsequent vision of 12:1–12 portraying the birth of Christ.[13] This is a recurring feature of

9. Despite the text's being written to a first-century audience, the dispensational futurist interpretation of Revelation as a whole in effect disregards the immediate audience altogether by attributing its contents from chapter 4 to post-rapture events. These chapters, therefore, are written to churches that would not be on earth to experience its contents and therefore would have no significant first-century relevance.

10. Poythress, *Returning King*, 46–47. "Bizarre and wild symbols dominate the main visionary sections of Revelation. But while these symbols may seem bizarre and wild from a modern point of view, they are not bizarre from the point of view of the original readers. . . . People living in John's own time understood this matter instinctively, because they recognized that John was writing in an 'apocalyptic' manner, a manner already familiar to them as a political cartoon is to us today." Bauckham, *Theology of Revelation*, 17. Bauckham writes, ". . . Revelation's readers in the great cities of the province of Asia were constantly confronted with powerful images of the Roman vision of the world. . . . In this context, Revelation provides a set of counter-images which impress on its readers a different vision of the world: how it looks from the heaven to which John is caught up in chapter 4." Beale, *Revelation*, 50–69. Beale provides a thorough analysis of symbolism as a predominant feature of the genre of Revelation. See also Riddlebarger, *Case for Amillennialism*, 197–200.

11. Primarily the word means "make known, report, or communicate," but can connote "signify." BDAG, "σημαίνω," 920. This connotation is most probable in Revelation 1:1 given the highly symbolic and apocalyptic nature of the book. For a thorough argument in favor of this understanding, see Beale, *Revelation*, 50–55.

12. Beale, *Revelation*, 122. "The clearest statement of consummative judgment and salvation is 11:14–18, where the eternal kingdom of God and Christ, as well as the final judgement of the impious and salvation of the faithful, is said to have been completely accomplished (v 18)."

13. Metzger, *Breaking the Code*, 71–72. Metzger notes, "If John had finished his

Revelation and suggests that the location of a particular vision within the book does not necessarily determine its historical and chronological order.[14] R. F. White notes, "Any historical relationship among the visions must be *demonstrated* from the *content* of the visions, not simply *presumed* from the *order* in which John presents them."[15] The symbolic nature of Revelation, as well as its unmistakable recapitulating structure, must be considered in one's hermeneutical approach to the text at hand.[16] Despite these features, dispensationalists assert that Revelation is structured in the form of a chronological end-times timeline. They say that the one thousand years of Revelation 20 must be understood literally and must chronologically follow the second coming of Christ as depicted in chapter 19.[17] This assumption, however, is challenged by the above example from among many recapitulations within the book.

The Thousand Years and the Bible's Two-Age Structure

It is equally necessary that Revelation be interpreted in a manner agreeable with the Bible as a whole and the progressive development of God's purposes for redemption, particularly with regard to the motif of fulfillment in Christ and the redefining of the people of God in Christ as the newer expression of Israel. In addition to the aforementioned, the characteristics of the "two ages" of time as discussed in chapter 3 similarly challenge the possibility of a future millennium as understood by

---

book here [11:15–19], we would have considered it properly terminated. But since there are eleven more chapters, the author will now go back to an earlier stage and repeat some of the teachings that he had previously set before the reader . . . the sequence in which John's visions are presented does not allow us to turn the book of Revelation into an almanac or time chart of the last days." See also Poythress, *Returning King*, 131–38; Hendriksen, *More Than Conquerors*, 132–37; Dumbrell, *Search for Order*, 341; Hoekema, *Bible and the Future*, 227.

14. Many scholars regard the book of Revelation to be structured in up to as many as seven or eight progressive cycles paralleling the same period of time, e.g., Beale, *Revelation*, 108–16; cf. 972–83. Poythress, *Returning King*, 60; Hendriksen, *More Than Conquerors*, 16–22; Metzger, *Breaking the Code*, 18–19; Riddlebarger, *Case for Amillennialism*, 200–206; McGuckin, "Book of Revelation," 117–18; Hoekema, *Bible and the Future*, 223.

15. R. F. White, "Reexamining the Evidence," 324 (emphasis original).

16. The concept of recapitulation will be addressed later in this chapter.

17. LaHaye and Ice, *Charting the End Times*, 125. From the chart "Revelation 19–20." The twelve novels in the Left Behind series sequentially follow this chronology as a tribulation timeline based on Revelation 6–20.

premillennialists. It was noted in that discussion that the characteristics of this age include marriage, death, natural human existence, things temporal, and the coexistence of both righteous and wicked persons. The age to come, in contrast, is characterized by no marriage, no death, resurrected human existence, things eternal, and the participation of only the righteous. Further, these two ages are separated by the second advent and together exhaust all time including eternity. It would appear inconsistent with all prior Scripture for Revelation 20:1–6 to introduce into time a one-thousand-year period, the nature of which according to the dispensational understanding cannot be placed in "this age" for it is to be *after* Christ's return. Yet, neither can it be placed in the "age to come," for that is the age of resurrection and eternal life, a time to which only the righteous attain. Dispensationalism, however, maintains that there will be both wicked and righteous un-resurrected people present during the millennium. A millennium such as characterized by premillennialists cannot be reconciled with the New Testament's representation of the two ages.

It would, moreover, be remarkable that such a crucial time period in the dispensational system, indeed *the* period of time that dispensationalists consider to be the climactic goal of Israel's existence and hopes, is never in any way or form mentioned by any other New Testament writer, even by those writing specifically to a Jewish audience. Similarly, it would seem most unlikely that *the* climactic time in Israel's existence would be first introduced in the latter part of the first century, to predominantly Gentile Christian churches in Asia, within a highly symbolic genre, and without any explicit reference to Israel and/or her prophetic hopes.

It has been shown above that the biblical narrative of redemption regards the church, through being in Christ, as presently being heirs of Israel's promises. For the writer of Revelation to introduce a future millennium in which national Israel's kingdom hopes are realized would contradict all prior New Testament teaching and would effectively constitute a denial of Jesus Christ's resurrection and exaltation as being his enthronement in fulfillment of Israel's kingship promises. The dispensational view of Revelation 20:1–6 is, therefore, as unconvincing as the essential tenets previously discussed. It remains now to consider this millennial text.

Seeing the Vision on Its Own Terms

> [1] Then I saw an angel coming down from heaven, holding in his hand the key to the bottomless pit and a great chain. [2] He seized the dragon, that ancient serpent, who is the Devil and Satan, and bound him for a thousand years, [3] and threw him into the pit, and locked and sealed it over him, so that he would deceive the nations no more, until the thousand years were ended. After that he must be let out for a little while.
> [4] Then I saw thrones, and those seated on them were given authority to judge. I also saw the souls of those who had been beheaded for their testimony to Jesus and for the word of God. They had not worshiped the beast or its image and had not received its mark on their foreheads or their hands. They came to life and reigned with Christ a thousand years. [5] (The rest of the dead did not come to life until the thousand years were ended.) This is the first resurrection. [6] Blessed and holy are those who share in the first resurrection. Over these the second death has no power, but they will be priests of God and of Christ, and they will reign with him a thousand years. (Rev 20:1–6)

The Thousand Years: Symbolic or Literal?

The visionary nature of this passage is clearly stated by the words "I saw" (20:1, 4), hence signaling the probability of its portraying realities couched within symbolism. This is made more than conjecture given that the dragon is interpreted to mean "the Devil and Satan." That is, a symbol seen in the vision refers to and portrays characteristics of a defined reality—a reality that does not necessarily look like a literal dragon.[18] Verses 1–6 are replete with symbolic images of a key, a chain, and an abyss into which the devil is thrown, then locked and sealed inside. There are "visible" souls of beheaded people, a beast, and a mark. It would, therefore, be hermeneutically inappropriate within such a context to assume *prima facie* a nonsymbolic understanding of the thousand years. The burden of proof, therefore, lies with literalists to evidence their case. In this regard, Walvoord asserts,

---

18. Poythress, "Genre and Hermeneutics," 42. "The symbolic clothing of the communication conveys something about the characteristics of the historical referent . . . understanding the significance of the imagery involves making a transition from symbols to actual historical significance."

where symbols are explained in the book of Revelation, they establish a pattern of interpretation which casts a great deal of light upon the meaning of the book as a whole. This introduces a presumption, that where expressions are not explained, they can normally be interpreted according to their natural meaning unless the context clearly indicates otherwise.[19]

Such a hermeneutical principle is simply, as Walvoord states, "a presumption"—a presumption without any reasonable hermeneutical warrant. It is, in fact, a principle that effectually denies the essence of symbolism by inferring that many symbols are to be understood literally and consequently that such symbols are not actually symbolic.[20] From Walvoord's assertion the question arises: Are interpreters to understand the unexplained key and chain to be tangible material objects, and that an actual "bottomless pit" exists somewhere? By understanding the thousand years literally according to natural meaning is tantamount to Walvoord ignoring his own principle of "unless the context clearly indicates otherwise." There is nothing in the context to indicate that the thousand years is to be understood literally. Instead, the contexts of genre, vision, and the abundance of symbolism as well as the content of that vision are indicators that the thousand years is also intended to be understood as symbolic. It will soon be shown that it is the *content* of the thousand years that will give meaning to the term—not the term itself.

Textual Clues Concerning the "When" Question

It is essential to observe that the primary meaning of the opening *kai* of Revelation 20:1 means "and," thus introducing a vision that was seen *in addition to* previous visions but without giving any indication of chronological sequence.[21] The word *kai* simply introduces the order by

19. Walvoord, *Revelation of Jesus*, 30.

20. Poythress, "Genre and Hermeneutics," 51–52: "many interpreters still are captivated by the principle of 'literal if possible.' Such a principle may seem safe, and indeed it works well as a first approximation for historical narratives and NT letters. But with respect to Revelation and other instances of apocalyptic literature it constantly inhibits interpreters in practice from doing justice to the pervasively visionary character of the discourses. . . . it fights the integrity of any literary genre that uses apocalyptic or symbolico-visionary style in its global structure."

21. English versions translating *kai* as "then" may unnecessarily imply temporal sequence rather than visionary sequence. For an analysis of *kai* in the book of Revelation, see Beale, *Revelation*, 974–76. "Elsewhere in the book, when "and" is directly followed by an angelic descent . . . or ascent, without exception it introduces a vision either

which the visions are recorded. It is not employed as an indicator that the contents of 20:1–6 are referring to a time historically subsequent to that of 19:11–21. Chronological sequencing is, nonetheless, evident within 20:1–10. This passage mentions the event that initiates the thousand years, that is, the binding of Satan for their duration (20:2), while "after that" (20:3) signals an event after the one-thousand-year period, that is, Satan being loosed for a little while. The phrase, "When the thousand years are ended" in 20:7 further indicates sequential chronology and clearly shows that the thousand years spoken of in 20:1–6 occur at a time prior to events spoken of in 20:7–10. That the writer makes use of such language to convey chronological sequencing of events suggests that his use of the simple *kai* in 20:1 is not intended to be read as meaning "historically subsequent to the events of chapter 19." Thus while 20:1–10 relates events that are historically chronological, it does not necessarily indicate that those events chronologically follow the event portrayed in 19:11–21. This in turn suggests two points for consideration: First, there must be a historically cohesive flow of events from 19:11 through 20:3 to support the dispensational view of the millennium as being subsequent to the second advent. Second, given the clear temporal chronology in 20:1–10, verses 7–10 will be helpful in locating the historical timing of the millennium, the one-thousand-years mentioned in verses 1–6.[22]

Revelation 19:11–21 tells of the gathering of all nations for "the battle" in which they are subsequently destroyed by Christ at his coming.[23] Dispensationalists insist that this is speaking about the battle of Armageddon at the end of the seven-year tribulation and of the second coming.[24] Verses 1–3 of chapter 20 then speak of Satan being bound in such a way as to prevent him from deceiving the nations during the thousand years. The chronological inconsistency is clear as noted by White, who says of this,

suspending the temporal progress of a preceding section to introduce a synchronous section or reverting to a time anterior to the preceding section."

22. R. F. White, "Reexamining the Evidence," 319–28. See also Kistemaker, "Hyper-Preterism and Revelation," 245; Venema, *Promise of the Future*, 182–86; Hendriksen, *More Than Conquerors*, 195; Waldron, *End Times*, 98; Poythress, *Returning King*, 179; Riddlebarger, *Case for Amillennialism*, 203; Dumbrell, *Search for Order*, 341–43.

23. R. F. White, "Reexamining the Evidence," 322–25. "[T]he visions of 19:11–21 . . . are demonstrably parallel to the visions of the second advent in 6:12–17; 16:12–21; and 20:7–10 (11)."

24. Pentecost, *Things to Come*, 231.

it makes no sense to speak of protecting the nations from deception by Satan in 20:1–3 after they have just been both deceived
by Satan (16:13–16, cf. 19:19–20) and destroyed by Christ at his
return in 19:11–21 (cf. 16:15a, 19).[25]

Through careful comparisons of the language and content of
Revelation 19:11–21 and 20:7–10 with that of Ezekiel 38–39, White
observes convincing similarities, noting that both Revelation passages
draw material from a single episode in Ezekiel, thus indicating that both
Revelation passages are a retelling of the same single event related by
Ezekiel. From this evidence, White demonstrates that 19:11–21 is re-
capitulated in 20:7–10, and as a consequence the latter should be also
understood as a retelling of events associated with Christ's return.[26] This
demonstrates that if 20:7–10 is related to the final battle associated with
the second advent, then the thousand-year period must occur prior to
the second advent.

---

25. R. F. White, "Reexamining the Evidence," 321. Harold Hoehner, in his critique
of White and in defense of the premillennial view of chronological progression in
19:11–2:3 suggests that *ta ethnē* in Rev 20:3 refers to the saints of the nations, having
been spared from the destruction of 19:19–21. White defends citing 17 occasions in
Revelation of *ta ethnē* being simply the nations as distinct from *tōn hagiōn*, the holy
ones. R. F. White, "Making Sense," 540. In fact, in 20:7–9 *ta ethnē* gather for the battle
against *tōn hagiōn*.

26. R. F. White, "Reexamining the Evidence," 326–30. Similarities include the angel's
message in 19:17–18 being a virtually verbatim quotation of Ezekiel 39:17–20, the use
of Gog and Magog in 20:8 and Ezekiel 38:2; 39:1, 6, and fire as the destroying agent in
20:9 and Ezekiel 38:22; 39:6. Further evidence is seen in Revelation's use of the definite
article with the noun *polemos*, i.e., the battle in 16:14; 19:19; and 20:8. "When πόλεμος
[*polemos*] appears without the article, it designates the activity of warfare in general.
But when it appears with the article, the noun refers to a specific episode of war. . . .
When we see the noun πόλεμος [*polemos*] with the definite article in 20:8, the article's
presence makes it all but impossible to avoid the conclusion that the battle mentioned
in 20:8 is the one previously described in 19:19 and in 16:14. . . . When writing about the
Gog-Magog revolt in 20:8, John uses precisely the same wording he uses in connection
with the Armageddon revolt in 16:14 and virtually the same wording he uses in 19:19
(N.B. 16:14 συναγαγεῖν αὐτοὺς εἰς τὸν πόλεμον [*synagagein autous eis ton polemon*],
"to gather them for the battle"; 19:19, συνηγμένα ποιῆσαι τὸν πόλεμον [*synēgmena
poiēsai ton polemon*], "gathered to wage the battle"; 20:8, συναγαγεῖν αὐτοὺς εἰς τὸν
πόλεμον [*synagagein autous eis ton polemon*], "to gather them for the battle"). Thus
when we notice the obvious verbal parallelism between 16:14; 19:19; and 20:8, we are
compelled to interpret John's reference to "*the* battle" in 20:8 as "the battle" in 16:14 and
19:19, i.e., as the age-ending battle at Christ's return" (emphasis original). A further parallel in content is seen in the use of cosmic destruction language in 16:17–21; 19:11–21;
and 20:9–11 (also 6:12–17). See also Riddlebarger, *Case for Amillennialism*, 223–26.

The preceding verses, Revelation 20:1–6, are in like manner a recapitulation of 12:7–11. The similarities between the two passages are clearly paralleled by Beale in the following table and provides additional understanding regarding the timing of the thousand years.[27]

Revelation 12:7–11	Revelation 20:1–6
1. Heavenly scene (v. 7)	1. Heavenly scene (v. 1)
2. Angelic battle against Satan and his hosts (vv. 7–8)	2. Presupposed angelic battle with Satan (v. 2)
3. The angel's evil opponent called "the great dragon, the ancient serpent, the one called the devil and Satan, the one deceiving the whole inhabited earth." (v. 9)	3. The angel's evil opponent called "the dragon, the ancient serpent, who is the devil and Satan," restrained from "deceiving the nations any longer" (vv. 2–3), to be loosed later to deceive the nations throughout the earth (vv. 3, 7–8)
4. Satan's expression of "great wrath because he knows he has little time" (v. 12b)	4. Satan to be "released for a short time" after his imprisonment (v. 3)
5. Satan's fall, resulting in the kingdom of Christ (v. 10) and his saints (v. 11; note the "conquering" theme)	5. Satan's fall, resulting in the kingdom of Christ and his saints (v. 4)
6. The saints' kingship, based not only on the fall of Satan and Christ's victory but also on the saints' faithfulness even to death in holding to "the word of their testimony" (v. 11)	6. The saints' kingship, based not only on the fall of Satan but also on their faithfulness even to death in holding to "the word of God" (v. 4)

This observation appears convincing. It seems evident, therefore, that 20:1–6 is portraying, by way of recapitulation, the same events as 12:7–11. The context preceding 12:7–11, that is, verses 1–6, tells of the birth of Christ and his exaltation and coronation as king.

---

27. Beale, *Revelation*, 992.

> And she gave birth to a son, a male child, who is to rule all the
> nations with a rod of iron. But her child was snatched away and
> taken to God and to his throne. (12:5)

The historical connectedness, either in time or by consequence (or both),
of 12:1–6 and 12:7–11 is indicated by *kai egeneto polemos ev tō ouranō*
(and *became* war in the heaven, v. 7)[28] resulting in Satan being "thrown
down" (12:7; cf. 20:3). Thus is established a correspondence between the
events of Christ's first advent and ascension to sit on his throne with
the restraining of Satan's deceptive activity (20:3). This exegesis demonstrates that if 12:1–6 is related to events of the first advent, then the
thousand-year period of 20:1–6 (as a recapitulation of 12:7–11) must
occur after the first advent, and, as just established above, prior to the
second advent.

I, therefore, put forward that, given the symbolic nature of the
book and of 20:1–10 in particular, the language of historical chronology within 20:1–10, along with the findings resulting from the above
episodes of recapitulation, and the overarching redemptive narrative of
Scripture as a whole, that the thousand years is a symbolic term and its
historical referent is the inter-advent era, the church age (at least up to
the time of the loosing of Satan to again deceive the nations, vv. 7–10).
Can such a conclusion be supported from the content of 20:1–6 and
from other passages of Scripture? An affirmative answer to this question
will now be offered.

THE BINDING OF SATAN

Verses 1–3 of chapter 20 indicate that the thousand years is initiated and
its duration characterized by Satan being bound (root: *deō*) and thrown
(root: *ballō*) into the pit so that he would "deceive the nations no more."
The "no more" implies that deception of nations is an activity Satan had
previously engaged in (cf. Acts 26:18; 2 Cor 4:4) and would again take
up after the thousand years are ended with the intent "to gather them
for [the] battle" (20:7–8, *ton polemon*, i.e., the battle). The beginning of
the thousand years is marked by the initial act of binding Satan and his
being cast down, thus ending his deception of nations for a season.[29] The

---

28. Note the lack of the definite article in this use of *polemos* thus differentiating
this *polemos* (occurring at the beginning of the thousand years) from "the battle" of
16:14; 19:19; and 20:8 (occurring at the end of the one thousand years). See R. F. White,
"Reexamining the Evidence," 328–30.

29. Contra Walvoord, *Revelation of Jesus*, 291. Walvoord's assertion that Satan's
binding was designed to render him inactive ignores the specific nature stated in the

question to be asked is this: Does anything in the narrative of Scripture relate such an event? The connection between the first advent and the restraining of Satan has already been identified above; however, a number of other passages present themselves to support the binding of Satan as concomitant with the historical events of Christ's earthly ministry.

Jesus, speaking of his action of casting out a demon, says, "how can one enter a strong man's house and plunder his property, without first tying up the strong man? Then indeed the house can be plundered" (Matt 12:29). It is evident from the preceding context (12:26) that Jesus understood his expelling demons to be *casting out Satan* (see "if Satan casts out Satan," root: *ballō*, cf. Rev 20:3) and as a result of having first bound ("tying up," root: *deō*, cf. Rev 20:3) the strongman. Thus Satan was bound at the time of Christ's earthly ministry. In a similar context, Jesus replies to the disciples' joyful declaration that demons submit to them, that in the course of their missionary activity he watched Satan fall from heaven like a flash of lightning (Luke 10:17–18; cf. Rev 12:9; 20:3). John's Gospel is also helpful. In chapter 12, prompted by the approach of some Greeks (i.e., non-Jews) wishing to see him, Jesus responds that "the hour has come" for him to be glorified (20–23; cf. Rev 12:5–9) and by saying,

> Now is the judgment of this world; now the ruler of this world will be driven out. And I, when I am lifted up from the earth, will draw all people to myself. (John 12:31–32; cf. 16:11)

Initiated by a desire of people from a nation not Jewish, this authoritative declaration of Jesus relates his crucifixion (v. 33), by which he would be glorified and would draw all (people/nations) to himself. Significantly, however, he reveals an explicit correlation of his crucifixion and glorification with Satan's being "driven out" (a form the same Greek word used in Rev 20:3, root: *ballō*). "The casting out of Satan is associated with the fact that not only Jews, as was the rule in the past, but 'all men [humanity]'—Greeks as well as Jews—shall be drawn to Christ."[30] This is congruent with the content of Revelation 20:1–3, where Satan's binding is specifically intended to prevent nations from being deceived. It is no coincidence that having come to destroy the works of Satan by the cross

---

text. Those holding a view of this binding as a future and complete curbing of Satan's activity due to evidence of him being at work in this age must also reconcile this with his being disarmed and triumphed over by the cross in Colossians 2:15, and with 1 John 3:8 where his destruction is the express purpose of Christ having been revealed.

30. Hendriksen, *More Than Conquerors*, 188.

(Col 2:13–15 1; Heb 12:14; John 3:8) the resurrected Christ then, as a consequence of his rule and authority, commissions the disciples to take the gospel to the nations.

> And Jesus came and said to them, "All authority in heaven and on earth has been given to me. Go therefore and make disciples of all nations, baptizing them in the name of the Father and of the Son and of the Holy Spirit, and teaching them to obey everything that I have commanded you. And remember, I am with you always, to the end of the age." (Matt 28:18–20)

THE FIRST RESURRECTION

Verses 4–6 of Revelation chapter 20 portray a further characteristic of the same period. As a consequence of Satan's binding, the saints "came to life" (*ezēsan*, root; *zaō*) and reign with Christ for one thousand years. Those participating in this "coming to life," described as the "first resurrection" (*hautē hē anastasis hē prōtō*) are those for whom the second death (explained in 20:14–15 as the lake of fire, cf. 21:8) has no power.[31] The rest of the dead do not come to life (*ezēsan*) until the one thousand years are ended. This latter event is seen by virtually all commentators as a physical resurrection, whereas the nature of the first resurrection is debated.[32] Premillennarians understand *hē prōtō* (the first) in a sequential sense: the first in a series of resurrections of the same kind, that is, physical resurrection.[33] It is probable that what John saw as the "first resurrection" of saints (Rev 20:4–5) was, at a visionary and symbolic level, a physical resurrection. However, this in no way demands an actual physical resurrection as its referent; he had just seen "visible souls" and what looked like a physical dragon, yet its referent was something quite different. "Mere appeals to an apparent literalness and vividness of the resurrection does not help. Such vividness is characteristic of the visionary form."[34]

Premillennialists argue that if the latter use of *ezēsan* (v. 5) is a physical resurrection, then its former usage concerning the first resurrection in the same context (v. 4) must also be understood as physical;

---

31. LaHaye and Ice, *Charting the End Times*, 121–23. LaHaye and Ice understand the first resurrection to be two distinct resurrections: that of the church at the rapture then of the Old Testament believers as well as all martyred tribulation saints at the second coming.

32. Beale, *Revelation*, 1003.

33. Kline, "First Resurrection," 366.

34. Poythress, "Genre and Hermeneutics," 52.

otherwise, "there is an end of all significance in language, and Scripture is wiped out as a definite testimony to anything."[35] This logic is deeply flawed, overstates the proposed outcome, and recalls the over-literalistic hermeneutic that we addressed in chapter 1 by failing to allow fluidity in the use of symbols and language, especially within the genre of the book of Revelation.[36] Other scholars, however, do not regard interpreting the first resurrection as spiritual and the latter as physical to have such extreme consequences and, so understand the first resurrection as coming to life in the sense of Ephesians 2:1–6:

> You were dead through the trespasses and sins in which you once lived, following the course of this world, following the ruler of the power of the air. . . . But God, who is rich in mercy, out of the great love with which he loved us even when we were dead through our trespasses, *made us alive* together with Christ—by grace you have been saved—and *raised us up* with him and *seated us with him in the heavenly places* in Christ Jesus. (emphasis added)

The idea of the saints (Eph 1:1) being made alive, raised up, and being seated in heavenly places, here applied to their present-age salvation experience, demonstrates remarkably similar parallels to Revelation 20:4 where the saints "came to life and reigned with Christ."[37] Of "coming to life" in Rev 20:4–5, Beale notes that

> ζάω ([*zaō*] or the cognate noun ζωή [*zōē*], "life") and synonyms are used interchangeably [elsewhere in the New Testament] of both spiritual and physical resurrection within the same contexts . . . [cf. Rom 6:4–13; Rom 8:10–11].[38]

---

35. Cited in Beale, *Revelation*, 1003, quoting Alford, *Greek New Testament IV*, 732.

36. Page, "Revelation 20," 36. "To infer . . . that the *ezēsan* of verse 4 must be understood of bodily resuscitation . . . is to interpret apocalyptic prophecy by methods of exegesis which are proper to ordinary narrative." Quoting Swete, *Apocalypse of St John*. The genre of the literature with which we are dealing is such that it is not at all certain that the most literal interpretation is to be preferred.

37. Poythress, "Genre and Hermeneutics," 47. Poythress writes, "Naturally the linguistic level, as a terse transcription of the visionary level, uses the usual words *anastasis* and *zaō* to describe the vision. . . . To put it another way, the words for resurrection and life in 20:1–6 are no less and no more 'literal' than are the words for beast and wound in 13:1–8. . . . The vocabulary is what it is because it describes a vision, not because it literally describes the referent of the vision."

38. Beale, *Revelation*, 1004–7. See also Dumbrell, *Search for Order*, 342.

The words of Jesus concerning resurrection in John 5:24–29 are also significant and provide a substantial contribution to understanding the meaning of resurrection in Revelation chapter 20.

> [24] Very truly, I tell you, anyone who hears my word and believes him who sent me *has eternal life*, and does not come under judgment, but *has passed from death to life*.
> [25] "Very truly, I tell you, *the hour is coming, and is now here*, when the dead will hear the voice of the Son of God, *and those who hear will live*. [26] For just as the Father has life in himself, so he has granted the Son also to have life in himself; [27] and he has given him authority to execute judgment, because he is the Son of Man. [28] Do not be astonished at this; for *the hour is coming* when *all* who are in their graves will hear his voice [29] and will come out—those who have done good, to the resurrection of life, and those who have done evil, to the resurrection of condemnation. (John 5:24–29, emphasis added)

Within this passage many scholars see two resurrections; the first being a *spiritual* resurrection (vv. 24–25). This first resurrection includes only "those who hear." It is the initial act of salvation and being brought to life. Based on believing one has passed from death to life. The hour is coming and is *now* here (i.e., present tense at the time Jesus spoke, v. 25) when *only some of the dead* hear and *will live*. The "dead" is a reference to being spiritually dead and then being given new life (i.e., it is a resurrection to life). The second resurrection is a *bodily* resurrection (vv. 28–29) and includes *all people* hearing his voice and responding. Of this resurrection Jesus says, "The hour is coming [v. 28; note the lack of "and now is"; cf. v. 25] when *all* who are in their graves will hear." This second resurrection is *both* to life *and* to condemnation. The first resurrection is present—the other is future; the first is spiritual—the other is physical; the first is restricted to only "those who hear"—the other includes everyone; the first is to life—the other is judgment to life or to death.

> Blessed and holy are those who share in the first resurrection [*tē anastasei tē prōtē*]. Over these the second death has no power, but they will be priests of God and of Christ, and they will reign with him a thousand years. (Rev 20:6)

The two resurrections of Revelation 20:4–5 can therefore be reconciled with the wider New Testament and understood to be different in kind without any loss of integrity in the text. In fact, Meredith G. Kline has, after a careful analysis of its usage in Revelation and other

New Testament passages, convincingly shown that *tē prōtē* (root: *prōtos*) should be understood to convey a different kind of resurrection rather than that of first in time.[39]

I have stressed the difference in the two resurrections, however, interpreters need not press this distinction too far by failing to recognize the essential connectedness of the two; participation in the second resurrection is inextricably linked to participation in the first. The reader is reminded of the essential continuity between the now but not-yet aspects of other salvific terms (salvation, eternal life, kingdom of God, and the age to come) as demonstrated in chapter 3. Such present and future aspects apply equally to resurrection.[40] As noted in that chapter, resurrection, being of the age to come but yet experienced in Christ as "first fruits" (*aparchē*), affirms that the age to come/kingdom of God has broken into the present as God's guarantee of its full arrival. It is possible, therefore, to regard the one thousand years as that period of the kingdom of God present now but in a not-yet consummated form.

A present consequence of participating in the first resurrection is to reign with Christ. Paul, in his lengthy treatment on resurrection in 1 Corinthians 15, states that Christ "must reign *until* he has put all his enemies under his feet. The last enemy to be destroyed is death" (vv. 25–26). According to Revelation 20:14, death is destroyed after the thousand years in the judgment associated with Christ's second coming, thus placing the time of saints reigning with Christ prior to the second advent. Resurrection life, reigning with Christ (cf. Eph 2:1–6 above) is a key characteristic of the millennium, a characteristic the New Testament elsewhere attributes to the present time.[41]

---

39. Kline, "First Resurrection," 366–75. After analysis of the wider use of *prōtos*, Kline notes in his conclusion, "The way 'the first resurrection' is identified with living and reigning with Christ a thousand years in Revelation 20:4–6 has the effect of connecting the qualifying force of *prōtos* quite directly to 'the thousand years.' The millennium as such is virtually called a 'first' age. It falls within the days of this present passing world characterized by 'the first things.' The Parousia with its concomitant consummative events of resurrection and judgment must then follow these 'thousand years.' The premillennial view of the Second Advent is excluded" (374).

40. Page, "Revelation 20," 38–40.

41. Ibid., 39. "Since the references to a thousand years in this pericope suggest a reign of limited duration, it could well be that this corresponds to the believer's present experience of reigning with Christ spoken of by Paul." Despite this Kline understands the first resurrection to be the physical death of believers by which they come to life and reign. He asserts that in order for the first resurrection to be a true counterpart to the

A future consequence of having experienced the first resurrection is to not participate in the second death, which is also associated with post-millennium judgment as symbolized by the lake of fire (20:14; 21:8). Indeed it is a person's salvation experience in the present age (first resurrection) that assures that one's name is "written in the book of life," and so spared from the finality of the second death.

Finally, 2 Thessalonians 2:1–10 is written to assure its readers that, despite rumor to the contrary, the coming of Christ had not yet happened.

> As to the coming of our Lord Jesus Christ and our being gathered together to him, we beg you, brothers and sisters, not to be quickly shaken in mind or alarmed, either by spirit or by word or by letter, as though from us, to the effect that the day of the Lord is already here. (vv. 1–2)

To evidence this, the writer tells of events that must occur prior to his arrival. These events have many similarities with Revelation 20:1–10, and if indeed both passages are referring to the same period, they suggest that the one-thousand-year period described in Revelation 20 must be prior to Christ's coming again.[42]

2 Thessalonians 2	Revelation 20
Man of lawlessness (by the activity of Satan v. 9) is restrained vv. 6–7	Satan bound vv. 2–3
Restraint lifted vv. 7–8	Loosed v. 7
Rebellion v. 3	Rebellion v. 8
Ability to deceive v. 11	Ability to deceive v. 8 (cf. v. 3)
Destroyed by Christ's coming v. 8	Destroyed v. 8, contextually, at Christ's coming

---

second death it must be a "first" death suited to normal death of this age. Kline, "First Resurrection," 372. Despite the evidences presented by Kline, I remain unconvinced, as it is not normal physical death in the present age that prevents one from the second death but a spiritual rebirth.

42. Adams, *Time Is At Hand*, 17–24. Page, "Revelation 20," 34. "The correspondence between 2 Thessalonians 2 and Revelation 20 is sufficiently close to raise the possibility that what John speaks of as a binding of Satan is nothing other than the present restraint upon evil described by Paul."

These New Testament passages together with the chronology of Revelation 20:1–10 collaborate to affirm the millennium being prior to the second advent and portray the present age of salvation. The understanding of the millennium as being the inter-advent age during which Satan is unable to prevent the taking of the gospel to the nations is validated not only from within Revelation but also from the wider testimony of the New Testament.[43]

CHAPTER CONCLUSION

This very brief study of the thousand years of Revelation 20:1–10 has, due to limitation of space, not been as thorough as I would have liked. A topic such as the millennium and the nature of the genre of the book of Revelation cannot be adequately addressed in the space available. It can be stated, however, that the millennium as understood by dispensationalists is questionable. Such a millennium is absolutely dependant on literalism, Israel as a distinct people of God who are still waiting for the parenthesis church period to come to a close via the rapture in order for her Davidic king and kingdom to come in fulfillment of her promises. The related hopes for a rebuilt temple and reinstating of the Old Testament sacrificial system during this one thousand years suggest a meaningless reversal to the shadows and copies of Christ's better ministry, rather than confidently living in the reality of what Christ's sacrifice has already accomplished. As such it disregards the narrative of Scripture as a whole, especially that Christ's life, death, and resurrection fulfilled these hopes once for all.

The dispensational view has also failed to treat the book of Revelation in terms of its highly symbolic form and has, counter to the genre, attributed a literalistic interpretation to the thousand years. No exegetical basis exists for such a conclusion, which appears to be controlled by the system of thought and the need to find a location, both in the Bible and in time, for the fulfillment of prophecy for Israel. Recapitulation is evident within the structure of the book, yet dispensationalism adheres to a strict chronological and futurist understanding.

The view presented in this chapter is most suited to amillennial and postmillennial views (especially the former) and has attempted to re-

---

43. Beale, *Revelation*, 988; Hoekema, *Bible and the Future*, 228; Mathison, *Postmillenialism*, 155; Hendriksen, *More Than Conquerors*, 188; Dumbrell, *Search for Order*, 341.

spect the integrity of the genre of Revelation. It further acknowledges the clearly evident recapitulatory nature of the text. As a consequence, this shows once again that the dispensational view is biblically inadequate. If literalism as an interpretive principle is unwarranted, if the church is the new Israel, if the person of Christ is the fulfiller of Old Testament hopes and bringer of the kingdom as previous chapters have defended, and if the millennium of Revelation 20:1–10 portrays the church age prior to the second advent as defended in this chapter, then the one thousand years of Revelation 20 cannot be understood to refer to glory days yet to come for the physical nation of Israel.

A present millennialism in which the saints reign with Christ during the church age in which the preaching of the gospel to the nations as a consequence of Satan being bound appears to be a more appropriate interpretation of the passage. An effect of this interpretation is to provide confidence for preaching the gospel based on Christ's victory on the cross and his effective binding of Satan from deceiving the nations.

The discussion this far has shown many ways in which the popular belief system known as dispensational premillennialism is inadequate. Eschatology is therefore a subject that needs to be better understood by Christians in order that they may better understand what it means to be Christian. As I have already stated, beliefs shape how Christians live their lives. Eschatology is no mere appendage at the end of the Bible with little to say to life in the present. Eschatology is the goal of God from the beginning of time; the Bible is eschatological from beginning to end. The past, present, and future of God's redemptive work is the context for coming to an understanding of who Christians are and of our participation in God's mission. To get that context wrong will see us not only mislead others but also misunderstand our role in effecting God's redeeming activity in the world.

6

Earthing Our Eschatology

THE FOREMOST AIM OF this book has been to test the reliability of dispensationalism. Previous chapters have sought to do this in some detail and have demonstrated that as a system of eschatological thought dispensationalism is inconsistent with sound principles of interpretation and the overall story of redemption as revealed in Scripture. This concluding chapter will briefly summarize key points from the preceding chapters and advance one further essential component of eschatological understanding (only hinted at in chapter 4) in order to point the way to a better understanding of the eschatological scope of redemption while providing some of the implications for life in the present time.

In chapter 1 the literalistic interpretive principle that leads to the formation of dispensationalism was shown to be both inappropriate and unsustainable. Despite this, dispensationalism as an eschatological belief system has gained widespread acceptance (though not so much within biblical scholarship), and as such it continues to shape the thoughts of a multitude of sincere Christians. The sad consequence for these Christian people is that they now live their lives based on what appears to be a nonbiblical worldview, and many are frequently distracted to misguided and unhelpful attention to events in the Middle East and to so-called signs of the times, such as wars, rumors of war, famines, earthquakes, and pestilences (Matt 24), in order to understand the times in which they live. Such signs have, however, in chapter 4, been shown to relate to the time leading up to the destruction of the temple in AD 70 rather than be harbingers of the second coming of Christ and an end of the world. End-time preaching has on countless occasions been used as a tool to encourage people to believe in Christ in order to be ready for the rapture and so escape the world before the fearful tribulation comes and the earth, in due course, is ultimately destroyed—that is, fear of what is said to lie ahead rather than hope for both the present and the future engender the responses of many people. The work of Christ on the cross has been diminished to his merely dying for the sin of humanity in order that they may one day go to heaven to walk on streets of gold and to live in a mansion prepared for them by Jesus.

Dispensationalism has likewise reduced the significance of the church to that of an interrupting "parenthesis" in God's primary purpose of establishing a kingdom for Israel, one that only exists because of Israel's rejection of Jesus as the Messiah; the church is the consequence of a great mistake. This belief system has failed to see Jesus as taking on the vocation of Israel, as being the light of the world, the true vine (Israel) in whom his branches, symbolizing his people, bear the fruit once required of ethnic Israel. Consequently, dispensationalism has failed to understand that the church of both Jew and Gentile is the true Israel through being in Christ, the true Israelite, and is what Israel was meant to be, a mediator of blessing to all peoples (Gen 12:1–3; Matt 28:19–20). As such, dispensationalism appears to have a diminished view of both the person and work of Christ and of the church, which in turn leads to a diminished understanding of mission.

It has also been shown that dispensationalism has misunderstood the nature of God's kingdom by understanding it as a nationalistic political kingdom for Israel, presently postponed, and yet to be fulfilled in a literal and still entirely future one-thousand-year period after the church has been raptured and Christ has returned. As noted in chapter 2, such beliefs, though being counter to a sound biblical understanding, have significantly influenced the foreign policies of governments (especially the United States) concerning Israel, giving rise to significantly distressing world-impacting events, and to what is often uncritical support for the modern state of Israel—despite her atrocious and dehumanizing tyranny of another people—by millions of people who profess to love God who himself abhors injustice. The kingdom of God is relegated to a future time rather than understood as a now in-part present phase of the redemptive and restorative reign of God in the world—a kingdom reign inaugurated in the person and work of Christ and continued by the gift of the Spirit as a deposit guaranteeing its full realization yet to come. It has been demonstrated, in contrast to dispensational thought, that as people of the kingdom, Christians as the Israel of God (made up of both believing Jews and non-Jews as one people in Christ), now live between the times of the kingdom in its present seed form and as yet to be fully realized. This implies an active participation by followers of Christ in the restorative work of God whereby life in the present experiences something of the future renewal of all things, rather than a passive waiting to be raptured off the earth to heaven.

Dispensationalism, as a consequence of its belief in a pretribulation rapture of Christians from earth and ultimate destruction of the earth, devalues the importance of the nonhuman created world and thereby effectively encourages a disengagement from seeking to redemptively cultivate, transform, and care for this world. I gladly acknowledge that many Christian people whose belief system is generally dispensational are actively engaged in many meaningful redemptive and people/earth caring activities. However, this often appears to be more a consequence of a commendable sense of Christian compassion than of a well-informed biblical understanding and its eschatological realities.

A COMPREHENSIVE ESCHATOLOGICAL WORLDVIEW

Behind every worldview, or understanding of life, lie the ever-pressing questions: (1) Who are we? (2) Where are we? (3) What's wrong? (4) What's the solution? And (5) what time is it?[1] In other words, humanity in every generation seeks to discover and understand their world and particularly the meaning or purpose of life in that world. Dispensationalism's answer to the first two of these questions is that Christians are aliens and exiles in the world (1 Pet 2:11); this world is not our home for the Christian's citizenship is in heaven (Phil 3:20). If we adopt "normal everyday usage" or "plain meaning" interpretation the language of Christians' being "aliens and exiles in the world" seems to affirm a non-earthly eschatological destiny for believers. However, Steve Graham has suggested that to attribute such an understanding to these metaphors is to introduce a meaning that is inconsistent with their wider biblical usage. These metaphors have their roots in the story of Abraham and recall the writer of the letter to the Hebrews as saying, "By faith he [Abraham] made his home in the promised land *like a stranger in a foreign country*" (Heb 11:9 TNIV). Graham writes,

---

1. N. T. Wright, *Paul*, 7.

In this case a man (Abraham) has been promised some land, but that land is currently under the control of another system so he must spend his life living there as an alien, waiting—not for deliverance *out* of that land but for a change of the system controlling the land—so that he may become the heir to it.

Here the person is not defined as an 'alien' because he is in a place in which he doesn't belong, but rather, he is an alien because he *belongs* in that place but it is currently under the control of another system. He is not waiting for deliverance out of the place, but for a change of system so that he may receive the place as his inheritance.[2]

Affirming this understanding, Genesis 28:4 records Isaac blessing his son Jacob by saying,

May he [God] give to you the blessing of Abraham, to you and to your offspring with you, *so that you may take possession of* the land *where you now live as an alien*—land that God *gave* to Abraham. (emphasis added)

Jesus, as with so many of the Old Testament images, widens the scope of "land inheritance" to reveal the greater reality to which its Old Testament usage points in shadowy form. He says, echoing the Psalm 37:11 mention of the meek inheriting *the land*, "Blessed are the meek, for they will inherit *the earth*" (Matt 5:5, emphasis added; see also Eph 6:3, where the writer expands the consequence of obedience to the fifth commandment (children obeying parents) from its original promised blessing of long life in the land (Exod 20:12; Deut 5:16) to long life on the earth[3] (cf. also Rom 4:13 with Gen 17:8). Thus, believers live as aliens and exiles on earth, not because they do not belong on earth, but *because they do belong there and are waiting for the full realization of their inheritance.* As such, Christians are compelled to see the earth in which they reside as an essential element of their eschatological worldview, inseparable from their eschatological hope, and therefore from their understanding of God's saving work. Being alien does not imply that Christians dwell temporarily on earth, but instead, speaks of a manner of life while waiting the possession of it. Herein lies the challenge for

---

2. Graham, "Aliens and Strangers," 17 (emphasis original).

3. Indeed, it would seem unreasonable to assure the Ephesian believers that adherence to this commandment would result in them having a long life far from Ephesus and in the Land of Promise.

God's people: to live now in a manner shaped by the values and ethics of the redeeming kingdom of God in the world while we wait the full realization of God's restoration of it, that is, to live Christianly within the prevailing culture. This is the essence of the metaphorical salt and light images required by Jesus to be characteristic of his people.

A comprehensive eschatological redemption including the restoration of all creation (Acts 3:19–21; Rom 8:19–23; Eph 1:9–10; Col 1:19–20; 2 Pet 3:10–13)[4] to its God-intended state and potential is perhaps one of the most crucial elements in the formation of a biblical eschatological worldview. Sadly, the study of the "last things" in popular eschatology (i.e., dispensationalism), appears to have been developed in a manner radically disconnected from the "first things" of Scripture. It is as if Genesis 1–11 records a history wholly unrelated to the story of the entire biblical narrative that follows. The biblical story beginning with God's creational intent, the creation mandate for humanity to look after God's very good world, the impediment of that intent through humanity exercising a desire for autonomy from God's sovereign rule (i.e., sin), and God's continuing love for his entire creation lie at the heart of eschatology.[5] The end of the biblical narrative is inextricably linked to its beginning. Rikk E. Watts notes, "Since eschatology recapitulates protology, salvation cannot properly be understood apart from creation."[6] Eschatological redemption is creation redemption; it is nothing less that God at work, motivated by his love for his entire creation, to restore it from the effects of sin and liberate it from its bondage (John 3:16; Rom 8:21).

It is not insignificant therefore that Revelation 21–22 reverberates with the scenery of Eden as depicted in Genesis 2, thus indicating an eschatological return to pre-Fall conditions in which the key features are harmonious relationships and humanity functioning as God's appointed caretakers and cultivators of creation, to develop and safeguard the environment in which we have been placed by the Creator, that is, in Yahweh's cosmic temple as his image-bearing stewards.[7] In Genesis 1–2 humanity was in harmony with each other, with God, and with their

---

4. See chapter 4, where this crucial aspect of eschatological thought is first addressed.

5. Middleton, "New Heaven and New Earth," no pages.

6. Watts, "New Exodus," 18.

7. Ibid., 19. "Isaiah 66:1 has Yahweh declare, 'Heaven is my throne and the earth is my footstool' . . . the heavens *and* the earth, are Yahweh's temple" (emphasis original).

environment as its managers. In Revelation 21–22, the images of the complete restoration of all things reveal that each of these relationships is restored. Further, and consistent with all of Scripture, Revelation 21 reveals that the direction of ultimate salvation is earthbound. As the new Jerusalem descends toward earth from heaven prepared as a bride, John hears a loud voice saying,

> Look! God's dwelling place is now among the people, and he will dwell with them. They will be his people, and God himself will be with them and be their God. "He will wipe every tear from their eyes. There will be no more death" or mourning or crying or pain, for the old order of things has passed away. (vv. 3–4 TNIV)

Reminiscent of the presence of God in Eden, the arrival of God to dwell with his people in the tabernacle and Solomon's temple (considered in the Ancient Near East to be a microcosm of creation),[8] the incarnation in Jesus as Emmanuel (meaning "God with us")—the Word becoming flesh to tabernacle among humanity (John 1:14)—and the presence of God by the indwelling Spirit within his church/temple, in this picture of consummate salvation, God is again portrayed as coming to dwell in the place where redeemed humanity lives. And it is there on the earth where God makes his dwelling place.[9] Nowhere in the Bible is salvation stated as redeemed humanity being removed from their God-given homeland and taken to somewhere else; such would be tantamount to the church being exiled—that is, a judgment similar to Adam and Eve's removal from the garden of Eden and Israel's exiles at the hands of the Assyrian and Babylonian armies. Instead, the Bible consistently portrays God as coming to his people where they are. Ultimately God comes to them in a restored (rather than a replaced) earth. However, as Middleton observes,

> Eschatological redemption . . . is not a simple return to primal origins. The Bible itself portrays the move from creation to the eschaton as a move from the idyllic garden (in Genesis 2) to a city (in Revelation 21–22). Redemption does not reverse, but rather embraces, historical development.[10]

8. Watts, "New Exodus," 24.

9. Watts, "On the Edge," 148. "the climax of the new creation is not the abandonment of the earth, but instead the coming of Yahweh himself to the earth to dwell among us. . . . The final goal is not the destruction of creation, but rather the unification of heaven and earth such that the renewed earth itself now becomes Yahweh's very throne room." Barbara Rossing calls this a "rapture in reverse." Rossing, *Rapture Exposed*, 147.

10. Middleton, "New Heaven and New Earth," no pages. See also Plantinga, *Engaging*

An eschatological system that fails to regard the all-creation-en-compassing scope of redemption as revealed in the story of Scripture is, therefore, enormously inadequate and serves to advance a worldview that in turn shapes a diminished meaning for Christian living. Through its excessive and at times strained literalism, dispensationalism has formed an unhealthy bifurcation, not only of heaven and earth, but also of God's people—giving to one (Israel) undue privileged status and a diminished significance to the other (the church). As discussed in chapter 2, the Abrahamic covenant (Gen 12:1–3), which the church comes to inherit through being in Christ (Eph 2:11–22; Gal 3:29), forms the basis for all that follows in Scripture and constitutes the beginning of restoring all things to God, that is, a comprehensive all-inclusive restoration of God's intended purpose for his creation as seminally portrayed in Eden and anticipated in the promised of land.

A theological system whereby the church's redemption is climaxed by its being raptured off the very placed where God intended humanity to dwell, where salvation is ultimately perceived as "going to heaven," re-veals the extent to which a Christian worldview, and as a result Christian praxis, has been influenced by Platonic dualism[11] and by ideas reminis-cent of Gnosticism. The earth, however, is not evil matter destined for destruction subsequent to Christians' being air-lifted off in a end-time rescue mission.[12] Rather, it, like the humanity who dwell on it, is equally loved by God (John 3:16) and is presently waiting and groaning in hope-ful anticipation of its redemption (Rom 8:19–23). This holistic redemp-tion hope is the essence of Christian faith and eschatology. It is a hope to one day live as fully human image-bearers of God, with God, in the place where God intended humanity to dwell and there to fully function in

---

God's World, 32. Plantinga writes, "Good urban landscape management is a godly oc-cupation. After centuries of urban crime and decay, the destination of the redeemed people is not a return ticket to Eden, but entry into 'the holy city, the new Jerusalem.'"

11. Walsh and Middleton, *Transforming Vision*, 93–96.

12. N. T. Wright, *Paul*, 141. He writes, "For some, alas, the very phrase 'second com-ing', and even perhaps the word 'eschatology' itself, conjures up visions of the 'rapture' as understood within some branches of (mostly North American) fundamentalist or evan-gelical Christianity, and as set out, at a popular level, in the 'Left Behind' series of novels by Tim F. LaHaye and Jerry B. Jenkins, and the theology, if you can call it that, which those books embody. The scheme of thought, ironically considering its fanatical though bizarre support for the present state of Israel, is actually deeply un-Jewish, collapsing into a dualism in which the present wicked world is left to stew in its own juice while the saints are snatched up to heaven to watch Armageddon from a ringside seat."

the human vocation of faithful stewardship of a renewed earth; thus the full effects of sin on all creation will be reversed. Restoration is the hope of Christian people, not the destruction of their God-given dwelling place and their escape to somewhere else that would remove forever the possibility of humanity functioning in a manner consistent with God's creational intent for them.[13]

Richard Middleton writes,

> The logic of biblical redemption, when combined with a biblical understanding of creation, requires the restoration and renewal of the full complexity of human life in our earthly environment, yet without sin.

"Renewal of the full complexity of human life in our earthly environment" carries significant implications. If restoration is indeed to God's creational intent, this must allow for an acceptance of the human ability to function as stewards of the earth by exercising their God-given ability to develop their environment. This development is seen in the image of

---

13. Despite this, dispensationalists in positions of the U.S. government deny the biblical eschatological significance of the earth except that the earth's environmental catastrophes are to be expected and even welcomed as signs of the coming rapture and therefore they are opposed to environmental care. Scherer, "Godly Must Be Crazy," no pages. "U.S. legislators backed by the Christian right vote against these issues [abortion, same-sex marriage, and stem-cell research] with near-perfect consistency. That probably doesn't surprise you, but this might: Those same legislators are equally united and unswerving in their opposition to environmental protection. . . . Many Christian fundamentalists feel that concern for the future of our planet is irrelevant, because it *has* no future. . . . They may also believe, along with millions of other Christian fundamentalists, that environmental destruction is not only to be disregarded but actually welcomed—even hastened—as a sign of the coming Apocalypse. . . . We are not talking about a handful of fringe lawmakers who hold or are beholden to these beliefs. . . . These politicians include some of the most powerful figures in the U.S. government, as well as key environmental decision makers. . . . Because of its power as a voting bloc, the Christian right has the ear, if not the souls, of much of the nation's leadership. Some of those leaders are End-Time believers themselves. Others are not. Either way, their votes are heavily swayed by an electoral base that accepts the Bible as literal truth and eagerly awaits the looming Apocalypse. And that, in turn, is sobering news for those who hope for the protection of the earth, not its destruction. . . . The social and environmental crises of our times, dispensationalists say, are portents of the Rapture, when born-again Christians, living and dead, will be taken up into heaven. . . . Natural-resource depletion and overpopulation, then, are not concerns for End-Timers—and nor are other ecological catastrophes, which are viewed by dispensationalists as presaging the Great Tribulation. . . . A plethora of End-Time preachers, tracts, films, and websites hawk environmental cataclysm as Good News—a harbinger of the imminent Second Coming."

a city in Revelation 21–22, whereas in the creation account of Genesis, God's presence with humanity is in a garden. Environmental development is therefore embraced in the restoration work of God in the world, yet only that which is good remains. Caird writes concerning the Holy City,

> The treasure that men find laid up in heaven turns out to be the treasures and wealth of the nations, the best they have known and loved on earth redeemed of all imperfections and transfigured by the radiance of God. Nothing is excluded but what is obscene and false, that is, totally alien to the character of God. Nowhere in the New Testament do we find a more eloquent statement than this of the all-embracing scope of God's redemptive work.[14]

This enduring feature of our present works can also be found in Paul's theology when he writes of godly human labors remaining on the Day when works are tested by fire (1 Cor 3:12–15) and affirming that human activity of building well in the present age carries over into the consummate restored age—quite consistent with the now and not-yet of God's kingdom. Such a truth implies that in the present age Christians should be functioning as faithful, creative and caring stewards of their world through God-honoring engagement and mission in every arena of society (e.g., politics, education, health, environment care, arenas of justice, aid organizations, arts, and so on). Watts highlights the importance of this in relation to creation care,

> If this creation is Yahweh's palace-temple, then we had best take good care of it. Far too many of us treat our homes far better than we treat this creation. We would never tolerate toxic waste or un-bridled pollution in our living rooms, and yet we seem happy to do so when it comes to God's palace-temple. While some have mistakenly read the apocalyptic language of purging fire as a *carte blanche* to do whatever they will to this present earth, we might do well to remember the warning in Revelation 11:18: God will destroy those who destroy his earth. Given that it is his palace-temple, and that far from people going to heaven, heaven is coming here (at least if Revelation 21 is to be believed), God's anger against violators of the earth is perfectly understandable. It is his palace-temple they are defiling, whereas he is committed to renewing it.[15]

---

14. Cited in Bouma-Prediger, *For the Beauty*, 115, quoting Caird, *Revelation of St. John*.

15. Watts, "On the Edge," 150–51.

In fact, God's displeasure has been seen before when his people engaged in the rituals of worship and yet failed to address the injustices and morally wrong acts they were committing in the world—particularly injustices against other image-bearers (Amos 5:21–24; cf. Isa 1:11–17).

Steven Bouma-Prediger, like Watts, writes to encourage Christians to active participation in creation care in the present, noting the eternal value:

> Christian Eschatology is earth-affirming. Because the earth will not be "burned up" but rather purified as in a refiners fire, we can act with confidence that our actions today are not for naught. Because we await and yearn for a renewed heaven and earth, we can work in expectation that our faithful deeds here and now will be gathered up in the eschaton.[16]

Jesus, in fact, defines his followers as those who actively participate redemptively in good works in order that others may glorify God.

> You are the salt of the earth; but if salt has lost its taste, how can its saltiness be restored? It is no longer good for anything, but is thrown out and trampled under foot. "You are the light of the world. A city built on a hill cannot be hid. No one after lighting a lamp puts it under the bushel basket, but on the lampstand, and it gives light to all in the house. In the same way, let your light shine before others, so that they may *see your good works* and give glory to your Father in heaven. (Matt 5:13–16, emphasis added)

The image of salt speaks of both Christian *identity* as an alternative community and of living in a manner consistent with the characteristics of Christ's restorative kingdom, whereas 'light' placed in a position of effectiveness speaks of the reign of God, "the light of God's salvation, presence, justice, and peace,"[17] and against any forms of disengagement from the world; the light of God's redemptive kingdom is not to be hidden but rather seen through the Christian's work in the world.

Stassen and Gushee note concerning these words of Jesus,

> Jesus taught that participation in God's reign requires the disciplined practices of a Christ-following countercultural community that obeys God by publicly engaging in working for justice and refusing to trust in the world's powers and authorities.[18]

16. Bouma-Prediger, *For the Beauty*, 126.

17. Stassen and Gushee, *Kingdom Ethics*, 470–71. They further write, "As such and only as such, can the church be a useful participant in God's kingdom building activity" (473).

18. Ibid., 467–68.

In an article titled, "Learning and Consummation: Mission and Peace in the Rhetoric of Revelation," Loren L. Johns defines the church's mission as a call to an *alternative way of life* in a manner that invites others, *indeed all creation*, to join in the life of redemption.[19]

These voices of encouragement for Christian involvement in the world, as related to its eschatological redemption, are reaffirmed in the parallelism of the Lord's Prayer, "your kingdom come, your will be done, on earth as it is in heaven" (Matt 6:10). Prayer for the redemptive reign of God is in parallel with a prayer for the will of God to be done on earth in the same way that it is done in heaven. Doing the will of God as modeled by Jesus in the Gospels is, therefore, an expression of a heavenly reality experienced on earth and each time bringing something of the "not yet" into the "now," in the assurance that one day Christ will return to consummate redemption, and heaven and earth will be indistinguishable in character—there will indeed be a new (*kainos*, i.e., renewed, not an altogether new replacement)[20] heaven and earth. Prayer and praxis, it seems, go hand in hand. In praying, "your kingdom come" the Christian is inviting oneself to participate in doing God's will on earth, and in so doing, heaven, where God's will is done, becomes a place on earth. This view of "proleptic anticipation" seems most suited to the eschatological hopes of the Christian faith.[21] Hoekema captures this well when he writes,

> As citizens of God's kingdom, we may not just write off the present earth as a total loss, or rejoice in its deterioration. We must indeed be working for a better world now. Our efforts to bring the kingdom of Christ into fuller manifestation are of eternal significance. . . . As we live on this earth, we are preparing for life on God's new earth. Through our kingdom building service the building materials for that new earth are now being gathered.[22]

Indeed, hope for a new creation is language presently applied to the Christian who is already being transformed in anticipation of his or her bodily resurrection:

> So if anyone is in Christ, there is a new creation: everything old has passed away; see, everything has become new! (2 Cor 5:15)

19. Johns, "Learning and Consummation," 249 (emphasis added).

20. Hoekema, *Bible and the Future*, 280.

21. Schwarz, *Eschatology*, 407.

22. Hoekema, *Bible and the Future*, 287.

In the same way that there is continuity with that person's physical body, the new earth is redeemed in continuity with the old earth that is passing away. Richard Bauckham and Trevor Hart write of this:

> it is clear that the biblical pictures of the destruction of the old creation and the appearance of the new (Isa. 65:17; 2 Pet. 3:7, 10; Rev. 21:1) do not really envisage the replacement of this old creation by another, but stress the radical transformation involved in God's creative renewal of the old creation.[23]

The goal of this book has been twofold: first and primarily, to test the trueness of dispensationalism. In so doing we have demonstrated the many inadequacies of this belief system—a system of thought that influences a substantial portion of the Christian church and hinders many Christian people from realizing the full extent of the eschatological redemption story and the important role they have in the redemptive mission as heirs, in Christ, of the Abrahamic mandate to mediate blessing to the nations.[24] Further, I want to point the way for many Christian people to rethink eschatology and to consider a biblical worldview that realizes the significance of Christian living in the present age and hope for the future in a manner more consistent with an eschatological worldview as narrated in the biblical story of redemption—a redemption that is so much more than merely human salvation but rather extends to the far-reaching salvific purpose of God to "reconcile to himself *all things*, whether on earth or in heaven, by making peace through the blood of his cross" (Col 1:20, emphasis added). In the words of N. T. Wright, I hope "to lift their eyes beyond the small horizons of their previous worldviews."[25]

My earnest desire is to promote an understanding of an all-creation inclusive eschatological redemption that is already experienced in Christ and the gift of the Spirit but not yet fully realized. It is also to encourage a manner of life that seeks to actively participate in the outworking of God's all-creation inclusive redemptive love for his creation, the creation that he called "very good"—including *all* humanity irrespective of race.

A number of conclusions have been presented throughout this study. Considered together, they suggest that dispensationalism may

23. Bauckham and Hart, *Hope against Hope*, 131.
24. Middleton, "New Heaven and New Earth," no pages.
25. N. T. Wright, *Paul*, 130.

not be regarded as a well-reasoned eschatological understanding of the biblical story. From the literalistic hermeneutic on which it is built, the bifurcation of God's people, the misinterpretation of kingdom, rapture, tribulation, and millennium through to the alleged destruction of the material world, dispensationalism radically distorts and diminishes the story of God's redemption of his creation.

The alternative eschatological view here presented has sought to be faithful to the biblical text and to the far-reaching, all-creation-inclusive restoration hopes inherent in the gospel of the kingdom. This is the hope of God's redeemed and restored humanity purchased from every tribe and language and people and nation as one people—one kingdom of priests, enjoying restored fellowship with God who is present with them, and reigning in the place that God intended for them to live, the new heaven and earth. This is the good news of the kingdom of God, experienced now in part; the full realization is yet to come.

> Then I saw "a new heaven and a new earth," for the first heaven and the first earth had passed away, and there was no longer any sea. I saw the Holy City, the new Jerusalem, coming down out of heaven from God, prepared as a bride beautifully dressed for her husband. And I heard a loud voice from the throne saying, "Look! God's dwelling place is now among the people, and he will dwell with them. They will be his people, and God himself will be with them and be their God. 'He will wipe every tear from their eyes. There will be no more death' or mourning or crying or pain, for the old order of things has passed away." (Rev 21:1–4 TNIV)

Bibliography

Adams, Jay. *The Time Is at Hand*. Phillipsburg, NJ: Presbyterian & Reformed Publishing, 1966.

Allis, O. T. *Prophecy and the Church*. Philadelphia: Presbyterian & Reformed Publishing, 1945.

Albertyn, Evan. "With God on Our Side." [DVD]. Directed by Porter Speakman Jr. Rooftop Productions, 2010.

Alexander, T. Desmond, and Simon Gathercole, eds. *Heaven on Earth: The Temple in Biblical Theology*. Carlisle: Paternoster, 2004.

Alford, H. *The Greek New Testament IV*. Cambridge: Deighton, 1866.

Baker, David W., ed. *Looking into the Future: Evangelical Studies in Eschatology*. Grand Rapids: Baker Book House, 2001.

Barr, James. *Escaping from Fundamentalism*. London: SCM Press, 1984.

Bass, Clarence B. *Backgrounds to Dispensationalism: Its Historical Genesis and Ecclesiastical Implications*. Grand Rapids: Baker Book House, 1960.

Bauckham, Richard. *The Theology of the Book of Revelation*. Cambridge: Cambridge University Press, 1993.

Bauckham, Richard, and Trevor Hart. *Hope against Hope: Christian Eschatology at the Turn of the Millennium*. Grand Rapids: Eerdmans, 1999.

Bauer, Walter. *A Greek-English Lexicon of the New Testament and Other Early Christian Literature*. Edited by William F. Arndt and F. Wilbur Gingrich. 2nd ed. revised and augmented by F. W. Gingrich and Frederick W. Danker from W. Bauer's 5th ed., 1958. Chicago: University of Chicago Press, 1979. [BAGD].

Walter Bauer, Frederick W. Danker, W. F. Arndt, and F. W. Gingrich. *Greek-English Lexicon of the New Testament and Other Early Christian Literature*. 3rd ed. Chicago: University of Chicago Press, 2000. [BDAG].

Beale, G. K. *The Book of Revelation*. New International Greek New Testament Commentary. Grand Rapids: Eerdmans, 1999.

Beasley-Murray, G. R. *The Coming of God*. Exeter: Paternoster. 1983.

———. *Jesus and the Kingdom of God*. Grand Rapids: Eerdmans, 1986.

———. *John*. Waco, TX: Word, 1987.

Behm, J. "καινός." In *Theological Dictionary of the New Testament*, edited by G. Kittel, translated by G. W. Bromiley, 3:447–54. Grand Rapids: Eerdmans, 1965.

Betz, O. "συμφωνέω." In *Theological Dictionary of the New Testament* on CD-ROM. Libronix Digital Library System, Version 1.0b, 2000–2001. Print edition: G. Kittel, ed. *Theological Dictionary of the New Testament*. Grand Rapids, Eerdmans, 1995, c1985.

Blaising, Craig A., and Darrell L. Bock. *Progressive Dispensationalism*. Grand Rapids: Baker Book House, 1993.

Blaising, Craig A., and Darrell L. Bock, eds. *Dispensationalism, Israel and the Church: The Search for Definition.* Grand Rapids: Zondervan, 1992.

Bouma-Prediger, Steven. *For the Beauty of the Earth: A Christian Vision for Creation Care.* Grand Rapids: Baker Book House, 2001.

Boyd, Allan P. "A Dispensational Premillennial Analysis of the Eschatology of the Post-Apostolic Fathers (Until the Death of Justin Martyr)." ThM thesis, Dallas Theological Seminary, 1977.

Brown, Raymond E. *The Gospel According to John.* New York: Doubleday, 1966.

Bruce, F. F. *The Epistle to the Colossians, to Philemon, and to the Ephesians.* New International Commentary on the New Testament. Grand Rapids: Eerdmans, 1984.

———. "Eschatology." In *Evangelical Dictionary of Theology,* edited by Walter A. Elwell, 362–65. Grand Rapids: Baker Book House, 1984.

———. *1 & 2 Thessalonians.* Word Bible Commentary. Waco, TX: Word, 1982.

Bruner, Frederick Dale. *The Churchbook: Matthew 13–28.* Grand Rapids: Eerdmans: 1990.

Burge, Gary M. *Jesus and the Land: The New Testament Challenge to "Holy Land" Theology.* Grand Rapids: Baker, 2010.

———. *Whose Land? Whose Promise? What Christians Are Not Being Told about Israel and the Palestinians.* Cleveland: Pilgrim Press, 2003.

Butler, Paul T. *Approaching the New Millennium: An Amillennial Look at A.D. 2000.* Joplin: College Press Publishing Company, 1998.

Caird, George B. *Jesus and the Jewish Nation.* London: Penguin Books, 1965.

———. *The Revelation of St. John the Divine.* New York: Harper & Row, 1966.

Chapman, Colin. *Whose Promised Land? The Continuing Crisis over Israel and Palestine.* Grand Rapids: Baker Book House, 2002.

Chilton, David. *The Days of Vengeance: An Exposition of the Book of Revelation.* Fort Worth, TX: Dominion Press, 1987.

Clayman, David. "The Law of Return Reconsidered." No pages. Online: http://www.jcpa. org/jl/hit01.htm.

"Clouds." In *Dictionary of Biblical Imagery,* edited by Leland Ryken, James C. Wilhoit, and Tremper Longman III, 157. Downers Grove, IL: InterVarsity Press, 1998.

Clouse, R. G. "Rapture of the Church." In *Evangelical Dictionary of Theology,* edited by Walter A. Elwell, 908–10. Grand Rapids: Baker Book House, 1984.

Cox, William E. *Amillennialism Today.* Phillipsburg, NJ: Presbyterian & Reformed Publishing, 1966.

———. *Biblical Studies in Final Things.* Phillipsburg, NJ: Presbyterian & Reformed Publishing, 1966.

———. *An Examination of Dispensationalism.* Phillipsburg, NJ: Presbyterian & Reformed Publishing, 1963.

Crenshaw, Curtis I., and Grover E. Gunn. *Dispensationalism Today, Yesterday, and Tomorrow.* Memphis: Footstool Publications, 1985.

Currie, David B. *Rapture: The End-Times Error That Leaves the Bible Behind.* Manchester: Sophia Institute Press, 2003.

Davies, W. D. *The Land and the Gospel: Early Christianity and Jewish Territorial Doctrine.* Berkeley: University of California Press, 1974.

Davis, John P. "Hermeneutical Issues in the Dispensational Understanding of the Abrahamic Covenant." *Quodlibet Journal* 3, no. 4 (Fall 2001). No pages. Online: http://www.quodlibet.net/davis-covenant.shtml.

DeMar, Gary. *Last Days Madness: Obsession of the Modern Church.* 4th ed. Atlanta: American Vision, 1999.

Dumbrell, William J. *The Search for Order: Biblical Eschatology in Focus.* Eugene: Wipf and Stock, 2001.

Dunn, James D. G. *The Theology of Paul the Apostle.* Grand Rapids: Eerdmans, 1998.

Fee, Gordon D. *1 and 2 Timothy, Titus.* Peabody, MA: Hendrickson, 1988.

———. *The First Epistle to the Corinthians.* New International Commentary on the New Testament. Grand Rapids: Eerdmans, 1987.

———. *Paul's Letter to the Philippians.* New International Commentary on the New Testament. Grand Rapids: Eerdmans, 1995.

Fromkin, David. *A Peace to End All Peace: The Fall of the Ottoman Empire and the Creation of the Modern Middle East.* New York: Holt, 2001.

Fruchtenbaum, Arnold. *The Footsteps of the Messiah.* Tustin, CA: Ariel Ministries, 2003.

———. *Israelology: The Missing Link in Systematic Theology.* Tustin, CA: Ariel Ministries Press, 1989.

Gerstner, John H. *Wrongly Dividing the Word of Truth: A Critique of Dispensationalism.* Brentwood: Wolgemuth & Hyatt, 1991.

Goldsworthy, Graeme. *Gospel and Kingdom: A Christian Interpretation of the Old Testament.* Homebush West: Lancer, 1983.

Graham, Steve. "Aliens and Strangers in the World: Reflections on a Biblical Image." *Reality,* June/July 2005, 16–19.

Green, Gene L. *The Letters to the Thessalonians.* Pillar New Testament Commentaries. Grand Rapids: Eerdmans, 2002.

Green, Joel B. *How to Read Prophecy.* Downers Grove, IL: InterVarsity Press, 1984.

Greer, Nick. "British-Israelism and the Revival Centres." (Copyright 1997, Nick Greer, P.O. Box 494, Glenside, South Australia, 5065). No pages. Online: http://www.preteristarchive.com/dEmEnTiA/British-Israelism/1997_greer_revival-center.html.

Grenz, Stanley J. *The Millennial Maze: Sorting Out Evangelical Options.* Downers Grove, IL: InterVarsity Press, 1992.

Grier, W. J. *The Momentous Event: A Discussion of Scripture Teaching on the Second Advent.* Edinburgh: Banner of Truth Trust: 1945.

Gutbrod, Walter. "Ἰσραήλ." In *Theological Dictionary of the New Testament,* edited by G. Kittel, translated by G. W. Bromiley, 3:386. Grand Rapids: Eerdmans, 1965.

Haddad, Mohanna. "Palestinian Refugees in Jordan and National Identity, 1948–1999." In *The Palestinian Refugees: Old Problems—New Solutions,* edited by Joseph Ginat and Edward J. Perkins, 150–68. Norman: University of Oklahoma Press, 2001.

Hays, Richard B., and Joel B. Green. "The Use of the Old Testament by New Testament Writers." In *Hearing the New Testament: Strategies for Interpretation,* ed. Joel B. Green. Grand Rapids: Eerdmans, 1995.

Hendriksen, William. *More Than Conquerors: An Interpretation of the Book of Revelation.* Grand Rapids: Baker Book House, 1940.

Hill, Craig C. *In God's Time: The Bible and the Future.* Grand Rapids: Eerdmans, 2002.

Hoekema, Anthony A. *The Bible and the Future.* Grand Rapids: Eerdmans, 1979.

Holwerda, David E. *Jesus and Israel: One Covenant or Two?* Grand Rapids: Eerdmans, 1995.

Ice, Thomas, and Timothy Demy. *Prophecy Watch*. Eugene, OR: Harvest House, 1998.

Johns, Loren L. "Learning and Consummation: Mission and Peace in the Rhetoric of Revelation." In *Beautiful upon the Mountains: Biblical Essays on Mission, Peace, and the Reign of God*, edited by Mary H. Schertz and Ivan Friesen, Studies in Peace and Scripture 7, 249–68. Elkhart, IN: Institute of Mennonite Studies, 2003.

Josephus, Flavius. *Wars of the Jews*. In *The Life and Works of Flavius Josephus*. Translated by William Whiston. Peabody, MA: Hendrickson, n.d.

"Judaism, Basic Jewish Beliefs." ReligionStudy.com. No pages. Online: http://www.religionstudy.com/religions/judaism/law.htm.

Kairos Palestine. "A Moment of Truth: A Word of Faith, Hope, and Love from the Heart of Palestinian Suffering." Kairos Palestine, 2009. Articles 2.3.3 and 2.3.4. Online: http://www.kairospalestine.ps/sites/default/Documents/English.pdf.

Kaiser, Walter C., and Moisés Silva. *An Introduction to Biblical Hermeneutics: The Search for Meaning*. Grand Rapids: Zondervan, 1994.

Kik, J. Marcellus. *An Eschatology of Victory*. Phillipsburg, NJ: Presbyterian & Reformed Publishing, 1971.

Kistemaker, Simon J. "Hyper-Preterism and Revelation." In *When Shall These Things Be? A Reformed Response to Hyper-Preterism*, edited by Keith A. Mathison, 215–54. Phillipsburg, NJ: Presbyterian & Reformed Publishing, 2004.

Kline, Meredith G. "The First Resurrection." *Westminster Theological Journal* 37 (1975) 366–75.

———. *Kingdom Prologue: Genesis Foundations for a Covenantal Worldview*. Eugene, OR: Wipf and Stock, 2006.

Kusmič, Peter. "History and Eschatology: Evangelical Views." In *In Word and Deed: Evangelism and Social Responsibility*, edited by Bruce Nicholls, 135–64. Exeter: Paternoster, 1985.

Ladd, George Eldon. *The Blessed Hope*. Grand Rapids: Eerdmans, 1956.

———. *Crucial Questions about the Kingdom of God*. Eugene, OR: Wipf and Stock, 2001.

———. *The Gospel of the Kingdom*. London: Paternoster, 1959.

———. "The Holy Spirit in Galatians." In *Current Issues in Biblical and Patristic Interpretation: Studies in Honor of Merrill C. Tenney*, edited by G. F. Hawthorne, 211–16. Grand Rapids: Eerdmans, 1975.

———. "Kingdom of God, Christ, Heaven." In *Evangelical Dictionary of Theology*, edited by Walter A. Elwell, 607–11. Grand Rapids: Baker Book House, 1984.

———. *The Presence of the Future: The Eschatology of Realism*. Grand Rapids: Eerdmans, 1974.

———. *A Theology of the New Testament*. Rev. ed. Grand Rapids: Eerdmans, 1993.

LaHaye, Tim, and Timothy Demy. *Prophecy Watch*. Eugene, OR: Harvest House, 1998.

LaHaye, Tim, and Thomas Ice. *Charting the End Times*. Eugene, OR: Harvest House, 2001.

Lange, J. P. *Commentary on the Holy Scriptures: Revelation*. New York: Charles Scribners, 1872.

Lindsey, Hal. *Late Great Planet Earth*. Grand Rapids: Zondervan, 1970.

Lindsay, Robert. "The Kingdom of God: God's Power among Believers." Jerusalem Perspective Online (Published January 1, 2004; revised June 13, 2010). No pages. Online: http://jerusalemperspective.com/Default.aspx?tabid=27&ArticleID=1440.

Marshall, Christopher. *Kingdom Come: The Kingdom of God in the Teaching of Jesus.* Rev. ed. Auckland: Impetus Publications, 1993.

Marshall, I. Howard. *The Gospel of Luke.* New International Greek New Testament Commentary. Grand Rapids: Eerdmans, 1978.

———. *New Testament Theology: Many Witnesses, One Gospel.* Downers Grove, IL: InterVarsity Press, 2004.

Mathison, Keith A. *Dispensationalism: Rightly Dividing the People of God?* Phillipsburg, NJ: Presbyterian & Reformed Publishing, 1995.

———. *Postmillennialism: An Eschatology of Hope.* Phillipsburg, NJ: Presbyterian & Reformed Publishing, 1999.

Mauro, Philip. *The Gospel of the Kingdom.* Boston: Hamilton Bros., 1928.

McClain, T. Van. "The Pretribulation Rapture: A Doubtful Doctrine." In *Looking into the Future: Evangelical Studies in Eschatology,* edited by David W. Baker, 233–45. Grand Rapids: Baker Book House, 2001.

McConville, J. Gordon. *Exploring the Old Testament.* Vol. 2: *A Guide to the Prophets.* Downers Grove, IL: InterVarsity Press, 2002.

McGuckin, John A. "The Book of Revelation and Orthodox Theology: The Theodrama of Judgment." In *The Last Things: Biblical and Theological Perspectives on Eschatology,* edited by Carl E. Braaten and Robert W. Jenson, 113–34. Grand Rapids: Eerdmans, 2002.

Mearsheimer, John J. "The Future of Palestine: Righteous Jews vs. the New Afrikaners." Transcript No. 327. A paper presented at the Palestine Center, Washington, DC, April 29, 2010. Online: http://www.thejerusalemfund.org/ht/display/ContentDetails/i/10418.

Metzger, Bruce M. *Breaking the Code: Understanding the Book of Revelation.* Nashville: Abingdon, 1993.

Michel. "οἰκουμένη." In *Theological Dictionary of the New Testament,* edited by G. Kittel, translated by G. W. Bromiley, 5:157–59. Grand Rapids: Eerdmans, 1965.

Middleton, Richard J. "A New Heaven and a New Earth: The Case for a Holistic Reading of the Biblical Story of Redemption." Paper presented at a meeting of Christian Theology Research Fellowship, Philadelphia, November 2005.

Moo, Douglas. *The Epistle to the Romans.* New International Commentary on the New Testament. Grand Rapids: Eerdmans, 1996.

Morris, Leon. *The Gospel According to John.* Rev. ed. New International Commentary on the New Testament. Grand Rapids: Eerdmans, 1995.

Motyer, S. "Israel, The New." In *Evangelical Dictionary of Theology,* edited by Walter A. Ellwell. 572. Grand Rapids: Baker Book House, 1984.

Osborne, Grant R. *The Hermeneutical Spiral: A Comprehensive Introduction to Biblical Interpretation.* Downers Grove, IL: InterVarsity Press, 1991.

Page, S. H. T. "Revelation 20 and Pauline Eschatology." *Journal of the Evangelical Theological Society* 23 (1980) 31–43.

Pappe, Ilan. *The Ethnic Cleansing of Palestine.* Oxford: Oneworld, 2006.

Pate, C. Marvin. *The End of the Age Has Come: The Theology of Paul.* Grand Rapids: Zondervan, 1995.

Pentecost, J. Dwight. *Things to Come : A Study in Biblical Eschatology.* Grand Rapids: Zondervan, 1958.

Peterson, Erik. "ἀπάντησις." In *Theological Dictionary of the New Testament*, edited by G. Kittel, translated by G. W. Bromiley, 1:380–81. Grand Rapids: Eerdmans, 1965.

Plantinga, Cornelius, Jr. *Engaging God's World: A Christian Vision of Faith, Learning, and Living*. Grand Rapids: Eerdmans, 2002.

Posner, Sarah. "Pastor Strangelove." In *The American Prospect*, May 2006. No pages. Online: http://www.prospect.org/cs/articles?articleId=11541

Poythress, Vern S. "Genre and Hermeneutics in Rev 20:1–6." *Journal of the Evangelical Theological Society* 36 (1993) 41–54.

———. *The Returning King: A Guide to the Book of Revelation*. Presbyterian & Reformed Publishing, 2000.

———. *Understanding Dispensationalists*. 2nd ed. Phillipsburg, NJ: Presbyterian & Reformed Publishing, 1994.

Preston, Don K. *Israel: 1948 Countdown to Nowhere*. Ardmore: Don K. Preston, 2002.

Ratnesar, Romesh. "The Right's New Crusade Lobbying for Israel." *Time*, May 6, 2003.

Ridderbos, Herman. *The Gospel of John*. Grand Rapids: Eerdmans, 1997.

Riddlebarger, Kim. *A Case for Amillennialism: Understanding the End Times*. Grand Rapids: Baker Book House, 2003.

Robertson, O. Palmer. *The Christ of the Covenants*. Phillipsburg, NJ: Presbyterian & Reformed Publishing, 1980.

———. *The Israel of God: Yesterday, Today, and Tomorrow*. Phillipsburg, NJ: Presbyterian & Reformed Publishing, 2000.

Rossing, Barbara R. *The Rapture Exposed: The Message of Hope in the Book of Revelation*. Boulder, CO: Westview Press, 2004.

Rushdoony, M. R. "The Christian and the Social Agenda." Frontline Apologetics. December 25, 2004. No pages. Online: http://frontlineapologetics.blogspot.com/2004/12/christian-and-social-agenda.html.

Ryrie, Charles C. *Dispensationalism*. Chicago: Moody Press, 1995.

———. *The Ryrie Study Bible: New American Standard Translation*. 1976, 1978. Chicago: Moody Bible Institute.

Sandy, D. Brent. *Plowshares and Pruning Hooks: Rethinking the Language of Biblical Prophecy and Apocalyptic*. Downers Grove, IL: InterVarsity Press, 2002.

Scherer, Glenn. "The Godly Must Be Crazy: Christian-Right Views Are Swaying Politicians and Threatening the Environment." October 27, 2004. No pages. Online: http://www.grist.org/article/scherer-christian.

Schwarz, Hans. *Eschatology*. Grand Rapids: Eerdmans, 2000.

Scofield, C. I. *The Scofield Reference Bible*. New York: Oxford University Press, 1917.

Shlaim, Avi. *Israel and Palestine: Repraisals, Revisions, Refutations*. London: Verso, 2009.

Sizer, Stephen. "Biblical Interpretation: Approaching Prophecy Today." No pages. Online: http://www.cc-vw.org/articles/wycliffehall.htm.

———. "Christian Zionism: Misguided Millennialism." No pages. Online: http://www.cc-vw.org/articles/coloradohistory.htm.

———. *Christian Zionism: Road-map to Armageddon?* Leicester: Intervarsity Press, 2004.

———. "Christian Zionism: True Friends of Israel?" Seminar given to the Centre for Jewish Studies, School of Oriental and African Studies, University of London, November 3, 1998. No pages. Online: http://www.christchurch-virginiawater.co.uk.

———. "Dispensational Approaches to the Land." In *The Land of Promise: Biblical, Theological and Contemporary Perspectives*, edited by Philip Johnston and Peter Walker, 142–71. Downers Grove, IL: InterVarsity Press, 2000.

Snodgrass, Klyne. "The Use of the Old Testament in the New." In *New Testament Criticism and Interpretation*, edited by David Alan Black and David S. Dockery, 409–34. Grand Rapids: Zondervan, 1991.

———. "The Use of the Old Testament in the New." In *The Right Doctrine from the Wrong Texts? Essays on the Use of the Old Testament in the New*, edited by G. K. Beale, 29–51. Grand Rapids: Baker Book House, 1994.

Speakman, Porter, Jr. "With God on Our Side." [DVD]. Rooftop Productions, 2010.

Stassen, Glen H., and David P. Gushee. *Kingdom Ethics: Following Jesus in Contemporary Context*. Downers Grove, IL: InterVarsity Press, 2003.

Stott, John. *The Gospel and the End of Time: The Message of 1 & 2 Thessalonians*. Downers Grove, IL: InterVarsity Press, 1991.

Strimple, Robert B. "Amillennialism." In *Three Views on the Millennium and Beyond*, edited by Darrell L. Bock, 83–129. Grand Rapids: Zondervan, 1999.

Strom, Mark. *The Symphony of Scripture*. Phillipsburg, NJ: Presbyterian & Reformed Publishing, 1990.

———. "Walking into One Conversation." Laidlaw College Forum, September 27, 2005.

Strombeck, J. F. *First the Rapture*. Eugene, OR: Harvest House, 1982.

Swete, H. B. *The Apocalypse of St John*. 3rd ed. London: Macmillan, 1909.

Tate, W. Randolph. *Biblical Interpretation: An Integrated Approach*. Peabody, MA: Hendrickson, 1991.

Theissen, Gerd. *The Miracle Stories of the Early Christian Tradition*. Translated by F. McDonagh. Philadelphia: Fortress, 1983.

Thigpen, Paul. *The Rapture Trap: A Catholic Response to "End Times" Fever*. West Chester: Ascension Press, 2001.

Thiselton, Anthony C. *New Horizons in Hermeneutics: The Theory and Practice of Transforming Bible Reading*. Grand Rapids: Zondervan, 1992.

Toussaint, Stanley D. "Israel and the Church of a Traditional Dispensationalist." In *Three Central Issues in Contemporary Dispensationalism: A Comparison of Traditional and Progressive Views*, edited by Herbert W. Bateman IV, 227–52. Grand Rapids: Kregel Publications, 1999.

Venema, Cornelis P. *The Promise of the Future*. Edinburgh: Banner of Truth Trust, 2000.

Waldron, Samuel E. *The End Times Made Simple: How Could Everyone Be So Wrong about Biblical Prophecy?* New York: Calvary Press, 2003.

Walker, Peter. Introduction to *Heaven on Earth: The Temple in Biblical Theology*, edited by T. Desmond Alexander and Simon Gathercole, 1–10. Carlisle: Paternoster, 2004.

———. *Jesus and the Holy City: New Testament Perspectives on Jerusalem*. Grand Rapids: Eerdmans, 1996.

———. "The Land and Jesus Himself." In *The Land of Promise*, edited by Philip Johnston and Peter Walker, 100–120. Downers Grove, IL: InterVarsity Press, 2000.

Walls, Jeannette. "Is Bush Getting Apocalyptic Advice?" In *MSNBC*, August 13, 2003. No pages. Online: http://www.unkownnews.net/apocalypsenow.html.

Walsh, Brian J., and J. Richard Middleton. *The Transforming Vision: Shaping a Christian World View*. Downers Grove, IL: InterVarsity Press, 1984.

Walton, John H. *The Lost World of Genesis One: Ancient Cosmology and the Origins Debate*. Downers Grove, IL: InterVarsity Press, 2009.

Walvoord, John F. "Amos 9:12." *The Bible Knowledge Commentary*. Libronix Digital Library System on CD-ROM. Version 1.0b 2000–2001. Print edition: *The Bible Knowledge Commentary: An Exposition of the Scriptures*. Wheaton: Victor Books, 1983.

———. *The Millennial Kingdom*. Grand Rapids: Zondervan, 1959.

———. *The Rapture Question*. Grand Rapids: Zondervan, 1957, ninth reprint, April 1972.

———. *The Revelation of Jesus Christ*. London: Marshall, Morgan & Scott, 1966.

Watts, Rikk E. "The New Exodus/New Creational Restoration of the Image of God." In *What Does It Mean to be Saved?* edited by John J. Stackhouse Jr., 15–41. Grand Rapids: Baker Book House, 2002.

———. "On the Edge of the Millennium: Making Sense of Genesis 1." In *Living in the LambLight*, edited by Hans Boersma, 129–51. Vancouver: Regent College Publishing, 2001.

White, Ben. *Israeli Apartheid: A Beginner's Guide*. New York: Pluto Press, 2009.

White, R. F. "Making Sense of Rev 20:1–10?" *Westminster Theological Journal* 37 (1994) 539–51.

———. "Reexamining the Evidence for Recapitulation in Revelation 20:1–10." *Westminster Theological Journal* 51 (1989) 319–44.

Williams, David J. *Paul's Metaphors: Their Context and Character*. Peabody, MA: Hendrickson, 1999.

Witherington, Ben, III. *Jesus, Paul and the End of the World: A Comparative Study in New Testament Eschatology*. Downers Grove, IL: InterVarsity Press, 1992.

———. *Revelation*. New Cambridge Bible Commentary. Cambridge: Cambridge University Press, 2003.

Wohlberg, Steve. *End Time Delusions*. Shippensburg, PA: Destiny Image, 2004.

———. *Exploding the Israel Deception*. Fort Worth, TX: Amazing Discoveries, 2000.

Wright, Christopher J. H. *Knowing Jesus through the Old Testament*. Downers Grove, IL: InterVarsity Press, 1992.

Wright, N. T. *The Climax of the Covenant: Christ and the Law in Pauline Theology*. Edinburgh: T. & T. Clark, 1991.

———. *Jesus and the Victory of God*. Minneapolis: Fortress, 1996.

———. "Jesus as the World's True Light." [Mp3 audio]. InterVarsity Press Conference, January 1999. No pages. Online: http://www.ntwrightpage.com.

———. "The Letter to the Romans: Introduction, Commentary, and Reflections." In *New Interpreter's Bible*, 10:395–770. Nashville: Abingdon, 2002.

———. *The New Testament and the People of God*. Minneapolis: Fortress, 1992.

———. *Paul: In Fresh Perspective*. Minneapolis: Fortress, 2005.

———. *The Resurrection of the Son of God*. Minneapolis: Fortress, 2003.

———. *Surprised by Hope: Rethinking Heaven, the Resurrection, and the Mission of the Church*. New York: HarperCollins, 2008.

Wright, Tom. *Acts for Everyone: Part 1 Chapters 1–12*. London: SPCK, 2008.

———. *What Saint Paul Really Said*. Oxford: Lion Publishing, 1997.

Young, E. J. *Daniel*. Geneva Series of Commentaries. Edinburgh: Banner of Truth Trust, 1972. First published, Grand Rapids: Eerdmans, 1949.

Made in the USA
San Bernardino, CA
20 July 2019